THE SWAN'S
WIDE WATERS

HAROLD W. FRENCH

THE SWAN'S WIDE WATERS

Ramakrishna and Western Culture

National University Publications
KENNIKAT PRESS • 1974
Port Washington, N.Y. • London

Library of Congress Catalog Card No. 74-77657
ISBN: 0-8046-9055-3

Manufactured in the United States of America

Published by
Kennikat Press Corp.
Port Washington, N.Y./London

To my Carolina students,
whose critical appetite for Eastern spirituality
has found much that is gratifying
in Ramakrishna

CONTENTS

ACKNOWLEDGEMENTS

I wish to express my profound appreciation to the persons and institutions whose support and counsel have been invaluable in the research, writing, and revision of this book. McMaster University, the Danforth Foundation, St. Andrews Presbyterian College, and the University of South Carolina have variously provided funds and facilities for the work. Dr. Paul Younger, Dr. David Kinsley, Dr. J. G. Arapura, and Dr. H. J. Mol, professors at McMaster University, offered very perceptive criticisms and suggestions that would bear more appreciative recognition than I can detail. Dr. Younger, my adviser, was also my host in Madras and Benares, introducing me to the larger Indian tradition. A number of colleagues at St. Andrews and the University of South Carolina have given helpful suggestions and encouragement, as have several students. A host of leaders and members of the Ramakrishna Movement extended extreme cordiality in providing facilities for study and opportunities for participant observation and discussion; they will, I fervently hope, receive a partial return from sharing this completed research. There are many others whom lack of space precludes specifically mentioning by name, but at whose recollection warm feelings of gratitude are evoked in me. However, a special citation must be tendered to some for their altogether exceptional helpfulness. Swami Bhashyananda of Chicago in 1966 served as my first contact with the Movement; his forceful leadership and gracious welcome to an outsider then and afterwards provided convincing evidence that this was a religious expression worth studying. In the Society of Southern California, the men of Trabuco followed a monastic life that seemed indeed exemplary; their openness and joy spoke volumes about the genuineness of their faith. Swami Vandananda in New Delhi, where I spent the first and final three days of my Indian sojourn, possessed a gift as interpreter of Vedanta East and West and a depth of spirituality which were extremely helpful at those crucial points. I passed thirty-two days in research at the Ramakrishna Mission Institute of Culture in Calcutta. While there were only occasional moments with the leaders, comfortable lodging, meals, and library resources were efficiently provided, enabling me to do my work. Daily encounters with the other guests provided in a most meaningful way the kind of transcultural encounter for which the Institute had been founded. Although the calendar of events was largely curtailed because of *puja* (worship) holidays, Calcutta itself was a research resource in those days. At one swiftly scheduled Institute event I read a paper, which was subsequently published in the Bulletin. Finally, I must thank my wife Rosemary and our children. They provided some change-of-pace activities and interests which were an invaluable respite from my labors. At the same time, they furnished a base of confident assurance that "Daddy would get the work done."

THE SWAN'S
WIDE WATERS

INTRODUCTION:
INDIA BETWEEN THE EAST AND WEST

Observers of the current religious scene in the West cannot escape being dazzled by the variety and virility of recently arrived Eastern imports. These seem quickly to take root in an alien soil and, despite their largely youthful clientele, to exhibit signs of mature "success." In fact, the maturity of certain of them is evidenced more authentically through their connection with ancient religious traditions. One of the hymns used in the Koyasan Temple of the Shingon sect in Los Angeles reads:

Who are these brave youths and maidens bearing torches in their hands?
These are Buddha's noble soldiers from far-off eastern lands. . . .
Ever forward they are marching, bearing treasures to the West,
Living waters to the thirsty, to the weary peace and rest.[1]

Although there are now thriving Buddhist organizations in Europe and America, it is perhaps surprising that Buddhism, which was strongly missionary in character even before the Christian era, was not the pioneering Eastern religious movement in the West in modern times. That distinction, strangely, belongs to a movement out of the Hindu tradition, and its emergence in the West marked also the first voicing by Hinduism to the claim of being a world religion. This book is a study of that pioneering movement, the Vedanta Society, or Ramakrishna Movement. Our understanding of the variety in the contemporary religious scene in the West may be enhanced by a study of how this alternative tradition first became available. What were the circumstances behind the first proclamation of its message? How did it become established and what has it had to offer to the West? To what degree is it responsible for and responsive to the new wave of interest in Eastern religions?

3

Beyond this, such a study may contribute to a larger knowledge of the Indian religious tradition itself, and the dynamics by which, specifically, Hinduism has become a world religion. Vedanta, as the Movement has interpreted its own usage of that term, is Hinduism universalized and made exportable beyond India's traditional cultural rigidities. It judges that the message of India's religious seers is relevant for all men. No longer is the foreigner outcasted and deemed unworthy to receive these teachings. The direct disciples of Ramakrishna may be credited with much of the responsibility for effecting this great transition. Ramakrishna himself, a village Hindu saint and a "local" in the extreme by most ordinary criteria, nevertheless had "cosmopolitan" insights and intuitions which were translated into institutional policy by Vivekananda and other disciples. This book attempts to explore the complex pattern of interaction with the West which followed. Ramakrishna was accorded the title "Paramahansa," or supreme swan, in his own lifetime, and in subsequent years this honorific title seems to have become attached to him almost exclusively, much as that of "Mahatma" has been to Gandhi. Again, in his lifetime, the waters of "the Swan" seemed no wider than those of the branch of the Ganges which flowed by the steps of the Kali Temple where he resided. We shall see how far those waters widened.

Patterns of Indian history may be charted around three themes: insularity, invasion, and expansion. From early times, the peninsula's cultural development bears the impress of these characteristics of interchange with other peoples. Geographical data readily confirm the feeling of extreme particularity which India conveys. Oceans combine with the Himalayas to create indeed formidable barriers. The Indian tradition thus reflects ways of thinking and behavior which flowered in relative isolation. But India was not impervious to alien influence; her isolation was relative. Waves of Aryans, Persians, Bactrian Greeks, successively moving into the north and west of India in ancient times, profoundly affected the course of the nation's history, as did Islamic invaders in medieval times and the British in the modern period. The response to these waves, obviously, was varied. The foreigner's cultural box was, on occasion, preserved relatively intact and segregated within the larger society. More typically, it was broken up and assimilated. Many observers have noted the vast absorptive capacities of India and, specifically, of Hinduism itself. The Bactrian Greeks, prior to the Christian era, may be cited as exemplifying the assimilative tendency, while the later Moslem conquerors may be characterized as having been largely compartmentalized within Indian society, with the essentials of Hinduism persisting without major alteration or accommodation.

Neither of the above responses adequately describes the results of the most recent invasion, that of the Europeans, primarily the British. India's cultural elite sensed the magnitude of the incipient challenge early in the nineteenth century, and India's subsequent history may be translated in terms of her multiple responses to Westernization. Religiously, the responsive movements have generally been categorized under the rubrics of reformist and revivalist. Another category, "renascent," has been devised to describe movements which arise from interaction of the two cultures. With reform the impetus is from extraneous factors and with revival from within the culture. Still another response, that of revolt, arises when the clash is felt to be too deep for reconciliation or compromise, even, perhaps, for co-existence.[2]

It may be questioned whether the term renascent is adequate to describe a phenomenon such as the Ramakrishna Movement. Before suggesting an alternative, a capsule description of the Movement is necessary. It was crystallized through interaction with the West, and that as the result of the personal experience of Swami Vivekananda. He received a Western education in Calcutta along with considerable exposure to Western influence before his initial residence in the West from 1893 to 1897. The invasion from the West was intensely real to him, and his life reveals an alternating pulsation of attraction-repulsion. But he was equipped with a powerful resource in the person of his guru Ramakrishna, who may be regarded as an embodiment of spiritual depth emerging from insular India. Ramakrishna's spiritual pilgrimage was polymorphic in character, personally validating the protean nature of Hinduism, and it was accomplished in virtual isolation from modern educational and Westernizing influences. His experiential verification of the essential truths of Islam and Christianity was accomplished without academic study of those faiths or personal encounter with their representatives.

The important conclusion here is that the Movement's desire to manifest a fidelity to its Indian roots was intense from its inception.

Moreover, this desire has been fulfilled with a large measure of integrity. The Movement, convinced of the richness of Hinduism generally and the representative stature of its own founders, early developed a strong missionary component. This illustrates the theme of expansion, which, religiously, had hitherto been little visible apart from the quiet march of Buddhist monks who had left India with a mission centuries earlier. While statistics of persons sent abroad by the new Movement are scarcely astounding, the expansive feature remains one of the Movement's most crucial components.

The term "satellite" occurs as best describing the Movement in its relation to the Indian tradition. The utility of this image from contemporary usage is readily apparent. The satellite movement is of the soil from which it has been launched, and its orbit continues with reference to its place of origination. But it feels the pull of other climes as well and is a communications device, maintaining liaison between them and its native locale. The sin of pressing the analogy to say more is obvious, but it may contribute useful suggestions which help us to understand the different facets of the Movement. "Satellite," then, graphically suggests the particular character of the Ramakrishna Movement. It especially conveys something of its strong claim for universality. Just as Ramakrishna's pilgrimage is interpreted as having demonstrated the validity of various paths to truth, his chief disciple Vivekananda is portrayed as exhibiting balancing tendencies towards Indian contemplation and Western activism. Thus the messages of each are judged to be religiously significant for men of disparate cultures. As their messages are concretized in the Ramakrishna Movement, therefore, institutional expression is given to the claim that they constitute the *sanatana dharma,* or universal religion.

Although the Movement has produced literally libraries of research on its leading personalities and teachings, the only significant study by any outsider is Wendell Thomas' *Hinduism Invades America,* written over forty years ago. This adds little to our knowledge of the early history and is of value chiefly for its assessment of the Movement in America in the late 1920's, when it was at a low ebb. While it has scarcely blossomed in the wake of the newly expanded interest in the East, the Movement is considerably more vital now than at that time. The fuller assessment, then, of both the earlier period and the more recent history presented here is appropriate.

Part I

The Ramakrishna Movement

History

Chapter One

RELIGIOUS FERMENT IN NINETEENTH CENTURY INDIA

The initiatives for nineteenth century religious and social reform in India came from two sources. First, British Evangelicals labored in concert with commercial interests and Utilitarian philosophy to civilize India. Second, a number of Indians sought, through a varying admixture of elements of Western culture and forgotten models from their own tradition, to break down the walls of poverty and superstition which blocked the entrance of India into the modern world. These forces shaped the setting in which the Ramakrishna Movement was born and established patterns which it could ponder in determining its own strategic response to the needs of India.

The British Stimulus to Reform

The policies of the British East India Company prior to the nineteenth century were largely determined by Britain's need for Indian exports. The Industrial Revolution, however, which vastly increased the output of manufactured goods in England, found her needing to develop a market for them. Insofar as her imperial subjects remained in peasant, agricultural societies, they had neither taste nor need for such products. Thus the earlier administrative romanticism which had been reluctant to impose the artifices of Western civilization upon the noble peasant and his immemorial culture began to be modified by Britain's economic situation.

At the start of the nineteenth century, however, the British were occupied in India with political problems and internal wars. Around

1818, however, with the defeat of the Mahratta powers, almost the whole of the coastline of the subcontinent was under British governance and, with the exception of certain central states, which cooperated more informally with the British presence, large sections of the interior as well. As warfare subsided, the dominant power could now set itself to the task of providing a stable and effective administration. This meant that pressures for policy change which had been building in England since the 1790's now demanded attention. The transition from merchant status to that of ruling caste imposed on the British a new set of responsibilities. Even though the transfer of rule from company to crown was not formally effected until 1858, following the Sepoy Mutiny, the need to provide a widened base of security for the expanding trade left the East India Company in virtual rule of the subcontinent long before that time.

The Evangelical interest in India was effectively initiated in 1792, when Charles Grant returned to England after twenty years of service with the Company in India. He brought with him some profound convictions about needed policy changes, first among which were the encouragement of English education and the presence of missionaries. He enlisted the influential cooperation of William Wilberforce in pursuit of these objectives, and the two became prime movers in the Clapham Sect, an Evangelical movement which also sought to secure the abolition of the slave trade. The manner in which, in Grant's mind, the civilizing influences of the West would also enhance Britain's commercial interests is indicated in the following passage:

In considering the affairs of the world as under the control of the Supreme Disposer, and those distant territories . . . providentially put into our hands . . . is it not necessary to conclude that they were given to us, not merely that we might draw an annual profit from them, but that we might diffuse among their inhabitants, long sunk in darkness, vice and misery, the light and benign influence of the truth, the blessings of well-regulated society, the improvements and comforts of active industry? . . . In every progressive step to this work, we shall also serve the original design with which we visited India, that design still so important to this country—the extension of our commerce.[1]

Education and Christianity were the keystones of the policy of assimilation whereby the gulf between British and Indian cultures could be bridged. "In this way," it was held, " 'the noblest species of conquest,' the spread of true religion and knowledge, would not forfeit its earthly reward; for 'wherever our principles and our language are introduced, our commerce will follow' "[2] Wilberforce echoed these sentiments in support of the clause in the East-India Bill for promoting the religious instruction and moral improvement of the natives of the British dominions in India; the measure, passed in 1813, permitted missionaries to be admitted to India. Having first proposed this step twenty years earlier, Wilberforce now believed that the most important battle of his life, affecting "the temporal and eternal happiness of millions, literally, millions on millions yet unborn," had been won.[3]

While some missionaries had been operating in South India and in small areas under the control of other foreign powers, for example, in the Danish colony of Serampore just north of Calcutta, the new measure largely opened India to the pent-up aspirations of many foreign mission boards. The Christian presence was to prove a powerful, if at times an irritating and intolerant, catalyst for social change. Shortly after the doors were opened to the missionary, the other side of the assimilative coin, English education, also was introduced. This, interestingly, was first begun by the efforts, not of the British, but of the Hindu elite in Calcutta, in the foundation in 1816 of Hindu College, the first European-style institution of higher learning in Asia.[4] The British, however, particularly under the leadership of Bentinck and Macaulay, were eager to expand this beachhead. In company with such leaders of the Indian elite as Rammohan Roy, they secured the enactment of Macaulay's Education Minute in 1835 as the culmination of their efforts.

The interests of Radicals and Utilitarian philosophers coincided with those of the Evangelicals. As Percival Spear notes, these had "a faith in reason as strong as the Evangelical confidence in the Gospel."[5] Thus they joined with the Evangelicals in denouncing customs which they regarded as offenses against humanity. Among the Utilitarians, James Mill was greatly influential. His *History of India,* written in 1817, gave him status among the Company's policy makers. With Bentinck he welcomed the initiatives of Macaulay in educational reform upon the latter's arrival in India.

Macaulay states how he conceived the Education Minute to be intimately related to the advance of British commercial interests and the Evangelical cause. "It is scarcely possible," he wrote, "to calculate the benefits which we might derive from the diffusion of European civilisation among the vast population of the East. . . . To trade with civilised men is infinitely more profitable than to govern savages."[6] In 1836, writing to his father, Macaulay stated his firm belief that, if the program for English education were pursued, there would not be a single idolater among the respectable classes in Bengal thirty years later.[7] Despite Macaulay's arrogant confidence in the superiority of British culture, the Indian historian and diplomat, K. M. Pannikar, has called his Education Minute the most beneficently revolutionary decision taken by the British government in India. "It is the genius of this man, narrow in his Europeanism, self-satisfied in his sense of English greatness, that gives life to modern India as we know it."[8]

When, therefore, the history of nineteenth century British India is charted in terms of social change, notable acts of legislation—such as the abolition of *sati* in 1829, Macaulay's Education Minute of 1835, the act allowing the remarriage of Hindu widows in 1856, and the Brahmo Marriage Act of 1872—might be cited as the most significant milestones. The mere recitation of these acts, however, might convey the impression that they were imposed by the British authorities, which is certainly incorrect. In each case, passage followed agitation by Indian reformers, who, in the large majority of the cases, acted as Hindus following their own carefully considered *dharma*. The British themselves, despite the adoption of a policy of assimilation based on a belief in the superiority of their own culture, nevertheless retained a balancing reluctance to interfere without indigenous pressure. When they did enact legislation to modify social practices which had become enmeshed in religious beliefs, as in Bentinck's suppression of *sati*,* the stand was taken on the premise that it was to purify the Hindu religion. Bentinck said, "I write and feel as a Legislator for the Hindoos, and as I believe many enlightened Hindoos think and feel."[9]

For the Evangelicals, the presence of a core of "enlightened Hindoos" meant that Christian ideals were already beginning to take root. They thus anticipated, not only moral and social advance, but, more tacitly, a broad turning to Christianity as this circle of enlighten-

Sati (also spelled *suttee*) was the practice in which the widow voluntarily (but, on occasion, under some duress) immolated herself on her husband's funeral pyre.

ment expanded. As late as 1902, the editor of the *Calcutta Review* expressed his strong belief that the process of Christianization of India was well under way, through the turning to Christ of "the most earnest seekers, . . . the moral heroes . . . who are the real salt, strength, and stamina of the nation. . . . When these," he confidently predicted, "have all been gathered into the Christian Church, the rest of the wavering and the careless, even though in the vast majority, will follow as a matter of course."[10]

While this generalized expectation was not uncharacteristic, many missionaries sought to stimulate a genuine transcultural interchange and to foster humanitarian objectives which were imperatives in themselves and not strategic instruments to advance the growth of the visible Church. William Carey and, to a degree, his associates at Serampore were so motivated. While encouragement to English education became official British policy after 1835, Carey's services as an Orientalist were helping to acquaint the British and the Indian people themselves with the Indian heritage. His primary linguistic contribution was in the vernacular languages, chiefly Bengali, in which his efforts have induced many historians to accord him the honorific distinction of father of modern Bengali prose. Linguistically, the Serampore Mission Press, as early as 1805, could print any work in Sanskrit, Bengali, Urdu, Oriya, Tamil, Kanarese, or Marathi, which seems a phenomenal achievement, and Fort William colleagues and facilities enabled Carey to derive the grammatical and lexicographical principles of these languages.[11] This was of inestimable value in promoting the systematic study of Hindu popular culture. William Jones, an earlier Orientalist, and H. H. Wilson, Friedrich Max Müller, and other later scholars, were part of this obverse intercultural dimension to that fostered by British Utilitarian, Evangelical, and commercial interests.

The Evangelical presence in the stimulation of social reform was also highly significant. K. Natarajan, the editor of *The Indian Social Reformer,* acknowledged that "the fear of the Christian missionary has been the beginning of much social wisdom among us."[12] The opening of schools and hospitals, the championing of the rights of women, widows in particular, quickened the conscience of Hindus. A partially defensive strategy began, then, to develop within Hinduism to meet the challenge of the Christian presence. A number of the movements which arose, even those superficially labeled "revivalist," incorporated "reform" elements within them, conscious that the magnitude of the confrontation with the West would not admit as viable any strategy calling merely for a rigid insistence on the adequacy of the social order.

The Hindu Response

A Christian, writing in the *Calcutta Review* in 1879, could make the insightful and prophetic observation, "It is . . . a peculiarity of Hinduism more calling for congratulation than surprise that . . . it has never ceased to engender attempts at regeneration and reform from the depths of its own consciousness."[13] The marvel is that, given the frontal character of the challenge from the West, so much of the cultural integrity of India survived. The Hindus quite rightly perceived that the total British presence and the specific programs of missionaries constituted a throwing down of the gauntlet before their own religion. Early in the nineteenth century the two faiths, Christianity and Hinduism, certainly seemed unequally matched. After describing the Hinduism of the day, Pannikar says, "As against this disorganized and inchoate mass of sects and creeds, with no defined dogma, no organized priesthood, no officially accepted scriptures, with its doctrines overgrown with superstition and primitive beliefs, stood Christianity—the accepted faith of the dynamic and expanding civilization of Europe."[14] The outcome of such an encounter would have seemed a foregone conclusion. And yet, by the century's end, Hinduism had discerned the nature of the threat, looked to its own most vulnerable points, and had begun to muster its own resources to effect the refinement of its practices and teachings. "The Hindu religion emerged stronger, more united, capable of meeting the challenge of other religions with complete self-confidence, ready in fact to carry the war into other camps."[15] The twentieth century has seen the elaboration of the tendencies even then being heralded.

Hinduism proved more pliable in certain respects than one might have anticipated. It was bound by no set of unchanging dogmas and, while the Vedas were often appealed to as revealed scriptures, their actual content, early in the nineteenth century, was so little known as to make them virtually useless in establishing a given position with regard to ethical practice. Research into the sacred texts was, however, stimulated by the reformers' zeal. Successful advocacy of any social change required that it be interpreted as restorative of an earlier, purer order. Thus the Orientalists found that their linguistic tools were readily put to use by reformers, seeking to establish precedents from scripture, and by the orthodox, hoping to find justification for practices hallowed by customary usage. This partially accounts for the difference in methodology between the typical Indian and typical British leader in India in effecting reform. The former, as represented by Rammohan Roy's dealings with Lord Bentinck, would make his case by searching the Hindu texts for relevant counsel from an earlier period. This was largely irrelevant for the representative of the British crown, whose decision would be made on the basis of what he felt to be universal human rights, some of which, such as the equality of all men before the bar of justice, were certainly not principles accepted by caste-structured Indian society.

The first name to be considered among modern Indian reformers must surely be that of Raja Rammohan Roy, rightfully accorded various ascriptions, such as "Pioneer of Modern Indian Renaissance," "the first really cosmopolitan type in India," "the Father of Modern India," etc. Cosmopolitan influences had been strong from an early period in his life. The larger Hindu culture from the centuries of its exposure to Islam had only become more resistant to change. Rammohan's education, on the other hand, beginning with the study of Persian in his native village and continuing at Patna, then a famous seat of Muslim learning, caused him to raise many questions about the religious practices of his people. While still in his teens he began to express his opinions against idolatry both verbally and in print, making it necessary for him to leave home for a time. But his intent persisted to purify Hinduism of what he regarded as its superstitious accretions. "He was banished from his father's house once or twice; he was insulted by his friends; his life was threatened, and even in the streets of Calcutta he had to walk about armed. Later in his life his relations (his own mother) tried to deprive him of his caste, and indirectly of his property." [16] Rammohan Roy never joined the Muslim or Christian communities with which he had so many cordial relationships, and which might have welcomed him openly as a convert, but remained to the end a devout Brahmin. Some missionary friends at Serampore became estranged because he favored dispensing with certain Gospel miracles that he felt lessened the credibility of the ethical message of Jesus.[17]

These difficulties mark Rammohan Roy as an almost solitary figure among his contemporaries in Indian society—as indeed he was for a time. He may be regarded as something of a counterpart to William Carey, however, in his services as champion for the freedom of the press, the rights of women (particularly in his unceasing campaign against *sati*), and the cause of education. Despite his appeal to the classics for precedents in support of reform measures, however, he definitely stood with the Anglicists against the Orientalists in his insistence that modern scientific education was much more a pressing need for India than further stress on Sanskrit. Having assisted David Hare in the establishment of the Hindu College, he regarded the opening of a Sanskrit College in Calcutta as a retrograde move. In a letter of protest he said, "The Sanskrit language, so difficult that almost a lifetime is necessary for its perfect acquisition, is well known to have been for ages a lamentable check on the diffusion of knowledge; and the learning concealed under this impervious veil is far from sufficient to reward the labour of acquiring it. . . . The Sanskrit system of education would be the best calculated to keep this country in darkness, if such had been the policy of the British legislature. . . ."[18]

As well as welcoming the promise of Western educational models, his cordiality to the Evangelicals was also striking, particularly to Alexander Duff, whom he greatly assisted in beginning his work in Calcutta in 1830.[19] Shortly thereafter Rammohan Roy was to travel to England, there to continue his pattern of close cooperation with British officialdom in effecting and cementing reform. Although he had not felt that Bentinck's legal act abolishing *sati* was the best way of dealing with the issue, once he saw that the desired effect was secured without disorder, he firmly opposed those who sought its repeal. This cause and the advocacy of other reforms attendant to the renewal of the Company charter in 1833 motivated his voyage to England; shortly after the reforms were adopted, Roy died and was buried at Bristol.*

*His death occurred within a few months of that of William Wilber-

Rammohan Roy's legacy to India was conveyed in part through the Brahmo Samaj, which he founded in 1828. It largely consisted of a simple worship directed toward Brahma. With Roy's absence from India and his death, the movement was to languish for a time, until the Tagores, Dwarkanath and his son Debendranath, were to emerge as leaders. The elder Tagore, while not a deep thinker, was nevertheless a colorful figure who followed Rammohan Roy's lead in coming to England in the next decade. He appreciated the magnitude of the Raja's contribution, and erected a monument to Rammohan Roy at the cemetery in Bristol, shortly before he himself was to die in England. Max Müller thought that the elder Tagore, observing his research on the Vedas in Paris, may have informed Debendranath, who shortly afterwards sent four scholars to Benares to study the Vedas and report back to him.[20] The study undertaken by the four scholars and subsequent discussion led to the Tagore group's abandoning the cherished doctrine of the infallibility of the Vedas.

While not possessing the statesmanlike qualities of Rammohan Roy, Debendranath seems to have had a more deeply pious nature. Reform came with more reluctance for him, and he was hesitant to impose the abolition of caste distinctions, e.g., the giving up of the sacred thread by Samaj (congregation) members from the three higher castes. While he did this at the behest of the zealous Keshab Chandra Sen, who had joined the Samaj in 1857 at the age of only nineteen, later, in 1860, he yielded to more conservative members and once more allowed the thread to be worn. Certainly less Westernized and less under Christian influence than Keshab, Debendranath and his young lieutenant seemed destined for a parting of the ways. The split came, then, over this immediate issue, and resulted in Keshab's founding of the Brahmo Samaj of India two years later, with Debendranath's group henceforth being known as the Adi (or original) Brahmo Samaj.

The New Dispensation of Keshab appears to have found an almost evangelical fervor in the proclamation of its message. Keshab

---

force, the English reformer. Their common cause in social justice, linking men of enlightenment from Britain to the ends of the Empire in India, finds testimony in the words engraved on the tomb of Wilberforce in St. Paul's Cathedral, London: "In an age and country fertile in great and good men, he was among the foremost of those who fixed the character of their times."

Chandra Sen's six-month visit to the West in 1870 enhanced for some his magnetism and strengthened his already warm feeling for Christianity. His influence throughout India multiplying, he made an all-India tour in 1873. Other missionaries were sent out, founding groups mostly in Bengal but beyond also, where clusters of persons welcomed the westernized religious message which the Brahmos had to share.

As an almost classic charismatic organization,[21] however, it was overly dependent on the personal leading of Keshab, whose development of Debendranath's doctrine of intuition made him almost a law unto himself. The movement contained few guidelines, and a new schism resulted when Keshab appeared to contradict his own earlier stance in allowing his daughter to be married in 1878 to the Prince of Cooch Behar although both were under the ages specified in the Brahmo Marriage Bill. His defenders, convinced of their leader's spiritual integrity, felt that he could not go against the express guidance which he claimed to have received on this occasion and cited other occurences which they thought had also been widely misrepresented.[22] The group separating from Keshab's movement called itself the Sadharan Brahmo Samaj and was generally of a more rationalistic and less theistic temper. Vivekananda later joined it before his meeting with Ramakrishna.

The influence of all of these groups was to wane as they moved into the twentieth century. The Sadharan Brahmo Samaj, while it developed rules, policies, and guidelines which had been lacking in the New Dispensation, was too coldly rationalistic for most Indians. The New Dispensation itself, borrowing from all traditions and committing itself to none, seemed like a cut-flower bouquet.[23] And the Adi Brahmo Samaj began to be restricted more and more to the activities of the Tagore family circle, having moved closer to orthodox Hinduism and lost much of its character as a reform movement.

The character of reform movements outside of Bengal is generally less radical, and the reform activities the Brahmos inspired in their missionary pursuits were usually more moderate in tone than their own in Bengal. Those calling for root and branch reform, however, were not always in possession of the most sophisticated understanding of the antecedent causes of the current religious situation.

The Maharastrian reformers were often more perceptive in their assessments of complex processes that had been at work for centuries. Justice Ranade says, listing ideas which had nurtured a general decline, "These ideas may be briefly set forth as isolation, submission to outward force or power more than to the voice of inward conscience, perception of fictitious differences between men and men due to heredity and birth, passive acquiescence in civil wrongdoing, and a general indifference to secular well-being, almost bordering on fatalism."[24]

Ranade and company in the Bombay Presidency seem to have held a greater feeling for national, as against regional issues, than did the Bengali Brahmos, who were also more characteristically emotional and volatile. The reformers in western India tended, also, to have more regard for tradition generally. Southern reformers, in brief, were educated but ritually orthodox Brahmins, while in the northwest, the Hindu-Muslim conflict imparted a dimension of militancy not found elsewhere.

In western India the **Prarthana Samaj** grew out of Keshab's missionary activities, but from its inception it seemed to exhibit less of a spirit of adolescent rebellion than the parent Brahmo organization. It was more concerned to preserve the historic ties which bound it to the ancestral faith than were most of the Bengalis. Thus there was nothing equivalent in the Bombay Presidency to the Brahmo Marriage Bill, which in Bengal in effect had created a separate caste or religion. Most of the movement in and around Bombay found its focus in the activities of Justice Ranade, whose long service on the bench gave a more judicial coloration to reform. Through the founding of the Indian National Congress and the Social Conference, which he hoped might prosper together, he was instrumental both in political organization and social reform. From the start of the Social Congress in 1887 into the 1900's its sessions were in fact concurrent with those of the National Congress.

Opposition to Ranade's program of social reform was expressed by Bal Gangadhar Tilak, who was forcefully advocating political action leading to *swaraj* (self-rule). The fascinating drama of the relationship between Ranade and Tilak and the tensions it led to among the reformers cannot be delineated here except in briefest outline. Tilak opposed the social reformers on two grounds, both of which had some credibility. First, he felt that the reformers did not consistently practice the new life style which they sought to impose on the larger society.* Second, activities in social reform were, he felt, an admission of weakness and, to alleviate the alleged short-comings of society, the reformers were both imitating the European overlords and cooperating with them to effect change. Political inde-pendence was the primary mandate for Tilak; efforts which appeared to him to compromise that mandate received his scorn. Tilak thus opposed the Age of Consent Bill, ultimately passed by the Viceroy's Legislative Council in 1891, because the social reformers were modi-fying Indian society and the Hindu religion by use of British law. Rigorously anti-Western, Tilak felt that this amounted to hand-in-glove collaboration.

But if Ranade and others seemed too temperate in political reform for Tilak and his associates, their middle path made them equally vulnerable to attack from more genuinely radical social re-formers. With the publication of *The Social Reformer,* first from Madras in 1890 and later from Bombay, personal vacillation and public concessions for the sake of diplomacy in the reformer's camp were subjected to harsh criticism. As an English language periodical, committed to rationalistic rather than Shastraic (scriptural) bases for reform, *The Reformer* largely ignored the conventions to which the earlier reformers in western India continued to feel amenable. When Ranade (and, interestingly, Tilak also) submitted to caste demands that he publicly repent for having taken food at a tea party given by Christian missionaries, it was a moment of genuine disil-lusionment for many in the movement and brought about a sharp censure in *The Reformer.* For Ranade the concession was too un-important to make him willing to alienate those whom he hoped to lead into reform in more crucial areas.[25]

The temper of the movement, however, as the century turned, was fired with a greater fervency. The causes of female education, widows' rights, and greater maturity before marital consummation

*Tilak's personal example often appeared more modern than that of certain of the reformers. He opposed governmental interference, though he was committed to going beyond the age limitations then being proposed for marriage legislation. He was one of the first five signators on a pledge in 1889 to educate his daughters and not marry them before the age of ten, and did not in fact marry them till they were over sixteen. Natarajan, *op. cit.*, p. 66, and Heimsath, *op. cit.,* p. 209.

still had gains to make, but the younger reformers wanted to break new ground. These older causes, championed for many years, did not threaten the caste structure itself, which was the aim of certain new causes. Among these would be the active promotion of intercaste dining—the issue from which Ranade and Tilak retreated—and the first stirrings of conscience about the plight of the untouchable. The mantle was to pass from Ranade to Narayan Ganesh Chandavarkar, who simply ignored the threat of caste excommunication for his reforming ventures.

Although in the decade before his death Ranade had been too tepid in his leadership for the younger zealots, he had been a prime mover in organizing both political and social reform into national movements through the National Congress Party and the Social Conference. Perhaps because he saw the need for orderly advance together in these two realms and, though with lesser emphasis, in religion also, he was not the one to provide the sharp thrust in any single realm.

The pace of reform in the south of India was generally slower than elsewhere, at least until the advent of *The Social Reformer* in Madras. Before that time, the leadership of Viresalingam, later to be associated with Vivekananda, was an almost isolated personal example. He could be, in the breadth of his concerns, at one moment a critic of British rule, at another pressing for widow remarriage. The slowness of the south was partly due to a larger social dominance by Brahmins than elsewhere. English language study had by the latter part of the century been more widespread here than elsewhere in India, but only a small percentage went on to the university education which produced much of the ferment for reform. The only issues in which the Madras Presidency gave significant leadership to the nation were those connected with a rather puritanical strain, such as the campaign against *nautch* dancing and usage of beverage alcohol. Reform was also intimidated in the south by the presence in Madras of the Theosophical Society after 1882. The Society became the bulwark for many years of the established social order, so that, even though orthodox Hindus did not actively relate to it for a number of reasons, they relied on it to defend the traditional positions against the often severe beleaguerment of the reformers. That Westerners were championing orthodox practice was a great conservative counteragency to social change.

The history of Theosophy in India is replete with colorful personalities, schisms arising between them, periodic scandals of various
sorts, and occult teachings which augmented those of the native faiths.
Colonel Olcott and Madame Blavatsky had established the Society
in New York City in 1875. Substantial activity began only with the
publication by Madame Blavatsky of her first book *Isis Unveiled* and
initiation of correspondence with Swami Dayananda Saraswati of the
Arya Samaj of India. In obedience to the leadings of the Tibetan
Masters, who were throughout the movement's history credited as
wielding a primary influence on its affairs, Madame Blavatsky and
Colonial Olcott came to India in 1879, landing in Bombay to a welcome
by members of the Arya Samaj, founded by Swami Dayananda. The
European pair's early efforts paralleled those of the Arya Samja in
reforming education, promoting Sanskrit learning, and generally seeking to counter the influence of Christian missionaries. The first few
years were spent mostly in Ceylon, espousing a revival of Buddhism,
but the movement established its headquarters in Adyar, just outside
of Madras, in 1882. Madame Blavatsky left India not long after when
she fell ill. An investigation of the Society's claims of letters from the
Tibetan Masters had been pressed by the Society for Psychical Research in London, and their report indicted Madame Blavatsky as a
fraud and the movement's claim to have received occult phenomena as
spurious. She then settled in London, where she died a few years later,
in 1891. In London Madame Blavatsky won the loyalty of Mrs. Annie
Besant, who had separated from her husband to become a leader in
free thought and socialism. She became the Society's leader upon
Madame Blavatsky's death and, shortly after having attended the
Parliament of Religions in Chicago, went to India in 1893. She developed a deep personal feeling for India, which she regarded as having been the place of her birth in a former incarnation, and swiftly
set about to instill a new vitality in Hinduism.

Until about 1915 in her public career Mrs. Besant was wholly
identified with the revival of Hinduism and not at all with reform. By
that time the questions which had been building in her for years could
no longer be contained, and she began to pursue a different course,
opposing caste restrictions and becoming politically active through
leadership in the Congress Party. That she could move so readily
from leadership in one realm to another is a clear tribute to her recog-

nized stature among the Indian people. She remained the President of the Theosophical Society in India from 1907 until her death in 1933, but her political influence began to wane in 1920, when she opposed Gandhi. Her earlier career as a revivalist was by no means solely negative in character, however. Perhaps her most noted contribution to the Indian scene will remain in the field of education, and this most strikingly through her part in the foundation of the Hindu University at Benares. Through her efforts, the Sanskrit tradition received a vital transfusion.

The Arya Samaj movement belongs largely to northern India. The founder, Dayananda, like his junior by a few years, Ramakrishna, had little exposure to Western influence. Unlike Ramakrishna, however, he was learned in Sanskrit, and the reforms which he advocated were based on his study of the Vedas and certain ethical teachings from the Code of Manu. He sought to restore a purer Hinduism after a Vedic model, for he believed that Puranic distortions had weakened Hinduism with idolatry and other corrupt influences. In temperament he exhibited nothing of the warm *bhakti* (devotional) strain that we witness in Ramakrishna.

The deaths of a sister and an uncle appear to have deepened his already serious nature, and he resisted his parents' efforts to stabilize him in a householder state by changing his name and leaving home on the day designated for his wedding to become a *sadhu* (ascetic mendicant). Fifteen years of wandering, during which he practiced yoga and became immersed in Vedanta philosophy, ended when at long last he was able to find a guru able to instruct him deeply in Vedic lore. The blind teacher Virajananda was a severe taskmaster, often applying physical discipline and, before the instruction could even begin, required Dayananda to throw some modern books into the Jumna River as a symbol of cutting himself off from all that was recent in scholarship. But Virajananda was a master of Sanskrit grammar, and the disciple stayed with him for two and a half years, perfecting his knowledge of the earliest and most authoritative literature of his people. Then Dayananda began to wander about, preaching against idolatry and debating with scholars about the essential teachings of Hinduism. His travels eventually took him to Calcutta, where he encountered Keshab Chandra Sen and other Brahmo leaders and

Ramakrishna.* He resisted the Westernization of the Brahmos, but
apparently followed Keshab's suggestion that he carry on his teaching
in the vernacular rather than Sanskrit to reach the people with his
message. These religious leaders admired Dayananda's enlightened
views on the caste system and even on idol worship, although his
opposition to that practice was decidedly more emphatic than that of
the Brahmos.

He moved on from Calcutta to Bombay, where he founded the
Arya Samaj in 1875. The relationship with the Theosophical Society
was soon initiated, but there were inevitable differences, and the two
organizations went their separate ways in 1881. One might suspect
that occult elements in Theosophy would have repelled Dayananda,
as we know that his sharp polemic against Christianity and Islam was
not acceptable to those in Theosophy. He wrote Madame Blavatsky,
"As night and day are opposed to each other, so are all religions
opposed to one another."[26] Perhaps his residence in the west and north
of India, where a history of militant opposition between Islam and
Hinduism was strongest, may have influenced him. At any rate, he
undertook the reconversion of those who had turned to Islam and
Christianity through counterpropaganda measures. There was no hint
of the universalism with which other reformers sought to clothe their
understandings of Hinduism. His call for classic education has, however, been answered by the movement which continued following his
death in 1883, though with the incorporation, doubtless, of more
Western models than he would have sanctioned.

To conclude this review of movements prior to and contemporary with that begun by Ramakrishna and Vivekananda, we note a
variety of responses to the Western presence which so began to
pervade the Indian atmosphere in the nineteenth century. Western
scientific rationalism, social practice, and organizational detail appeared to many, particularly in Bengal, to provide the models by
which India might be remade. They were eager to adopt Western
ways, in their enthusiasm often offending their elders and creating

*Ramakrishna recorded his impressions of Dayananda to his disciples,
as follows: "I went to see him in the garden of Sinthi: I found that he had
acquired a little power; his chest was always red. . . . He misapplied grammar and twisted the meanings of many words. He had in his mind the
egoism, 'I'll do something, I'll found a doctrine'." Swami Saradananda, *Sri
Ramakrishna, The Great Master* (Madras: Sri Ramakrishna Math, 1952),
p. 551.

sharp divisions in society. Others sought to insure continuity with the past through a respect for tradition, but by the close of the century their timidity in reform cost them the allegiance of younger militants. Theosophy's revivalism had what appeared to many Indians to be preposterous added teachings, and the Arya Samaj seemed overly severe, advocating a kind of fictionalized Vedism rather than Hinduism and lacking in religious warmth. No movement appeared to satisfy Justice Ranade's criteria for social, political, and religious idealism, and none was to emerge. But in this situation a personality appeared who seemed to incarnate many of the deepest aspirations of the Indian soul, and the subsequent interpretations of this man's genius sought to relate his insight to the particular problems raised by the encounter of India and the West as the twentieth century dawned. The movement which bears his name continues to be significant. We meet Ramakrishna.

Chapter Two

RAMAKRISHNA'S PILGRIMAGE
AND TEACHINGS

"If one takes into consideration Ramakrishna's life only up to 1875 or so, when he first came into contact with modern educated Bengal, it is difficult to place him in any particular age: he seems so immune from any contemporary influences."[1] At the time, his *sadhana* (spiritual pilgrimage) complete, it seems particularly auspicious that his meeting with Keshab Chandra Sen should have occurred, for by that acquaintance the circle of his influence began to expand. The first public notice of Ramakrishna in a periodical of the time appears to have been in an article by Keshab in *The Indian Mirror* of March 28, 1875, titled "A Hindu Saint." Describing their first encounter, Keshab reported, "We met a sincere Hindu devotee and were charmed by the depth, penetration and simplicity of his spirit. The never-ceasing metaphors and analogies in which he indulged were as apt as beautiful."[2] It was no momentary fascination, for the relationship between them deepened; each was to have a significant influence upon the other.

While Keshab's circle before this time had become broadly cosmopolitan, Ramakrishna had been immersed in village India, in the vast sea of its saints and sages, its ancient myths, legends, and customs. Ramakrishna's pilgrimage had taught him to treasure the wealth of the Hindu tradition by personally striving to realize truth through its varied paths. As we trace the steps of his *sadhana* we are impressed with the tradition's breadth and with the comprehensive character of Ramakrishna's experience of it.

Gadadhar (Ramakrishna) was born late in the marriage of Kshudiram and Chandradevi Chatterjee, a poor, pious farming couple living in the village of Kamarpukur in Bengal. They were worshipers

26

of the boyhood form of Rama, the family deity for many years, made more venerable by the discovery by Kshudiram of a salagrama stone (fossilized shell) associated with Rama. There were auspicious visions and portents before the birth of Gadadhar in 1836, particularly vouchsafed to his mother, who had a warm, generous nature.[3]

The boy early attracted the attention of others by his winning, playful spirit, his gift of mimicry, and his extreme sensitivity to beauty. He went into his first trance at age six or seven on the sight of a flock of snow-white swans in the sky. This stimulation to his already strong disposition for worship, enactment of the sacred stories, and meditation made progress in school difficult. His brother Ramkumar, thirty-one years his senior (there were five children; Ramakrishna was the fourth), used his talent for conducting ceremonies and teaching the scriptures to augment the family income for a time, especially after the father's death when Ramakrishna was seven. But Ramkumar's talents were not enough in demand in the village, so he went to Calcutta to start a Sanskrit school. At sixteen Ramakrishna, partly to further his schooling, joined Ramkumar. Ramakrishna, however, was still averse to what he termed "bread-winning education" and much of his time was spent in spiritual pursuits little reached by the more modern aspects of Calcutta culture.

When the new Kali temple at Dakshineswar just north of Calcutta was dedicated in 1855, its donor, the wealthy widow Rani Rasmoni, had considerable difficulty in finding a priest to officiate. Like her husband, who had helped Rammohan Roy in his fight against *sati*, she was given to charitable deeds for religious and humanitarian causes. But for the Dakshineswar complex, conceived as an ecumenical expression of Hinduism with separate temples for Shiva, for Radha-Krishna, and—the largest of all—for the goddess Kali—for this product of eight years of work and six lakhs (hundred thousands) of rupees—no Brahmin would serve as priest. For Rani Rasmoni was of the *shudra* (or *sudra*) caste (the lowest), and no orthodox Brahmin could offer worship for a *shudra* or accept gifts from him. She asked various pandits for suggestions on how to meet this impasse, and from Ramkumar came the counsel that if she were to deed the property to a Brahmin, he might then see to the conduct of the worship and she continue to provide for the maintenance without transgression of scriptural injunctions. The Rani, impressed with

Ramkumar for his apt suggestion, prevailed on him to accept service there as priest, and the image of the goddess was duly installed amidst great festivities in the year 1855.

Ramkumar's catholicity, in striking contrast to that of current Brahmin opinion, was also beyond that of his younger brother. Gadadhar attended the inauguration but he remonstrated with his brother for taking service from a *shudra* woman, refused any of the *prasad* (food which had previously been consecrated in worship), and returned to Calcutta that same day.[4] His love for his brother caused him to return and stay a week later, but for some time, finding that he could not dissuade his brother, he followed his own disposition by taking uncooked food from the temple stores down to the Ganges to cook it with the purifying water from the sacred river, and then ate beneath the *panchavati* (five trees, sacred to Tantric practice) outside the temple precincts. Official biographies, beginning with that of Saradananda, do not disguise the Brahmin mentality which formed a part of Ramakrishna's heritage. He was to ignore caste restrictions at various times during his *sadhana* and much of his larger religious vision was certainly catholic, yet his identity as a Brahmin returned to impose certain limitations upon him socially after the time of his *sadhana,* the twelve years of his most arduous experimentation with the different roads to realization. First asked to attend to worship preparations in the Radha-Krishna temple, Ramakrishna was soon requested, perhaps with the decline of Ramkumar's health, to perform the more demanding duties attached to the Kali temple. Ramkumar's death occurred only a year after the dedication of the temple.

One can only speculate on the impact of this loss on Ramakrishna, but it appears that the fervency of his devotion, which had already so impressed the temple authorities, now flamed still more brightly; he became almost incapacitated for the conduct of the worship. Despite the complaints made about his frequent trances during worship and his irregular attendance, his benefactor believed in him and felt that his depth of spirituality had already fulfilled the purpose of the new temple. More of the duties of conducting worship devolved to Hriday, Ramakrishna's nephew, and others.

Ramakrishna entered upon his *sadhana,* which was to last twelve years. For the first four years he was without a guru, except an inner one whom he saw in a vision and whose teachings the later gurus largely served to clarify and corroborate. Ramakrishna assumed various classic modes of worship in the early years of the *sadhana,* each time immersing himself completely in the role. His earlier talent for mimicry and dramatic role playing now served him religiously in a manner almost unparalleled in spiritual history. Although the tradition gives abundant precedent for seeming madness accompanying spiritual practice, the disorienting character of his devotion gave rise to concern for both his mental and physical well-being. His own testimony confirms that he was at the point of ultimate despair before he received his first vision of Kali. He relates his extremity one day in the temple:

There was then an intolerable anguish because I could not have her vision. Just as a man wrings a towel forcibly to squeeze out all the water from it, so I felt as if somebody caught hold of my heart and mind and was doing so with them. Greatly afflicted with the thought that I might never have Mother's vision, I was dying of despair. Being in agony, I thought, there was then no use in living this life. My eyes suddenly fell upon the sword that was there in the Mother's temple. I made up my mind to put an end to my life with it that very moment. Like one mad, I ran and caught hold of it, when suddenly I had the wonderful vision of the Mother and fell down unconscious. I did not know what happened then in the external world—how that day and the next slipped away. But, in my heart of hearts, there was flowing a current of intense bliss, never experienced before, and I had the immediate knowledge of the light that was Mother.[5]

He returned to his home in Kamarpukur for over a year in response to the concern expressed, and his health improved. While at home he obediently married a girl of five years to whom, through a vision, he had directed his family in their search. She remained with her family for some years when he returned to Dakshineswar.

In the second four years of his *sadhana* he had two gurus. The first, the Bhairavi Brahmani, a noted woman Tantric practitioner, led him for three years through the sixty-four disciplines of the Tantric path. She regarded him from an early meeting as an incarnation of Chaitanya (or Caitanya), a Bengal religious reformer born in the late fifteenth century. He says that by the Mother's grace it did not take him more than three days to succeed in any of the disciplines and that he had not needed the physical accompaniment of a woman in the practices as do weak persons destitute of self-control. Indebted though he was to the Tantric path, he later opposed its view that yoga and *bhoga* (discipline and enjoyment) could exist in the same person, and felt that the *vamamarg,* or left-hand path of Tantrism, had dangers so great as to make it inadvisable for most persons to follow.[6] Much of the ritual practice, it should be noted, seeks to transcend the senses through exposure to the most explicit and often revolting sensual stimuli. Death and the cremation grounds are regarded as particularly auspicious to spiritual realization. Other Tantric practices, sexual in nature, are often undergone symbolically, as was the case with Ramakrishna. The temple grounds at Dakshineswar were holy through earlier having been a cremation ground, and the *panchavati* there was the site of many experiences in Ramakrishna's *sadhana.*

The other guru of these second four years was Jatadhari, an itinerant devotee of Ramachandra, who came to Dakshineswar and initiated Ramakrishna, perhaps at the urging of the Brahmani, into Vaishnava (Vishnuite) *sadhana.* From his boyhood days, he had been habituated to the worship of Rama, an avatar of Vishnu, and he vividly responded to these memories in his play with the image of the god given him by Jatadhari before the latter's departure. He also adopted another Vaishnava pattern, the *madhura bhava* or sweet mood, worshiping Krishna, another of Vishnu's avatars, as his female consort, the shepherdess Radha. Once more his genius in merging into the adopted role is evidenced in his having assumed the dress and manner of life of a woman for some months to relate to the beloved Krishna, and also, by his own account, to overcome the idea of sexual difference.

But while the Brahmani may have encouraged Ramakrishna's assumption of the Vaishnavite path, she definitely discouraged his experience of Advaita worship, which, we are told, was rather rare in Bengal before Ramakrishna. But Mother Kali gave her sanction, which would seem to indicate that the interiorized deity remained more authoritative than any personal guru. In Advaita worship, the teacher was Tota Puri, "the naked one," who guided him for a year. It was difficult for Ramakrishna to pass into *samadhi* (enlightenment) through the realization of Brahman beyond name and form, so intense was the reality of Kali's image, but the insistent Tota Puri led him into a prolonged state of *samadhi* which astonished even that guru. Ramakrishna became convinced through this experience that all the *sadhanas* took the aspirant toward the nondual plane, which in turn produced in his mind a still wider catholicity. He soon desired to know something of spirituality beyond his native Hindu tradition and was initiated by Govinda Ray into the practice of Islam, attaining *samadhi* with Islamic visions after three days of seeking to divest his mind of anything Hindu. Still later, after having a fellow Hindu read the Bible to him for a certain period, he also received a vision of Jesus.*

His mother was with him in Dakshineswar for the last twelve years of her life, from 1865. And when he returned for a time to his village he again saw his wife, now fourteen, and spent some time in teaching and educating her, again against the counsel of the Brahmani, who felt that he should have no contact with her. His wife, Sarada Devi, came to Dakshineswar four years later and lived with him for over a year, sharing his vision of what their relationship should be. During this time neither experienced desire; instead, as the final stage of his *sadhana,* called the *shodasi,* Ramakrishna learned to worship the divine through the body of a woman, whom he continually sought to think of as Mother.

A brief account by Ramakrishna of his *sadhanas* is recorded in *The Gospel of Sri Ramakrishna,* a rare, intimate account of the last few years of his life as witnessed by M (Mahendranath Gupta), a lay disciple. Ramakrishna relates that he had attained the highest spiritual goals through the various stages of his *sadhana* and all the attendant graces, including acts of healing. His extraordinary insight into the minds and needs of other persons is detailed, but he felt

*A tribute to Ramakrishna's catholicity is recorded from Bengal's Nobel Prize winning poet:
To the Paramhansa [again, the Swan which soars to spiritual heights]
Ramakrishna Deva
Diverse courses of worship
from varied springs of fulfillment
have mingled in your meditation.
The manifold revelation of joy of The Infinite
has given form to a shrine of unity
   in your life
Where from far and near arrive salutations
   to which I add mine own.
               Rabindranath Tagore
(From the inside cover of *Prabuddha Bharata,* Sri Ramakrishna Centenary Number, February, 1936, in reproduction of Tagore's handwritten tribute.)

that supernatural powers, while he could have exercised them, were obstacles on the road to salvation and contributed to the swelling of the ego.[7] In this insight he followed the thought of India's great teachers from the time of the Buddha, although certain strains of the tradition, such as the *Yoga Sutras* of Patanjali, give prescriptions by which such powers may be attained.

Many persons came to recognize the vast spiritual magnetism which Ramakrishna radiated and began to regard him as an incarnation of deity. While we do not know when he adopted the name Ramakrishna, his self-consciousness is manifest in his statement, repeated many times, "One who was Rama and Krishna is now Ramakrishna."[8] Among those through whom he was introduced to modern Bengal, Keshab's name, once more, is crucial. The richness of their relationship is unfortunately somewhat diminished by the persisting partisan claims by the followers of each as to who influenced whom. This tendency was already noted in 1893 in a Vaishnava journal, which cites a mutual irradiation:

> Keshab Chander Sen used to tell his friends that he was gradually making him [Ramakrishna] a convert to Brahmoism; Ramakrishna, on the other hand, told us that he was gradually bringing Keshab Chandra back to Hinduism! And this was the motive which led them to meet so often. As a matter of fact, both were right and they influenced one another. It was Ram Krishna, who with his powerful mind, succeeded in convincing Keshab Chandra that there was much in Hinduism that was not to be found in other religions. And it was Keshab Chandra who taught Ramakrishna to take every good thing of every religion. At first, Ramakrishna was a pious Hindu devotee; under Keshab Chandra's teaching, he became a cosmopolitan in view.[9]

It may be plausibly objected that Ramakrishna's experiments with Islam and Christianity antedate his relationship with Keshab. Both men had a disposition to inquire beyond the limits of their own tradition; however, their inquiry certainly led them to a different manner of appropriation of the truths resident in other faiths. Ramakrishna's was almost exclusively mystical, based on his intuition of the nature of Islam and Christianity with very little personal interaction with its representatives, their institutions, or literature. This is in no way to question the depth of the experience, for the observer must have regard for the specific character of his intention, i.e., to experience the truth in these faiths. However one may assess the authenticity of these experiences, his resolution in pursuing them is clear. Keshab's education, use of English, travels to the West, etc., brought him into intimate association with organized Christianity. Max Müller relates how he and Keshab conversed with the learned Dr. Pusey, a conservative Christian at Oxford, who seemed finally to make at least a personal concession that a man of Keshab's faith, though remaining in the Hindu tradition, might claim "salvation."[10] Keshab's relations with liberal Christianity were far less grudging, and he established close working ties with Unitarianism. The Vaishnava newspaper would seem eminently credible in suggesting that Keshab could have communicated a measure of his personal experience of ecumenicity to Ramakrishna, just as it seems beyond refutation that Keshab's own devotional nature began to blossom, and with more characteristically Hindu expression, from his association with Ramakrishna. Some of the later more partisan claims by the followers of each may have stemmed from the ill feeling that developed between Vivekananda and Protap Chander Mazoomdar following the 1893 Parliament of Religions.

A single significant contact with Western Christianity—the only direct one recorded for Ramakrishna—was shared by Keshab and Ramakrishna. This was a brief encounter with the Rev. Joseph Cook, a representative of New England Protestant orthodoxy, on a tour of the Orient in 1882. Research reveals that it was the same Rev. Cook to whom Vivekananda apparently responded at the Parliament of Religions in Chicago in 1893. On February 23, 1882, Ramakrishna went by steamer from Dakshineswar to Calcutta as the guest of Keshab. The New Dispensation of February 26 of that year records that the missionaries Rev. Joseph Cook, Miss Pigot, and other Brahmos were present. "In the presence of all and to their wonder Paramahansa 'successively went through all the phases of spiritual excitement which characterizes him. Passing through a long interval of unconsciousness, he prayed, sang, and discoursed on spiritual subjects.' Rev. Cook who represented Christian theology and thought, seemed much impressed and interested."[11] *The Indian Mirror* in 1886 elaborated: "Mr. Cook, the American evangelist, who came to this country a few years ago, once witnessed Ramakrishna's divine exercises. He expressed his great surprise and remarked that he was not aware before that a man could become so immersed in divine spirit as to lose all perception of the external world."[12]

Cook's book *Orient* tells of his journey to the East, which had taken place during a period of over two years. He mentions leaving Calcutta, after a series of lectures, on February 26, 1882. While in that city he had a close association with Keshab, who impressed him greatly. "On invitation," he records, "I made an expedition with him and his pupils up the river Hooghly,"[13] apparently the incident referred to above. No mention is made of Ramakrishna, although a long chapter is devoted to Keshab and another brief one is added in the appendix, after Cook had heard of Keshab's death. It was Keshab, according to Cook, who moved a vote of thanks at Cook's last lecture in Calcutta. Despite his warm appreciation of his friend from India, Cook's assessment of him was not uncritical. He pointed out to his hearers the eclectic character of Keshab's thought and the excesses of the doctrine of personal inspiration which other observers had noted. Characteristically, as we shall discuss in Chapter Four, Cook also faulted the Brahmo Samaj for its failure to deliver men from sin.

Nevertheless, his tribute contained these words: "The news from the Ganges that Keshab Chander Sen is dead overwhelms me with a more profound sense of personal bereavement than I can now remember to have felt before at the departure of any public man.... Oh, my brother, my brother, how lonely the world seems without thee!"[14] Keshab's spirituality reached the heart of this champion of orthodox Christianity.

The cosmopolitan Keshab was warmly appreciative of Ramakrishna's spirituality, and three years after their meeting he published a ten-page Bengali booklet of Ramakrishna's sayings entitled *Paramahanser Ukti*. Among numerous references to Ramakrishna in the *New Dispensation* is one that says, "Paramahansa is serving as a marvellous connecting link between the Hindus and the New Dispensation Brahmos. Representatives of both are seen blended together in common meetings."[15] The official biographies of Ramakrishna, however, express the feeling that Keshab was too westernized to follow Ramakrishna fully, and look to other, more qualified persons who also began to associate with him, beginning in about 1879. These were the disciples for whom Ramakrishna had longed, and whose coming seems to have been preceded by a vision, as the story is told. The vision was particularly intense in the case of Naren (later Vivekananda), whom Ramakrishna first met when Naren was the singer of some devotional songs at the home of a friend. While an elaboration of their relationship will follow in the next chapter, we should here note in brief the nature of the association which developed between Ramakrishna and his followers. It seems not to have been a formal guru-disciple relationship, for Ramakrishna appears to have had a reluctance to initiate others or to assume the direct responsibility of the guru. Nevertheless, there was a definite circle of persons whom the sources term his disciples and a great deal of direct, personal spiritual guidance was imparted to them by Ramakrishna. Several, like M, as noted above, were householders, but the inner circle, who appear to have received his still more intimate, esoteric teaching, began early to adopt a monastic life style.

In Ramakrishna these persons found, in a very deep sense, the mother lode of Bengali religion. He seemed to embody the ecstatic devotion directed to the goddess Kali which had been current in Bengal since Ramprasad, whose exuberant poetic outpourings formed the language of so much of Ramakrishna's spiritual utterance. The latter's ecstatic mood is vividly conveyed in accounts of his devotion to Kali during the Kali Puja festival at Dakshineswar and a nearby Brahmo home in 1884. *The Gospel* records the home observance as follows:

Presently Trailokya [a Brahmo] began to sing to the accompaniment of drums and cymbals. Sri. Ramakrishna danced, intoxicated with divine love. Many times he went into *samadhi*. He stood still, his eyes fixed, his face beaming, with one hand on the shoulder of a beloved disciple. Coming down a little from the state of ecstasy, he danced again like a mad elephant. Regaining consciousness of the outer world, he improvised lines to the music:

O Mother; dance about Thy devotees!
Dance Thyself and make them dance as well.
O Mother, dance in the lotus of my heart;
Dance, O Thou the ever blessed Brahman!
Dance in all Thy world-bewitching beauty!

An indescribable scene. The exquisite and celestial dance of a child completely filled with ecstatic love of God and identified heart and soul with the Divine Mother! The Brahmo devotees danced around the Master again and again, attracted like iron to a magnet. In ecstatic voices they chanted the name of Brahman. Again, they chanted the name of the Divine Mother. Many of them wept like children, crying, "Mother, Mother!"[16]

The attitude of an abandon of joy is illustrated again in an incident in which, while riding in a carriage with two disciples in Calcutta, Ramakrishna came across a noisy group of drunkards. Rather than express disapproval, he entered into their inebriated mood himself and swayed from the carriage, muttering indistinctly, till one of his disciples feared for his safety. Certainly there is kinship in this note of ecstatic celebration with the rapturous lyrics of Ramprasad:

Make me mad, O Divine Mother!
There is no more use of knowledge and discrimination.
Make me intoxicated with the wine of Thy love.
O Mother; enchanter of the devotee's hearts!
    immerse me in the ocean of love.
In this Thy lunatic asylum, some laugh, some cry,
    and others dance in excess of joy.
Jesus, Moses and Chaitanya were, O Mother, unconscious
    in ecstasy of love.
Alas! O Mother! when shall I be blessed, mixing
    with them?
In heaven there is a fair of lunatics; there Master
    and disciple are alike.
Who can fathom the mystery of the play of love?
Thou art mad with love, O Mother, crown of lunatics!
Make poor Prasada rich, O Mother, in the treasure
    of love.[17]

Yet certainly there were moments of serious and sober reflection. We see him in one such mood the evening of Kali Puja at the temple, the day before the festive occasion cited above. He directed a disciple, "Perform the worship carefully. There is a sheep to be slaughtered." Yet, when the sheep was being taken to the block, Ramakrishna returned to his room. "He could not bear the sight."[18]

It was to this deeply sensitive man that a few representatives of educated, westernized Bengal now began to turn. What did they find in Ramakrishna, the illiterate little man in the Kali temple on the banks of the Ganges? In a province whose leaders had been struggling to raise the economic status of the people, to develop in them the first signs of political awareness, who were seeking to purify the social order of long-standing affronts to human dignity, Ramakrishna was almost wholly uninterested in social reform. His was purely a spiritual genius, couched in emotional, often unorthodox expression which seems peculiarly Bengali in character. Any integration of his message and the needs of the whole of India, striving to move into the modern age, must have seemed impossible to most. But a few began slowly, with great difficulty, to discern the possibility of such a synthesis.

Chapter Three

VIVEKANANDA: THE YEARS OF PREPARATION

The Hindu tradition in which he was reared gave shape to many of the archetypal expressions which guided the life of Vivekananda, born as Narendranath Dutt on a Hindu festival day, January 12, 1863. His devout mother, after having seen a vision of Shiva, in which he agreed to be born as her son, dedicated him to Shiva, the god of ascetics. Something of this identification may have been openly impressed upon him from an early date, for he relates that when he was naughty as a small child, his parents would say something such as "Dear, dear, so many austerities, yet Shiva sent us this demon after all, instead of a good soul!" A particular mode of correction is still more graphic. When he was very rebellious (which, by the accounts, occurred rather often) a can of water might be emptied over him, with the invocation, "Shiva! Shiva!" which, he reports, would immediately quiet him. The impression was sufficiently vivid that, as he later said, "Even now, when I feel mischievous, that word keeps me straight."[1]

But if the tradition conveyed to him a model of renunciation, it also sanctioned *bhoga* (enjoyment or indulgence), and both of these alternative pulsations were communicated through his immediate male ancestors. His grandfather had followed the pattern of the *ashramas* or life stages, and had become a *sannyasin*, or wandering ascetic, after the birth of his first son, having fulfilled the duty befitting the householder stage. Naren's father, however, was a lawyer, a cultured man of affairs, sophisticated in his knowledge of the arts, with a particular interest in Islamic culture. He was generous to a fault, fond of creature comforts, especially enjoying travel. He was little interested in religion. The mother in the household is described, in

37

contrast, as deeply religious, tranquil, and dignified. The brief portraits of her in the biographies seem formalized, as though depicting Sita, the ideal wife of Indian mythology. Vivekananda paid tribute to her many times in his messages on Indian womanhood in the West.

The alternative paths of enjoyment and renunciation are also said to have appeared to Naren in a vision which repeatedly came in his youth. "Every night just as I fell asleep two dreams took shape. In one I saw myself among the great ones of the earth, the possessor of riches, honours, power and glory; and I felt that the capacity to attain all these was in me. But the next instant I saw myself renouncing all worldly things, dressed in a simple loincloth, living on alms, sleeping at the foot of a tree; and I thought that I was capable of living thus, like the Rishis of old. Of these two pictures the second took the upper hand and I felt that only thus could a man attain supreme bliss. . . . And I fell asleep in the foretaste of that bliss."[2] Again, the alternate paths form a common paradigm in the Indian tradition from the time of the Buddha, who seems to have been a strong influence in his choice of the path of the *sannyasin*. The diary of another disciple relates still another vision, this one singular and overpowering. Vivekananda beheld a serene, shaven-headed figure, with staff and begging bowl. The image so frightened the astounded Naren that he rushed from the room. Yet he reported to the disciple an almost instantaneous feeling of regret in having done so, for the figure never appeared again, and Naren felt that it might have communicated something to him verbally. Later, reflecting, he seemed to make an identification. "I now think that it was the Lord Buddha that I saw."[3] In any case, Vivekananda was later to draw on the Buddha's example for his own understanding of the role of the monk in the Ramakrishna Order.

That his parents, despite his mother's earlier dedication of him, felt that the *sannyasin* model might exert too strong an influence upon the child is evidenced in an experience which he related to Sister Nivedita. As a child of perhaps two, playing in rags, he recalls having been locked in to prevent his giving away too much when a beggar came. Later there did not seem to be a wholehearted acceptance of his celibate state by his family, either, for they urged him to take a bride.

His more serious nature was usually hidden from public view

during his school days. His friends often marveled at his preparation in classes, for he was always ready for active games, seemingly little given to study. In fact, however, he would pore over his books late at night, isolated in his room. There seemed to be a certain reluctance at this stage to expose the scholarly image. But the athletic disposition was clearly evidenced. With a strong build and physical courage, he excelled in a variety of sports, chiefly boxing, swimming, rowing, and horsemanship. Strength became a cardinal virtue, and he abhorred the bodily weakness in many of his countrymen which he felt contributed to a spineless condition of the nation as a whole. At times he could wish for the diet of Vedic days, in which the eating of meat was not prohibited. He could say later to the young men of India, "You will be nearer to heaven through football than through the study of the Gita."[4] Their bodies must become strong vessels, fit to contain the strong spiritual wine of their inheritance. Nationally, a new sense of nerve had to be grafted into the heart of India, whose people, under British rule, had become a servile, bootlicking race.

From the above language we may discern something of the warrior spirit which caused him to be spoken of on occasion as "a true-born *Kshatriya.*" In fact he belonged to the *Kayastha* caste, rather numerous in Bengal, which on occasion sought to claim *Kshatriya* origins. Their traditional occupations, however, were those of clerks and letter writers. These gave them special access to English education, as they were often found in service to British officials, as earlier to Mohammedans. Other occupational choices found them generally as a part of the Bengal *bhadralok,* or cultural elite, seldom engaged in manual labor. Education and occupation, then, gave them some status in Bengal society, but they were still ranked as upper class *shudras.**

As a child, Vivekananda reports that he was considerably given to the practice of meditation. He relates that he would see a bright light upon closing his eyes when retiring. This happened so regularly that he regarded it as something which everyone experienced, and

*Something of the *Kshatriya* militancy surfaced in the nationalist agitation in Bengal a few years after Vivekananda's death, in which they were the most numerous caste represented among those convicted of revolutionary crimes or killed in commission of such crimes. Nirmal Kumar Bose, *Culture and Society in India* (Calcutta: Asia Publishing House, 1967), pp. 334–37.

was surprised to find that this was not so. Ramakrishna explicitly asked him whether he experienced this or not, evidently regarding it as the mark of a great spiritual past and an inborn habit of meditation.

With his entrance into the Scottish Presbyterian College in Calcutta (founded by Duff), Naren's intellectual nature began openly to mature; he avidly immersed himself in the exploration of such varied fields as astronomy, philosophy, mathematics, medical science, and music. He wrote tunes and published a documented essay on the science and philosophy of Indian music. There was something of a reverence for the scientific model, and much of his understanding of religion later would be conveyed in scientific terminology. In music, his beautiful baritone voice was conspicuously used in singing the sacred music of his people, and biographies of Ramakrishna are replete with references to Naren's breaking into song spontaneously and at the request of Ramakrishna and others.

His diverse interests caused a series of intellectual crises during his student days. The surface theism of the Brahmo Samaj was fashionable, and for a time this appeal alternated with a philosophical skepticism. None of his scholastic pursuits, immersed as he became in them, seemed able to give him the satisfaction which he sought. His own identity was still to emerge beyond the maze of fascinating paths which beckoned.

In one of the two accounts of his initial meeting with Ramakrishna the explicit religious character of his search is evidenced. He states that he addressed to Ramakrishna the question which he had put to many a religious sage, "Sir, have you seen God?" Instead of the usual evasions or qualified responses, Ramakrishna's was amazingly direct: "Yes, my son, I have seen God, just as I see you before me, only much more intensely."[5] Stunned by the prompt and unambiguous reply, he was drawn to discover the source of such assurance. In another account, however, their first acquaintance came when Ramakrishna asked Naren to come to Dakshineswar after having heard him sing in the home of a friend. Naren, who was eighteen and had just begun his university career, brought some of his fellow students with him. Ramakrishna, deeply moved by his singing, passed into ecstasy. Naren continues:

After I had sung he suddenly got up, and taking me by the hand, led

me to the north verandah, and closed the door behind us. We were alone.
Nobody could see us. . . . To my great surprise he began to weep for joy.
He held me by the hand and addressed me very tenderly, as if I were
somebody he had known familiarly for a long time. He said, "Ah! You
have come so late. Why have you been so unkind as to make me wait so
long? My ears are tired of hearing the futile words of other men. Oh! how
I have longed to pour out my spirit into the breast of somebody fitted to
receive my inner experiences! . . ." He continued thus sobbing the while.
Then standing before me with his hands together he said, "Lord, I know
that you are the ancient sage Nara, the incarnation of Narajana, reborn
on earth to take away the misery of humanity." I was amazed. "What have
I come to see?" I thought. "He ought to be put in a strait-jacket!" . . .
But I remained outwardly unmoved and let him talk. He took my hand
again and said, "Promise me that you will come to see me again alone,
and soon!"

    Naren promised in order to free himself from his strange host, but
he vowed within himself never to return.[6]

    The rest of the visit was quite normal. Ramakrishna treated his
visitor with simple and familiar kindness as if nothing had happened.
Ramakrishna discoursed on spiritual matters to the total group, and
the wisdom of his words appeared to modify Naren's earlier resolve
not to come again to Dakshineswar, for a month later he was back.
Once more, the account is so striking as to merit quotation:

    I found him [Ramakrishna] alone sitting on his small bed. He was
glad to see me and called me affectionately to sit near him on one side
of the bed. But a moment later I saw him convulsed with some emotion.
His eyes were fixed upon me, he muttered under his breath, and drew
slowly nearer. I thought he was going to make some eccentric remark as
on the previous occasion. But before I could stop him, he had placed his
right foot on my body. The contact was terrible. With my eyes open I saw
the walls and everything in the room whirling and vanishing into nothing-
ness. . . . The whole universe and my own individuality were at the same
time almost lost in a nameless void, which swallowed up everything that
is. I was terrified, and believed I was face to face with death. I could not
stop myself from crying out, "What are you doing? I have parents at
home. . . ." Then he began to laugh, and passing his hand over my breast,
he said, "All is well. Let us leave it at that for the moment! It will come,
all in good time." He had no sooner said these words than the strange
phenomena disappeared. I came to myself again, and everything, both
outside and in, was as before.[7]

    Successive visits, despite the defenses which Naren indicates,
were of similar character. The following visit saw Naren passing into
a trance at Ramakrishna's touch as before. When he came to himself
he saw Ramakrishna looking at him and stroking his chest. While
Naren did not speak of what he experienced upon losing conscious-

ness, Ramakrishna later related that he had probed the depths of Naren's consciousness at the time concerning his spiritual past and the work he had been born to do. He was satisfied with his young friend's potentiality for greatness.

The powerful dynamic of these encounters convinced Naren that he was in the presence of a spiritual giant, but he was still not ready to become his disciple. As one detesting all forms of sentimental piety, such as tears or anything which seemed effeminate, he felt threatened by emotional excess. Yet, while he was often embarrassed and irritated by Ramakrishna's oversolicitous affection and concern, the spiritual magnetism was drawing him. He would visit Ramakrishna once or twice a week, with Ramakrishna seeking him out if he were absent for a longer time. Gradually the testing became mutual, with Naren coming again and again, finding that Ramakrishna would not speak to him, but still returning. When this period passed, another long one followed in which Ramakrishna urged Naren to express his doubts. Naren soon discovered that Ramakrishna possessed a great intellect underneath the emotional nature which had seemed overpowering at first. "Outwardly he was all Bhakta [devotional temperament] but inwardly all Jnanin [intellectual temperament]. . . . I am the exact opposite."[8] Naren felt that, as he had passed into the life of the serious scholar from a boyhood given to mischief and active frivolity, now through his relationship with Ramakrishna his own deeply emotional nature began to surface.

It was a perplexing transition for some of Naren's fellow students to behold. One, later a noted Indian educator, expressed his feelings at witnessing the growing attachment of Naren to Ramakrishna, with participation in the cult of Kali worship:

> I watched with intense interest the transformation that went on under my eyes. The attitude of a young rampant Vedantist—cum Hegelian—cum revolutionary like myself towards the cult of religious ecstasy and Kali-worship may be easily imagined; and the spectacle of a born iconoclast and free-thinker like Vivekananda, a creative and dominating intelligence, a tamer of souls, himself caught in the meshes of what appeared to me an uncouth, supernatural mysticism, was a riddle which my philosophy of the pure reason could scarcely read at the time.[9]

But for Naren there was no complete acceptance of Ramakrishna and Kali until he had suffered severe hardships and spiritual anguish after the death of his father, which followed the completion of his college course. The sudden heart attack which felled his father left the family ill prepared to meet debts which had been mounting. Naren, unable to find permanent employment and finding his friends less than helpful, began to question a deity which could allow such suffering as his family, along with millions of others throughout India, was experiencing. When he asked Ramakrishna, who had never lost belief in him despite his doubts, to pray for his concerns, Ramakrishna said that he should do so himself. Entering the temple of Kali, Naren went into a spiritual ecstasy; this was repeated twice again as, upon emerging, he would realize that he had forgotten his purpose in going and would be told by Ramakrishna to return. It became his decisive transformation, in which he was delivered from his own private concerns to worship the Mother. Connected as it was with circumstances surrounding his father's death, this may be viewed as a sudden assumption of a mature identity partially occasioned by the loss of the father. One may speculate that there was no such urgency before, because of filial dependence, to make decisions crucial in determining his adult destiny. His lack of success in finding a position through which he might have been able to provide for the needs of his family may have influenced his choice of the alternate path of the *sannyasin*.

Observers of Indian family life note a long period of family pampering, with particular dependence on the father, though with little familiarity toward him.[10] If his father had lived, could Naren have withstood family pressures to marry and secure a job? Filial obedience might have dictated acceptance of that course, but in the father's absence Naren and the other young men sought another nurturing environment. At Dakshineswar they found one free of family pressures but which nevertheless fulfilled their dependency needs.[11]

Other studies may yield additional understanding of Vivekananda's development at this stage. It has been suggested that the indulgence of the Indian male child results in a narcissistic behavior pattern in contrast to the Western oedipal model. A strong ego ideal may thus develop in the absence of a punishing superego, and in the exceptional person the resultant moral energy, when attached to the available abstract and absolute goals, may sharply separate him from ordinary men. Heroic models of the ascetic and the warrior are exalted for such persons. Girls, who are treated with less indulgence than boys, often demonstrate a more practical character as a result.[12]

One incident from the life of Vivekananda would seem to illustrate the strength of the ego ideal conjoined with the strong wine of the doctrine of the Atman (the supreme universal self). His biographer, Romain Rolland, notes that Naren, in some of his more juvenile moments, seemed to have been intoxicated with the fumes of the Atman. Sensitive to possible excesses, Rolland adds, "The air of great heights must be treated with caution. When all the gods have been dethroned and nothing is left but the 'Self,' beware of vertigo!"[13] The incident which he cites in support of this observation is contained in the following dialogue between Naren and Nag Mahasya, one of Ramakrishna's devoted household followers:

Nag: "Everything happens according to the will of the Mother. She is the Universal Will. She moves, but men imagine that it is they who move."

But the impetuous *Naren* replied, "I do not agree with you, with your He or She. I am the Soul. In me is the Universe. In me it is born, it floats and disappears."

Nag: "You have not power enough to change one single black hair into a white one, and yet you speak of the Universe! Without God's will not one blade of grass dies!"

Naren: "Without my will the Sun and Moon could not live. At my will the Universe goes like a machine."

And *Ramakrishna* with a smile at his youthful pride, said to Nag: "Truly Naren can say that, for he is like a drawn sword." And the pious Nag bowed down before the young Elect of the Mother.[14]

Naren carried with him, nevertheless, a sensitivity to suffering which enabled him to identify with the oppressed and downtrodden in his mature message. His later mission to the West, besides its spiritual motive, was intended to secure food for his people. "I do not believe," he was to say, "in a God who will give me eternal bliss in heaven, and who cannot give me bread here. Thus it does not follow that I am to accept the indignities of the world. Rather it is my business to abolish them."[15]

While according to the records Ramakrishna had recognized Naren from the first as his successor, only a few months or a year before Ramakrishna's death could Naren wholly accept him as master. In a memorable kind of Elijah-Elisha scene a few days before Ramakrishna's death from throat cancer, he bequeathed his spiritual powers to Naren. Naren, called to his side, heard Ramakrishna softly say, "Today I have given you my all, and now I am only a poor fakir possessing nothing. By this power you will do infinite good to the world, and not until it is accomplished will you return."[16] Still earlier, Ramakrishna had indicated to his favorite disciple that his mission was not to be that of the lonely, isolated *sannyasin*. When Naren implored his master to show him the way to *nirvekalpa samadhi* or ultimate bliss, he was given a surprisingly sharp rebuke by his gentle master. "Shame on you!" Ramakrishna exclaimed. "I never thought you to be so mean as to be anxious for your own salvation only whereas you have powers to do so much good to mankind!"[17] The earlier vision of the Buddha seemed confirmed by the Master's own instruction.

Naren interpreted the parting gift of Ramakrishna as also the conveying of the power of Kali, for he regarded Ramakrishna as her incarnation. She became, from his eyes, the energizing force in his life. But his own rebel temperament, rather reflecting that of the goddess, persisted even in his relationship with Kali as he described it. In a letter written in 1899, he could confide, "I fight and do not give in. Ravana got his release in three births by fighting the Lord Himself! It is glorious to fight Mother."[18] Kali's own tempestuous character he recognized in the conscious embracing of life's most vexing problems. "How few," he would say, "have dared to worship death or Kali! Let us worship Death! Let us embrace the Terrible, because it is terrible; not asking that it be toned down. Let us take misery for misery's own sake!"[19] The goddess thus became interiorized as a component of Vivekananda's own manliness. "This is my new gospel. Do even evil like a man! Be wicked, if you must, on a great scale!"[20] If his rhetoric seems excessively flamboyant, it may perhaps be best understood in relation to his nationalist sentiments. India had, in his thought, become timid and must have the courage of Mother Kali instilled into her national fiber as Mother India.

The Mother's dictates were also communicated interpersonally through individuals other than Ramakrishna, particularly certain women whose counsel became important to him and who had the effect of drawing him into life. While he could reject his family's urging that he take a bride because of the conflict of this counsel with the model of the *sannyasin*, his family members seem to have continued to exert an influence upon him. On his long, lonely pilgrimage in the

Himalayas, when he received word of his sister's suicide, it reminded
him of his mission to minister to human suffering and recalled him
to the world.[21] Ramakrishna's widow, the Holy Mother of the Order
which was to develop, also incarnated the guiding principle of the
Mother Goddess. Except for occasional meetings, Vivekenanda had
been removed from his brother monks in Bengal for a number of years
before departing for America in 1893. Yet before making the journey,
by letter he sought the counsel of Sarada Devi rather than that of his
fellow disciples of Ramakrishna and received her endorsement. Still
later, we observe certain of his female followers in the West—particularly Mrs. Hale and her daughters in Chicago and Mrs. Ole
(Sarah) Bull, the wealthy widow of a noted violinist, whom he was
to call Dhira Mata (the steady mother)—exercising something of a
mothering role toward him.

The important task, at this point, would be to recognize how
the Mother Goddess and her representative, Ramakrishna, helped
Naren to assume his mature identity in contrast to that urged on him
by his natural mother and other family members. Here it seems to
me that western psychological categories are of little relevance in
explaining the developmental choice which he made at this stage.
Any attempt at application of an oedipal conflict would appear to
belong wholly to the realm of conjecture, partly because he says so
little about his father.[22] It may be somewhat more tempting to attempt to see manifestations of Jungian archetypes, particularly those
of the *anima,* the seductress element in the unconscious which seeks
to draw one into life, as exhibited in rather irrational, emotional
behavior which surfaces in contrast to the more typically ordered,
"masculine," image.[23] This, however, seems artificial, just as does the
naive judgment that Vivekananda at this point was simply retreating
from the vexing responsibilities which had suddenly been foisted
upon him with the death of his father.

A more fruitful attempt at understanding may follow from a
look at a few of the complexities implicit in the Indian concept of
dharma. Each person has the task of discerning his own *dharma* and
performing it, in conjunction with the counsel of the Gita: "Better
one's own *dharma,* (tho) imperfect, than another's *dharma* well-
performed;/Better death in (doing) one's own *dharma;*/Another's
dharma brings danger."[24] Within the social order, caste affiliation

obviously has a great deal to do with the discernment of one's *dharma,* as this in turn reflects tendencies accumulated in previous births. Variables of temperament, interests, and abilities which emerge in one's development in this lifetime may, within limits, modify the inherited social and vocational role. There are also the tasks which prescribe the *dharma* fitting to the four traditional *ashramas* (life stages), so that the *dharma* of one stage is not appropriate to another. Complexity becomes intense for some as they confront alternate models by which certain of the *ashramas* may be prolonged or others bypassed altogether. What are the social and psychological dynamics by which the transition is normatively made from the *dharma* of the *brahmacharya,* or student, to that of the *grihastha,* or householder? One can well imagine a difficult transition for many.

Even if the alternate choice of the *sannyasin* path is well authenticated within the tradition, it would seem to require a strong legitimation by an internalized or interpersonal authority figure, particularly when the family needs one's bread-winning services so crucially as did Naren's family at the time. In this case, the mother surrogate who issued the more dominant imperative was that of Ramakrishna-Kali.* Significantly, before fully committing himself to his new course, Naren required the assurance of Ramakrishna, gained through spiritual insight and not through a material guarantee, that the needs of his family would be met. Although Ramakrishna sought and gained this assurance with some reluctance, on receiving it Naren felt free to pursue the dictates of the vision which came to him in the Kali temple. His new Mother had pledged the sustenance of the other, so that he could feel that he was honoring both of what had appeared as the contrary urgings of his *dharma.*

Following Ramakrishna's death, there was a period of consolidation by his monastic disciples, largely under Naren's leadership, but then each seemed to feel an urgency to pursue a private path for a time. Naren remained for two years at the rented, dilapidated house which they were able to secure for their monastic life, supervising the

*Erickson, *op. cit.,* p. 63, reports that Anasuya Sarabhai, who was early orphaned, when asked what the essence of Gandhi's presence was to her, replied with the words, "Oh, he was my mother." The culture would seem to permit a freer symbolic expression of a relationship, in which the term, "Mother" may be diffused, and applied without threat to a nurturant person of either sex. Certainly Ramakrishna, interpersonally, was Kali for Vivekananda.

training and sharing with his fellow disciples the very real poverty in which their early corporate life was passed. They did not at this time establish any formal rules, nor did they undertake any of the social service which was later to characterize the order. But there was a richness of shared memory of their days with their master which prevented a total dispersion in spite of their periodic wanderings.

Naren's first ventures from the Calcutta vicinity were brief ones, to Benares and other holy places; but in 1890, chafing at the regimen of the settled life, he left on a journey of almost seven years that was to take him throughout India and then to North America and Europe. Northern India, with its honored shrines and places of pilgrimage, first beckoned, and at times Naren would have the companionship of fellow disciples. The solitary urge grew still more intense, however, and he indicated forcefully his desire to go his own way. That there was a continuation of his search for identity is apparent in the different names which he assumed during this period. Ramakrishna had given him one, Kamalaksha (lotus-eyed), which he had dropped immediately, and other names were used briefly and then changed, partly for reasons of privacy, for other disciples, feeling the need of his leadership, kept wanting to attach themselves to him. He vacillated for a few weeks as to whether he should affiliate with another guru, Pavhari Baba, a teacher of *hatha* yoga, which uses physical exercises as a means to attaining spiritual enlightenment; his motive may have partly been to overcome a certain illness attendant on the deprivations endured during this ascetic period. But Pavhari Baba had a larger appeal. He was an extremely learned man who had retired into a hermit life and practiced severe austerities. On the verge of accepting initiation by the new guru, Naren was deterred by visions of Ramakrishna each night for up to three weeks, and finally gave up the notion of such an attachment. Disloyalty to the Master seemed to be implied, and perhaps also compromise with a growing feeling that private mysticism was not to be his path. Pavhari Baba's saintliness was widely acknowledged, and he had been visited by Keshab Chandra Sen and also by Naren himself when Ramakrishna was still alive. Several years later Pavhari ritually anointed his body, sat in a sacrificial pit, and set fire to himself. Vivekananda grieved for the only near rival as guru which Ramakrishna was to have.

During his three years of wandering in India, Naren moved

increasingly into contact with the needs of the modern country, seeing its struggles and suffering, searching for a way to apply his people's ancient insights to their present bereft condition. It was a time for meeting the illiterate and the educated, the masses and the maharajas, for learning and teaching. Occasions for teaching became more frequent as his intuition of his message began to take shape. Encouragement came from influential sources, such as the Maharaja of Khetri whom he met in his travels through western India. He heard reports of the Parliament of Religions which was to take place in Chicago in 1893; a plan began to emerge in his mind.

This crystallized in a moment of rare vision when, his Indian travels complete, he stood at the tip of the Peninsula, at Cape Comorin. Rapturously he rushed into the temple of the Virgin Goddess, Kanyakumari, to worship. But one more act remained before his native pilgrimage was perfected. A short distance out in the ocean, he saw a small rock to which he resolved to swim through the shark-infested waters. Reaching it, he looked northward to Mother India. Standing outside it, a new measure of objectivity enabled him to see his homeland as never before. His arms outstretched, a great intuition of compassion began to well up within him. How, where was he to secure help for his people? The West seemed to hold the key to the world's storehouse of material goods, but what did he have to give in exchange? India's unmined treasures lay in the depths of her religious truths. The young educated *sannyasin* felt that he could share that with the people of the West, perhaps as no other could.

He traveled directly to Madras, the nearest city of consequence, and started to see how his own people would respond to his vision. A following gathered; some who now urged him to go to the West apparently had more certainty than he as to the wisdom of the venture. Some members of the Hindu community gathered to appoint him as their spokesman to the Parliament of Religions, although other more officially designated representatives had already been chosen. Monetary sponsorship was also forthcoming, chiefly from his friend, the Maharaja of Khetri, who wanted Naren to come again to western India to bless the new-born son for whom he had prayed. There, almost on the eve of his departure for the West, Naren assumed the name Vivekananda at the Maharaja's request. The name referred to the power of discrimination which the Maharaja saw so strongly evidenced in his young friend. And, while it may (like earlier names) have been assumed only provisionally at the time, his swift rise to fame in the West would permit no later alteration. It is interesting to note that although shortly before he had told two of his brother disciples, Brahmananda and Turiyananda, about his impending voyage, they and the others in Bengal were not certain for some time after reports began to come back from the Parliament of Religions that the colorful Swami Vivekananda of whom they read was their own Naren.

The young man who now began to travel west was just over thirty years of age. Educated in a Presbyterian College in Calcutta, he had nevertheless developed some quite strong feelings of resentment against western, and particularly Christian, influences. He admitted almost no direct indebtedness to missionaries, singling out only Mr. Hastie, the old Scottish headmaster at the College whom he had deeply admired, but who seemed to be cast in a quite different mold from that in which he saw other representatives of Christianity in India. Mr. Hastie, instead of seeking to convert him to Christianity, first suggested that he go to see Ramakrishna.

Vivekananda's relationship with Islam appears to have been substantial during his wanderings, particularly in northern India, and his reflections from that period indicate a much warmer appreciation which is difficult to fathom historically. Islam presented no current challenge to Hinduism, however, and its earlier invasions by the sword could be effectively allowed to recede in one's consciousness. By this time Islam had been generally incorporated into the Indian stream, whereas Christianity still seemed an alien force.

Despite his fervent pride in the sublime spiritual insights of the ancient *rishis* (seers) of India, Vivekananda retained something of a fascination for the West, which must partially account for his decision to travel there. This had been his legacy from the Brahmo Samaj. At that time no sea voyage could be undertaken lightly by a Hindu. Those who traveled west were judged by orthodox Hinduism to incur contamination from *mllechchan* (foreign) influences which could be purged only through strenuous ritual countermeasures upon return. His act in no sense could have been seen as that of a revivalist at the time, although he was later to be so labeled generally. His example as a champion of Hinduism journeying to the West was implicitly an act of reform. We shall see that it was so evaluated and felt to be highly offensive to those who retained oversight of the place most dear to Vivekananda, the Kali Temple at Dakshineswar.

Both revivalist and reformer traveled west in the single psyche of Vivekananda, whose task, in accordance with his newly acquired name, would be to discriminate between the false and the true, the eternal and the ephemeral in cultures East and West. The revivalist was informed by Ramakrishna; the reformer, more than Vivekananda and his followers would customarily concede, was instructed by the Brahmo Samaj and the Christian missionary.

Chapter Four

VIVEKANANDA IN THE WEST

At 1415 North Dearborn Avenue in Chicago there stood, until 1966, a large, formerly fashionable dwelling with the figure of a bear seated upright atop it. Like many other such buildings, it has since been torn down to make room for a high-rise apartment complex. Yet this structure's demolition was lamented by a few residents of Chicago, and by others visiting there from their native India. Certainly lacking in symmetry and utility by mid-twentieth century standards, it was nevertheless something of a shrine. For it was here that, seventy-three years earlier, one of India's most colorful interpreters, a stranger in a foreign land, met with unusual hospitality. Arriving late by train, with no one to meet him, and having lost the address of the place where the Parliament of Religions was to meet, Swami Vivekananda asked directions in the station. Receiving no help, he slept in a large, empty box in a corner of the railroad station. The next morning, wandering as a *sannyasin* from door to door, he was rudely treated and dismissed from a number of homes. "He was in a city that knows . . . a thousand and one ways of making money— except one, the way of St. Francis, the vagrancy of God."[1] Exhausted but not in despair, he sat down on the curb, accepting whatever might come to him.

He did not have long to wait, for a woman across the street, from a window in the house on North Dearborn, noting his strange appearance, asked if he were not a delegate to the Parliament of Religions. He was invited in, given refreshment, and taken to be introduced to the President of the Parliament, who was a personal friend of his hostess, Mrs. G. W. Hale. The Swami resided for a time with the Hale family, who became some of the most faithful followers of this "cyclonic monk of India." This was only one of a series of seemingly fortuitous circumstances in America which served Vivekananda; he had come without credentials, representing no organized body, seemingly unaware that delegates from India had been selected nearly two years previously. And yet, through doors being opened by persons of influence who recognized that he had a message, he now stood on the threshold of his impressive debut at the Parliament.

The Chicago Parliament of Religions, removed from it as we are by about eighty years, remains an amazing ecumenical achievement. Nothing of its magnitude had been attempted before and seldom since has a like gathering approached its dimension. The idea had originated with Charles C. Bonney, a lawyer, in 1889, and his liberal vision began swiftly to enlist support. It was conceived as one of a series of congresses recognizing human achievement in government, jurisprudence, finance, science, literature, education, and religion, all to be held in connection with the Columbian Exposition or Chicago World's Fair. All of the congresses were outlined by Mr. Bonney as Chairman and were held from May 15 until October 28, 1893, in the newly erected Art Institute on the shores of Lake Michigan.

The Parliament of Religions was actually one of two parts of the Congress on Religion. The separate denominations, sects, and movements held their own meetings from August 27 to October 15. But it was the later feat which captured the world's imagination, the coming together of representatives of the great religious traditions. This, also, was organized by Christians, although Jewish, Unitarian, and Swedenborgian representation on the central committee was included. The committee sent out its invitation to the world's faiths in June of 1891, and they responded.

The representation from India alone is sufficient to indicate the magnitude of the response; the following addressed the Parliament:

Professor G. N. Chakravarti of Allahabad (Theosophist).
Narasima Chaira of Madras—gave a Vaishnava message with a criticism of missionary tactics.
Manilal Ni Dvivedi of Bombay—his was one of the longest addresses printed, a detailed, orthodox outline of Hinduism (read by Gandhi).
Virchand A. Gandhi of Bombay—honorary secretary to the Jain Association of India.
Protap Chander Mozoomdar of Calcutta—minister and leader of the Brahmo Samaj of India.
B. B. Nagarkar of Bombay—minister of the Brahmo Samaj of India.

Miss Jeannie Serabji of Bombay—formerly Parsee, now Christian.
Swami Vivekananda—"A monk of the orthodox Brahminical religion."

Two lawyers, Siddhu Ram and Jinda Ram, the latter representing a temperance society, were also present on the platform on the opening day of the Parliament.

H. Dharmapala was listed as General Secretary of the Maha Bodhi Society of Calcutta, though he actually resided in Ceylon.

Jinanji Jasmshodji Modi gave an extensive paper on the Parsee faith.

Lakeshnie Narain spoke as secretary of the Kayasth Community.

Other Western Christian missionaries then living in India were among the speakers.

Mrs. Annie Besant, who was to leave shortly after for India for the first time, spoke at the Congress of Theosophists. Miss Henrietta Muller of London, who was later to be associated with Vivekananda in India after being his hostess for a time in London, also spoke in the Congress of Theosophists.[2]

A listing of the speakers from North America would read like a Who's Who for the period. The attention of the world, and certainly of the people of the United States, was fastened on this great gathering. A complex of hopes were invested in it; some saw it as a platform in which the clear superiority of Christianity would vanquish all rival faiths. Others anticipated that a larger measure of fellow feeling would emerge from the lifting up of the noblest aspirations of the world's religions. Some sense of a world community, with a humanitarian imperative to respond to the rising demand for education, economic justice, and political freedom, lay at the heart of those who now gazed in hope towards Chicago.

Many dignitaries, including President Bonney and Chairman J. H. Barrows, had addressed the Parliament on the day of its opening. Vivekananda had been pressed several times to speak by one in charge but had demurred till late in the afternoon, being, by his own testimony, devoid of assurance and having no written text. Finally he consented to speak, and, invoking the goddess Sarasvati, he strode to the platform. In the turban and brilliant orange robe given him by the Maharaja of Khetri, he was an impressive sight. Hardly had he pronounced the ringing, impassioned words of his salutation, "Sisters and brothers of America!" when hundreds arose from their seats and applauded what seemed to be the real keynote of the assembly. The message which followed was brief, but the popular appeal which it stimulated became a mandate for further appearances. In addition to his first message, he spoke ten times at the Parliament.

With his unique gifts and commanding presence Vivekananda, by many accounts, was an electrifying figure. *The New York Herald* termed him "undoubtedly the greatest figure in the Parliament of Religions."[3] Merwin-Marie Snell, Chairman of the Scientific Section of the Parliament, later said, "No religious body made so profound an impression upon the Parliament and the American people at large, as did Hinduism. . . . And by far the most important and typical representative of Hinduism was Swami Vivekananda, who, in fact, was beyond question the most popular and influential man in the Parliament."[4] A few such superlative tributes might intimate that the Parliament was a one-man performance, which was most surely not the case. A number of others also became favorites, and among the Indian representatives, similar tributes to Protap Chander Mozoomdar and Dharmapala, who also spoke on a number of occasions, are recorded.[5] A reading of the accounts of the proceedings during those historic days cannot fail to convey a profound impression of the vast array of wisdom which assembled in Chicago.

It was clearly, however, not the intent of those planning the Parliament to advance the cause of an alien faith nor to promote one of its representatives. There were certainly sectarian and parochial assumptions behind many of the Christian conveners and speakers at the Parliament. Patronizing concessions were often thinly disguised beneath a mantle of harmony. These in turn evoked defensive responses to charges made by missionaries concerning moral practices in nations where faiths other than Christianity were dominant. Most histories of the Ramakrishna Movement understandably highlight the dramatic role played by Vivekananda in the Parliament, but they do not display the tendencies found in one to exalt their representative by attributing prejudiced and bigoted attitudes uniformly to the Christian clergy present and to indulge in belittling references to the other Indian representatives.[6]

One apparent confrontation is nevertheless of particular interest because of the personalities involved, Vivekananda and the Rev. Joseph Cook of Boston. Cook rather personifies one of the religious currents operative in America in the late nineteenth century, *i.e.,* the orthodox reaction to the Unitarian and Transcendental thought which had been so strongly influential earlier in the century. It is surprising to read the classic utterances of men such as Channing, Emerson, and Theodore Parker from the vantage point of current religious plural-ism and to appreciate that a storm of controversy had originally attended their statement. Channing's principles of Biblical criticism have become almost axiomatic; Emerson's call for a broader human basis for morality and for a doctrine of miracle which "is one with the blowing clover and the falling rain,"[7] do not alarm us; Parker's delineation of the transient status of seeming absolutes of Christian doctrine simply remind us that our grasp of the ultimate is always relative. But in the nineteenth century the backlash was strong. One of the bulwarks of orthodoxy was Joseph Cook who, as related in Chapter Two, met Ramakrishna and Keshab in India in 1882. Cook, armed with a scholarly mind and educated in Yale, Harvard, Andover Newton Seminary, and Germany, had settled to teach in Boston, the center of the liberal movement.

In an address in Japan on his world tour in 1880-82, Cook had said, "Boston, under Channing, Parker and Emerson, has three times tried to found a new religion, but each attempt is now a last year's bird's nest."[8] He obviously conceived of his mission in Boston partially in terms of a refutation of the pervasive heresies of this Unitarian trinity. Whereas many comparisions had been noted between Unitarianism and the Brahmo Samaj under Keshab Chandra Sen, Cook drew the following analogy: "The progressive Brahmos are in the vestibule of Christianity, with their faces turned toward the inner doors; while radical Unitarians in the Occident are in the same vestibule, but often with their faces turned toward the outer doors."[9]

Cook rather prided himself on having no sectarian commitments, and his primary platform was a series of Monday lectures, in Tremont Temple and Old South Meeting House over a twenty-five year period; these were published in eleven volumes. One volume in the series, *Conscience,* indicates the direction of Cook's mind with respect to the issue which so characterized his utterances in the Parliament of Religions: "How am I to keep peace with myself, my God and my record of sin . . .?"[10] In the Parliament, Cook asked, "What religion can wash Lady Macbeth's right hand?" and he affirmed, "It is clear that we cannot escape from conscience and God and our record of sin. It is a certainty and a strategic certainty that, except Christianity, there is no religion under heaven or among men that effectively provides for the peace of the soul by its harmonization with itself, its God, and its record of sin."[11]

We cannot be certain, as some interpreters contend, that a part of
Vivekananda's address on Hinduism, given on the ninth day of this
Parliament, was in response to Cook's on the fourth day. But the con-
trasting emphasis is clear. Vivekananda exhorted:

> Allow me to call you, brethren, by that sweet name, heirs of immortal
> bliss—yea, the Hindu refuses to call you sinners. Ye are the children of
> God, the sharers of immortal bliss, holy and perfect beings, ye are divinities
> on earth. Sinners? It is a sin to call a man so; it is a standing libel on
> human nature. Come up, Oh, live and shake off the delusion that you are
> sheep. . . .[12]

There was only this possible rejoinder; we do not know of any
personal relationship between Vivekananda and Cook, who, alone of
all the persons he might meet in the West, had seen Vivekananda's
Master. Because he wished not to personalize the message of Vedanta,
Vivekananda did not refer to Ramakrishna in his recorded utterances
at the Parliament, and seldom during his visits to the West; conse-
quently, there would have been no opportunity for Vivekananda and
Cook to establish a personal association on the basis of their shared
relationship with Ramakrishna.[13] However much Cook may have been
impressed by his meeting with Ramakrishna, he maintained the
emphasis on sin which Ramakrishna and Vivekananda alike found
offensive in the teachings of the Brahmo Samaj and Christianity.

Prior to the Parliament, Vivekananda had the opportunity to
sample the atmosphere of Boston briefly, but the acquaintances which
he made there were among the religious liberals whom Cook opposed.
He had first come to Chicago in July, only to find that the Parliament
did not open until September. He wandered in childish delight through
the World's Fair for a few days, but found that his money was rapidly
depleting. He had made no close acquaintances in this initial visit,
but was advised by someone that he could live more cheaply in
Boston, so he traveled there by train, to live until the Parliament
would open.

On the train he providentially met a wealthy woman, Miss
Katherine Sanborn, who invited him to stay at her country estate. She
had a number of acquaintances among prominent persons, and speaking invitations for her Hindu guest were soon forthcoming. The first of
these was at the Boston Ramabai Circle, one of a number of groups
founded to advance the status of widows in India by an Indian widow,
Pandita Ramabai, who had become a Christian in her visit to the

West. More will be said later of the conflict which developed between
Vivekananda and the followers of Pandita Ramabai in Brooklyn in
1895. Vivekananda was also to meet the Hellenist professor at
Harvard, J. H. Wright, who was much impressed with the intellectual
capacity of the young Swami. Upon learning that he had no credentials to attend the Parliament, Wright is quoted as having said,
"To ask for your credentials is like asking the sun to state its right to
shine." Wright then addressed a letter to the Chairman in charge of
delegates, saying, again extravagantly, "Here is a man who is more
learned than all our learned professors put together."[14] The letter
along with Mrs. Hale's personal introduction, secured the desired
result and, after a number of lectures in New England, Vivekananda
returned to Chicago for his impressive debut at the Parliament of
Religions.

Following the Parliament, Vivekananda determined to pursue
his original intention of raising funds through public lectures. He remained briefly in the Chicago area and then secured the services of a
lecture bureau, which busily booked him across the east and midwest
for several months. This became exhausting, and Vivekananda was
particularly disenchanted when he discovered that the bureau was
withholding a part of the attendance receipts which were to have come
to him. Accordingly, at considerable sacrifice, he broke the contract
with them.

A further disenchantment was developing in Vivekananda with
the nation whose circus atmosphere and material achievements had so
dazzled him initially. On occasion his invectives against audiences were
unaccountably harsh, as in Boston when he was to have spoken on the
subject of his master, Ramakrishna. Even before he began to speak
the sight of the crowd, composed of persons of wealth and position
so repelled him that he changed his subject and raged furiously against
a civilization represented by such foxes and wolves. Hundreds noisily
left the hall and the press was furious. Nikhilananda records the re-
morse Vivekananda felt on reflecting on what he had done. "His
Master had never uttered a word of condemnation against anybody,
even the most wicked person; yet he, while talking about Ramakrishna, had criticized these good-hearted people who were eager to
learn about the Master. He felt that he was unworthy of Sri Ramakrishna and resolved not to discuss him in public or even to write about
him again."[15]

The strain of public appearances was doubtless partially responsible for outbursts such as occurred in Boston, but a developing role conflict was also in evidence. Vivekananda had come to secure money for work among his people. Yet he found himself driven more and more to the position of a defender of India and of Hindu society. Missionary opposition, particularly in Detroit early in 1894, accused him of misrepresenting actual conditions in India in his messages. The cross-purposes of the Swami and the missionaries are apparent without, in retrospect, drawing caricatures of heroes and villains in the scene. The missionaries, in attempting to enlist support for their ministries in India, were naturally required to depict the needs of the people, often in dramatic language. This became increasingly offensive to Vivekananda, who although he also had intended to launch a massive appeal for funds for India, was driven to underplay those conditions whose portrayal might have earned a visible financial response. The zeal of the missionaries resulted at times in clear distortions. Vivekananda's contrary descriptions were in contrast, also, with his dedicated attack on the evils of Indian society upon his return.

At the time, his course of action may be understood to have been dictated by feelings of national pride and loyalty. Rather than to abase himself by appealing for financial help from the West, the source of maligning attacks on his own society, he sought to defend India by a counterattack from strength. This strength he deemed to lie in India's wisdom, and the zenith of this wisdom for him was the philosophy of Advaita Vedanta. As a Brahmo in his youth, he had held to Theism, but under Ramakrishna had been initiated into the mysteries of Advaita. Ramakrishna had been certain that the path for Naren was that of the intellect. Despite his own predilection for devotion, Ramakrishna felt that the consummate course for his intellectual disciple was in pursuit of realization through Advaita philosophy. Accordingly, despite the possibility of gaining succor for his people through political means, a secularized strategy of social action, or an appeal to the West to "come over and help us," Vivekananda rather asserted more strongly India's preeminence in the realm of the spirit. The unitive teachings of Vedanta into which he had been initiated by his Master now more than ever constituted the burden of his message, as the quintessence of Indian spiritual insight.

One of Vivekananda's statements in 1894 expresses his *sannyasin's* reluctance to touch money; if this is taken at face value, it is difficult to fathom just why it surfaced at the time apart from the other dynamics.[16] A more credible explanation would seem to lie in the difficulty in reconciling a financial appeal with a recognition of certain failures within Indian society. A coordinate factor, the developing stereotype of the East as spiritual and the West as material, led Vivekananda to seek to divest himself from the taint of that which represented Western materialism.

These dynamics come into sharpest focus as we explore Vivekananda's controversy with the Ramabai Society in Brooklyn in the early days of 1895. By way of background, Pandita Ramabai belonged to the same Chitpavan Brahmin caste which produced Ranade, Gokhale, Tilak, and other social and political leaders of the Bombay Presidency. Her father was an itinerant Puranic scholar and in her wanderings over India with her parents, she saw the current status of women, their subjection to men, and lack of education. She became a recognized Sanskrit and Puranic scholar in her own right, thus earning the appellation Pandita. She married out of her cast in Bengal; her husband died of cholera after a year and a half, leaving her destitute with an infant daughter.

The Pandita came to Poona, the center of reform in western India, in 1882 to work for women's education. Her fame as a scholar and lecturer had preceded her, but her marriage and her ideas on women's education caused opposition from Brahmins. She started an organization for women's rights but, disappointed with the response she began to seek support elsewhere. Encouraged by missionaries, she traveled to England, where she openly became a Christian. In England and the United States she toured to gain financial backing for the home she planned for widows. A part of her indictment against the treatment of women in India was contained in her book, *High Caste Hindu Women*. Various Ramabai Associations were formed in the West to help her with her work.

Upon returning to India in 1889, the Pandita began the Sarada Sadan for widows. Replying to criticism of her having become a Christian, she censured her opponents in return for their dog-in-the-manger attitude, saying that it was because she could not get help from Hindus that she went to Christians. The Sarada Sadan was soon avowedly Christian. It has been charitably said of Pandita Ramabai "Like Mrs. Besant, [she was] one of those rare souls who, born in one religion and driven by their past Karma into another, feel instinctively at home there and find in it perfect satisfaction for all their spiritual needs as well as full scope for their ambitious personalities."[17]

No such charitable assessment was forthcoming in the conflict which emerged in Brooklyn newspapers between Vivekananda and Dr. Lewis Janes, President of the Brooklyn Ethical Association, on the one hand, and Mrs. James McKeen, President of the Brooklyn Ramabai Society, on the other. Accusations and counteraccusations of misrepresentation appeared in *The Brooklyn Eagle* from January until April of 1895. Vivekananda did mildly acknowledge certain needs in the area of women's education, however, and offered the proceeds of one of his lectures—not to the Ramabai Society, since the Pandita had converted to Christianity—but to the widows' home founded by Sasipada Banerjee near Calcutta.[18]

This appears to be the last public controversy in which Vivekananda was involved during his ministry in the West. Indeed, from this point another chapter began, in which the Swami began to solidify his work through the training of disciples in smaller, more intimate circles, and through the foundation of the first of the Vedanta Societies in the West, in New York City in 1895. The large lecture platform was largely abandoned. Vivekananda began a series of lectures; with the assistance of Miss Ellen Waldo, who became a very useful disciple, they were developed into a series of small books on the yogas. Other intimates gathered, among them two rather eccentric personalities whom Vivekananda, in the summer of 1895, was to initiate as his two first Western *sannyasins* at Thousand Islands Park. They were Madame Marie Louise, a Frenchwoman by birth, whom he called Swami Abhayananda, and Leon Landsberg, a Russian Jew, whom he named Swami Kripananda. That one of the *sannyasins* was a woman was a source of some consternation to persons in India, as will be later developed. Other persons were initiated out of the relationships which developed in the New York work and the setting in Thousand Islands Park.

His public lectures had enlisted a following for the Swami of much larger consequence than might have appeared from a brief delineation of the controversies which for a time surrounded him. The Parliament of Religions had provided an excellent entree into intellectual circles. In Vivekananda's 1894 stay in the Boston area, although his intemperate address alienated many, other personal encounters were much more fruitful. He pursued his Parliament acquaintance with Colonel Thomas Higginson, the advocate of women's rights, whose Parliament address conveyed with a strong, virile humor a warm welcome to the representatives of the Eastern faiths.[19] On a later visit, in 1896, Vivekananda was offered chairs in Oriental religions at Harvard University and then Columbia. A rather close relationship developed with William James. That with Dr. Lewis Janes of the Brooklyn Ethical Association, which furnished the Swami a speaking platform, provided him earlier an opportunity to address the conferences in Greenacre, Maine, sponsored by Dr. Janes. His talks there, beneath a tree which was to become known as "Swami's pine," were an important part of the 1894 Conference. The Greenacre Conference later became a platform for two of his brother monks who were also to come to the West, Swami Saradananda and Swami Abhedananda. These Conferences, gathered specifically for the study of comparative religions, were one of the concrete results of the Parliament of Religions. Another, perhaps more lasting achievement, was the introduction of the study of world religions into the curricula of theological seminaries and later of colleges and universities.

Letters to Vivekananda kept him in communication with friends in Madras and western India almost from the time of his arrival in America. Yet, when the first reports of the Parliament of Religions began to filter back to Bengal, the Indian press and his own followers were not certain for a time of the identity of the monk Vivekananda. The first letter from Vivekananda to any of his brother monks in Bengal was written to Ramakrishnananda on March 19, 1894, nine months after the Swami had first come to America. The reason for this lack of communication can only be speculated, but there is some evidence of estrangement due to Vivekananda's impatience with some of his brother monks for having, as he thought, followed him after he had expressed a desire to go alone. He had not been in close communication with them for a while before leaving, and, since it is doubtless true that there had been little sharing of his vision of what his mission to the West might involve, a greater intimacy with more recent associates who had been a part of that maturing vision might have developed.

Persons in Bengal attached to Ramakrishna did, however, learn about his American activities before the letter cited above. It is not possible to determine if this was through his writing to other monastic disciples of Ramakrishna located at Alambazar. A letter to the editor of *The Indian Mirror* relates how, on the occasion of Ramakrishna's birthday in 1894—which would have been held, presumably, in early March—5,000 copies of a pamphlet entitled "Swami Vivekananda at the Parliament of Religions, Chicago" were distributed free to the public. The pamphlet was described as containing a reprint of the presidential address and some of the addresses of the Swami, together with the opinions of the English and American press on the Swami's utterances.[20] It is somewhat of a surprise to discover that at this early date Vivekananda and his followers had developed this degree of sophistication in public relations, but a promotion of this nature helps to account for the way in which the Swami moved so swiftly into public consciousness.

The initial letter to Ramakrishnananda criticized the traditional role of the holy men of India: "A million or two of Sadhus and a hundred million or so of Brahmins suck the blood out of these poor people, without even the least effort for their amelioration—is that a country or hell?" The Swami went on to speak of his vision at Cape Comorin, where, "I hit upon a plan: we are so many *Sannyasins,* wandering about, and teaching our people metaphysics—it is all madness. . . . Suppose some disinterested *Sannyasins,* bent on doing good to others, go from village to village, disseminating education and seeking in various ways to better the condition of all down to the Chandala, through oral teaching, and by means of maps, cameras, globes. . . ."[21] Soon after this letter, Vivekananda apparently asked the monks to gather at Calcutta from their various places of wandering to begin together to discover their new monastic role.

At this point another personality entered the scene. Dharmapala, with whom Vivekananda had had cordial relations at the Parliament of Religions, did not remain long in the West. This representative of Buddhism, on coming to Calcutta, was entertained by Vivekananda's fellow monks at their Alambazar monastery, on April 19, 1894, almost certainly before Vivekananda's March 19 letter had reached Ramakrishnananda. It was the first direct contact which the monks had apparently had with anyone who had been with Vivekananda in the West, and we can imagine the eagerness with which they greeted him. The event is not mentioned in the biographies. It may well have been Dharmapala who reinforced Vivekananda's new ideal for the monastic life, or actually, out of Buddhism's long history of missionary and monastic activity, first introduced certain aspects of it. Re-

maining for a time in Calcutta, Dharmapala gave a public address
on May 14, 1894, and from its contents we are not left in doubt as to
what may have been the burden of his words to the men at
Alambazar:

There is not only Swami Vivekananda, I have seen his colleagues in
the Dackinesore Math, and I say if five or six men go abroad with the
liberal ideas of that great master Ram Krishna, I am sure, you will soon
bring about a great revival of Hinduism among the millions of human
beings in this country. If you organize a missionary propaganda, millions
will join you in your great work. Send them to all parts of the world. You
have got the key, and the success is in your hands. The best men of
England and Germany are now learning the Indian philosophy. Let the
great men of Bengal, Rajahs and Maharajahs, help them to form a missionary propaganda. Thus you will have done your duty to Bengal, and your
duty to India.[22]

Perhaps it was the force of these words of the young General
Secretary of the Maha Bodhi Society which helped to persuade the
Alambazar monks to follow the leads which Vivekananda was to
convey in the following months and years. Reports of Vivekananda's
own successes in the West would have helped, certainly, to enforce
his authoritative interpretation of the way that their Master Ramakrishna would have had them go; but from a reluctance which
periodically asserted itself after Vivekananda's return, we know that
there would have been no unquestioning acceptance of his counsel.
The Swami was to pay great tribute to the example of the Buddha
and his early followers; it may well have been true that his friend
Dharmapala, as a contemporary representative of Buddhism, played
a significant role also in the adoption of the new path for the
sannyasin followers of Ramakrishna.

While much of Vivekananda's correspondence with his friends in
Madras and western India and his fellow monks in Bengal was occupied with the transmission of his vision of the new religious task
which he envisioned for India, there is another aspect which for a time
was crucial. Christian missionary opponents, along with certain representatives of the Brahmo Samaj and Theosophy, in 1894 were calling
into question the authenticity of Vivekananda as a spokesman for
Hinduism. Their charges, of a varied character,[23] resulted in a certain
threat of falling away among some of the Swami's Western followers.
Even Professor Wright of Harvard, who had with such extravagance
commended Vivekananda to the Parliament officials, seems to have

entertained doubts for a time. Vivekananda was at some pains to counter these charges and from America he appealed for supporting statements from Madras and Calcutta. These were slow in coming, and his annoyance with his friends in India grew, but finally testimonial gatherings were held, first in Madras, then in Calcutta, and word was conveyed to the press in the United States. Once the flow of supporting testimony had begun, Vivekananda actually had difficulty in shutting it off!

One of the crucial periods in Vivekananda's Western period was his gathering with intimates at Thousand Islands Park. His hostess, Miss Dutcher, went to such lengths of hospitality as to enlarge her dwelling for her guests. She is described as a devout Methodist who had some difficulty with some of Vivekanada's frontal assaults on her orthodoxy. Others who came were those to be ordained Swamis —Marie Louise and Leon Landsberg, already mentioned, and Ellen Waldo, Ruth Ellis, and a Doctor Wight.[24] The last three had known each other in New York for some time. These new Swamis and Miss Dutcher had been in Vivekananda's New York classes. Another person was a rather mysterious figure named Stella. She seldom came to classes, being, by Sister Christine's account, too engrossed in ascetic practices. The group seemed to feel that this former actress was using yoga to restore her fading beauty. Late arrivals were Christine Greenstidel and Mrs. Mary Funke from Detroit; they had heard the Swami lecture in their city. Three others are not named in the available accounts.

Vivekananda apparently arrived on June 6, 1895, and gave instruction from the 19th until August 6. During this seven-week period, we have one of his most illuminating series of lectures, as recorded by Ellen Waldo in the book *Inspired Talks*. Sister Christine also gives a vivid impression of the relationships which developed among the colorful personalities present. The Swami, however, did not initially feel the possibilities which were to emerge from this interlude at the Thousand Islands. In a letter to Mary Hale on June 26, he said, "Nothing noticeable has happened during this visit to the Thousand Islands. The scenery here is very beautiful and I have some of my friends here with me to talk about God and soul ad libitum. I am eating fruits and drinking milk and so forth, and studying huge Sanskrit books on Vedanta which they have kindly sent me from India."[25] Another letter a short time later reveals a changing mood.

This is also addressed to Miss Hale. The Swami says, "I am enjoying this place immensely. Very little eating and good deal of thinking and talking and study. A wonderful calmness is coming over my soul."[26] Chapter Six elaborates on the Thousand Islands period, so important for its encapsulated portrait of the dynamics which evolved between Vivekananda and his Western followers.

Shortly before, the Swami had visited the Percy, New Hampshire, country estate of Francis Leggett, another friend from New York, for a brief period. Leggett and two other guests, Mrs. William Sturges, a widow, and her sister, Miss Josephine MacLeod, had attended the Swami's lectures in New York. The four were to develop a close relationship. While at Percy, Leggett and Mrs. Sturges announced their engagement and invited Vivekanada to attend the wedding ceremony, to be held in Paris in early September. Invitations to visit London were extended by Miss Henrietta Muller, a speaker at the meetings of the Theosophical Society at the Parliament of Religions who had met Vivekananda there, and by E. T. Sturdy. The coinciding invitations seemed a divine leading and, following the Thousand Islands stay, the Swami left for Paris.

Remaining there but briefly for the wedding, he left for London, where he stayed until early December. Sturdy—a student of Sanskrit who had been engaged in religious practices for a time in the Himalayas—and Miss Muller swiftly spread the word of the Swami's presence, and he began classes which rapidly outgrew the quarters in which they were offered. The heroism of England impressed itself on Vivekananda and the hatred which he acknowledged he entertained for the English upon landing there changed to a feeling of deep admiration. He felt also that in Europe the knowledge of India was more sophisticated than in the United States, largely through the scholarly pursuits of men such as Max Müller and Paul Deussen, both of whom he was to meet during his visits the following year. The Swami's affection for England was expressed in a letter to an Indian friend on November 18, 1895, as he made the assessment: "In England my work is really splendid. I am astonished myself at it. The English do not talk much in the newspapers, but they work silently. I am sure of having done more work in England than in America."[27] This judgment did not subsequently prove accurate in terms of organizational continuity, but it was here that Vivekananda acquired his most noted Western follower, Miss Margaret Noble, who was later to come to India as Sister Nivedita to work for women's education. She relates how little she knew of Vivekananda personally until she later traveled with him in India. Still there was a magnetism which made her regard him as master less than a month after first hearing him.

Vivekananda returned to New York on December 6, 1895, leaving Sturdy to continue the work in London until another swami arrived. In New York he reassumed the teaching ministry, which Swamis Abhayananda and Kripananda, with Ellen Waldo, had continued in his absence. The acquisition of another disciple of English descent was soon effected in an unexpected manner. Someone capable of recording the messages given by the Swami was thought to be urgently needed, and after one or two volunteers proved inadequate, an advertisement was printed in both the New York *Herald* and *World:* "Wanted—A rapid shorthand writer to take down lectures for several hours a week. Apply at 228 W. 39th Street."[28] J. J. Goodwin, a professional stenographer, appeared, and after serving to record the lectures, became one of the Swami's devoted disciples and went with him to India in 1896.

The work of consolidation continued in New York and Boston through the spring of 1896, and public lectures, including three in Madison Square Garden, alternated with more private shepherding of those who had become attached to him. Vivekananda also returned briefly to Detroit, where his devotional theme aroused less opposition that the earlier messages. In Boston he was the guest of Mrs. Ole Bull, who soon after accompanied him to England and then to India. The relationship with his great friend Miss Josephine MacLeod developed to the point that she too joined his entourage. On returning to England in 1896, he wrote to her brother-in-law, Francis Leggett, to whom he attached another of his pet names, "Frankincense," his appreciation of Miss MacLeod's services: "The Galsworthys have been very kind. Joe brought them around splendidly. I simply admire Joe in her tact and quiet way. She is a feminine statesman or woman. She can wield a kingdom. I have seldom seem such strong yet good common sense in a human being."[29]

Vivekananda also relates that the swami whom he had requested from Bengal had by this time arrived in London: "We have a nice little family, in the house, with another monk from India. Poor man!

a typical Hindu with nothing of that pluck and go which I have, he
is always dreamy and gentle and sweet! That won't do. I will try
to put a little activity in him."[30] This was Saradananda, whom Vivekananda shortly dispatched to Boston, accompanied by Goodwin, who
remained briefly to help Saradananda get started before returning
to Europe. The American work had moved into the dominant position in the consciousness of Vivekananda. A letter from this period
says: "It is to Amerique—there is where the heart is. I love the
Yankee land. I like to see new things. I do not care a fig to loaf about
old ruins and mope a life out about old histories and keep sighing
about the ancients. I have too much vigour in my blood for that.
In America is the place, the people, the opportunity for everything.
I have become horribly radical. I am just going to India to see what
I can do in that awful mess of conservative jellyfish. . . ."[31]

Vivekananda's mood upon anticipating his return to India is
apparent. While many of his Western utterances had been "revivalist"
in character, the "reformer" was now emerging as he faced home-
ward. There was so much to be done, so much organization to be
set in motion in order to effect the changes which he had in mind.
Still he traveled at a leisurely pace, through Switzerland and Italy,
with those who were to accompany him to India, Captain and Mrs.
Sevier and Goodwin. The Seviers had become attached to him in
London and in their travels with him in Switzerland had first for-
mulated the idea of the monastery in the Himalayas which they
were soon to establish in Mayavati.

The work in London was enhanced with the coming of a second
assistant from India, Swami Abhedananda, whose first public lecture
in London convinced Vivekananda of his great future in the West.
Abhedananda did not remain long in London, but traveled to Boston
and then to New York City, where he had a ministry for some time.
The cultural exchange which had now begun between East and
West through Vivekananda was to be enlarged still further in the
months to come as Mrs. Ole Bull, Miss MacLeod, and Henrietta
Muller traveled to India. They were joined there in 1898 by Margaret Noble, who came to further the educational ministry to the
women of India which Henrietta Muller wanted to begin. Christine
Greenstidel was to associate herself with Miss Noble still later in
that work.

Vivekananda returned to hero's welcomes of a tremendous magnitude in Colombo, Madras, and Calcutta. The word of his triumphs had spread throughout India, and he was widely acclaimed as one who had vanquished the West. *The Indian Mirror* of July 18, 1896, had quoted an English newspaper, "The Swami boasts of having converted nearly 4000 persons to Hinduism in the States." An editorial on January 21, 1897, in the same journal offered this enthusiastic estimate: "The tide of conversion seemed to have rolled back from the East to the West—the tables were completely turned—and the Hindu mission to the West was crowned with a greater and more glorious success than what has ever been vouchsafed to Christian mission in the East." The Rajah of Ramnad, who had first given Vivekananda the idea of attending the Parliament, was quoted in this tribute to him: "Your Holiness has crossed boundless seas and oceans to convey the message of truth and peace, and to plant the flag of India's spiritual triumph and glory in the rich soil of Europe and America." That India had learned the language of imperialism and here used it to interpret the achievements of Vivekananda should not be surprising, nor should Vivekananda's own assessment of his work, couched in terms such as conversion and proselytization, astound us except by comparison with his later, more refined, interpretation developed in contrast to methods attributed to Christianity. At this stage, when asked in an interview, "Does the spirit of Hinduism permit proselytism of strangers into it?" the Swami replied directly, "Proselytism is tolerated by Hinduism."[32]

The tumultuous adulation in Madras seemed excessive to part of the Bengal press, which felt that a certain psychological inflation which it induced in Vivekananda contributed to some rather intemperate references to Theosophists and social reformers. A more modest approach, consonant with the spirit of his Master and in contrast to his pugilistic manner in Madras, was evidenced when he returned to Calcutta. There his public address contained this tribute to Ramakrishna: "If there has been anything achieved by me, by thoughts or words or deeds, if from my lips ever has fallen one word that has helped any one in the world, I lay no claim to it, it was His. But if there have been curses falling from my lips, if there has been hatred coming out of me, it is all mine, and not His. All that has been weak has been mine, and all that has been life-giving, strengthening, pure, and holy, has been His inspirations, His words, and He himself." *The*

Mirror felt that a more natural response in Calcutta, without the excessive deference given him in Madras, elicited a better performance from Vivekananda. "He who had been dubbed your Holiness by his countrymen in the South felt no less honored by being received and talked to as dear brother by his own people in Calcutta. . . . Here he was no longer His Holiness but the old Calcutta boy."[33]

Yet even in Calcutta, extravagant as we can imagine was the warmth of his welcome by his fellow monastic followers of Ramakrishna, he experienced rejection in the place most sacred to him, the shrine at Dakshineswar. The proprietor of the temple, Troilochhya Nath Biswas, in a letter to *The Mirror* sought to clarify reports which had circulated about Vivekananda's visit to the temple where he had known Ramakrishna. He refused, as the temple proprietor, to see Vivekananda or to have anyone else welcome him. "I thought that I should not have any, the least, intercourse with a man who went to a foreign country and yet calls himself a Hindu."[34] The continuing force of orthodoxy must have powerfully impressed the Swami after so long a time in the West. It seems possible that, with money from Mrs. Ole Bull and Miss Muller, the decision to locate the new center of the Math and Mission just downstream across the river from the Dakshineswar shrine may have been prompted by this rejection. Whatever the reason, the location at Belur proved auspicious, and the headquarters of the Movement has remained at that site to the present day. The purchase was effected in February of 1898.

There are many warm reunions recorded in the official life of Vivekananda besides tensions which were resolved only with difficulty. The authenticity of Vivekananda's interpretation of Ramakrishna as having commanded the *gurubhais* (disciples) to dedicate themselves to social service was particularly called into question. It took time for Vivekananda's Western disciples to develop real fellowship with the monks, who had scarcely been touched by the earth-shaking jolts to the tradition which Vivekananda had experienced in the years since they had first known him. A few, however, had caught his vision before his return. Swami Akhandananda, the first of these, began educational work as early as 1894 and later was a prime mover in plague and famine relief.

Vivekananda's Western disciples had some large adjustments to make upon coming to India, as he had warned them they would. He is reported to have exclaimed to Miss MacLeod, before her trip:

"Come if you wish to see poverty, degradation, dirt, and men in rags who speak of God! But if you want to see anything else do not come! For we cannot bear one criticism the more!"[35] In 1898 three Western women disciples also met with the refusal of welcome at Dakshineswar; however, in reporting the incident, they warmly related the shy, yet eloquent way in which a few of the aged women followers of Ramakrishna made their acquaintance.

The Swami's Western friends traveled extensively with him to the cooler Himalayan regions, where his health required him to spend much time. This became for them a period of training of matchless value. Shortly after the arrival of Margaret Noble in January of 1898, Vivekananda introduced her to Calcutta as a "gift of England to India," and initiated her into the role of *brahmacharya* (student) as Sister Nivedita. The Swami, the Seviers, Goodwin, and Miss Muller had traveled in northern India in 1897, with the Westerners settling for a time in Almora. Now, in June of 1898, the Swami journeyed again towards Almora with another contingent of Westerners and fellow disciples, including Mrs. Ole Bull, Josephine MacLeod, and Sister Nivedita.

The work at Almora had by now begun under the Seviers; with Swami Swarupananda as editor, they revived the *Prabuddha Bharata*, which had been published from Madras by Vivekananda's friends until the death of the former editor. Mayavati, where the Math was relocated in 1899, was conceived as an Advaita shrine, wholly devoted to the worship of the absolute without benefit of rituals or symbols. The serenity of this peaceful retreat was soon disturbed with the news of the death in Ootacamund of enteric fever of J. J. Goodwin, who had recently become attached to the staff of *The Madras Mail*. The deeply affected Swami wrote a moving tribute to Goodwin's mother in England. Restless and impatient, he soon journeyed with the Western women to Kashmir, where he had traveled with Goodwin the previous year. This pilgrimage included the Ice Cave of Amarnath, with its shrine to Siva. It was an unforgettable experience for the small group, but the exertion took its toll on Vivekananda, whose health was anything but robust as he arrived back at Belur with the group in October.

Nivedita's school for girls opened in November of 1898 in Calcutta. Her expected role as assistant for Miss Muller did not materialize, and Miss Muller separated herself from the Ramakrishna

Movement in December, 1898. *The Indian Social Reformer* of December 25, 1898, recorded this severance in an interesting manner:

> To our Christian brethren we beg to offer a Christmas present in the shape of the news . . . that Miss Muller has completely severed her connection with Swami Vivekananda's movement to spread Hinduism and that she has returned to her Christian faith. She believes that the future of India lies in a radical reform from those errors and superstitions of the past which have brought her nearly to death. She agrees with our views that social reform must accompany religious reform. Nothing has been able to move her from that conviction and we hope her sincerity and earnestness may be productive of much good to this part of the Empire to which she and we, Christians and Hindus alike, belong.[36]

Vivekananda, as will be explored in Chapter Six, gave a different interpretation to Miss Muller's decision. Yet, while Miss Muller turned towards reform to be effected through the social dynamic which she saw operating more freely within Christianity than Hinduism, Nivedita's reaction to India's needs was to embrace Hinduism and all its customs, while seeking to undertake service activities which would not threaten the structures of society. Women's education was her forte, but her ministry in Calcutta during the plagues of 1898 and 1899 was widely noted in periodicals of the day. Much of this ministry was also educational in character, as Nivedita and other disciples of Vivekananda helped to teach people better sanitation practices. With Sister Nivedita as Secretary of this program and Sadananda, Vivekananda's first Indian disciple, as officer-in-chief, many of the bustee (slum) areas were cleansed of cartloads of filth and then thoroughly disinfected.

Descriptions of Sadananda portray an almost Saint Francis character in his pure joy and his deep identification with suffering. He gathered about him a group of untouchable sweeper boys when the plague broke out and lived with them during the few short days which remained to him. They would go together to their sanitary work of cleaning in the neighborhood. According to Christine Greenstidel, writing years later, the sweeper boys had continued to keep his shrine alive on Bosepara Lane in Baghbazar.

Vivekananda, having imparted something of his *rajasic* or energetic vision to his followers in India, and having welcomed Swami Saradananda back from the West to organize the internal affairs of the monastic order, felt that he could now be spared for another visit

to the West. In the interests of her girl's school, Nivedita was to accompany him as far as England, and he sought to persuade Swami
Turiyananda, a fellow monk, to go as well. Turiyananda, as a man
of meditation, had a certain reluctance to undertake a public mission,
particularly to the West, but was at last persuaded by Vivekananda's
deeply moving appeal to lighten his burden. Vivekananda perceived in
Turiyananda a complement to his own representation of the *sanatana
dharma* (universal religion): "They have seen the Kshatra power;
now I want to show them the Brahmana!"[37] Vivekananda himself was
to display less of the combative spirit of the warrior on this second
visit.

This Western visit was to be of considerably shorter duration
than the first; Vivekananda left on June 20, 1899 and returned December 9, 1900. The major part was occupied with revisiting his
earlier friends and striving to encourage his Western disciples and
his Indian colleagues, Abhedananda and Turiyananda, in carrying
out the work. Following a short stay without public work in London,
Vivekananda and Turiyananda left for the United States, accompanied by Mrs. Funke, who had been with Vivekananda in Detroit
and the Thousand Islands, and another woman. He arrived in August
in the United States and went to Ridgely Manor, the home of the
Leggetts in the Catskills; with the exception of a few days of public
ministry in New York City in November, he stayed there with his
friends, resting and gaining strength. The work in New York was
now under the direction of Abhedananda; Vivekananda seems to
have been reluctant to intrude on work in another's charge.

An occasion to break new ground of his own came through
Miss MacLeod, who had left Ridgely Manor in early November to
be with her dangerously ill brother in Los Angeles. The brother died
soon, in the home of an elderly woman, Mrs. Blodgett, who had kept
Vivekananda's picture since she heard him at the Parliament of
Religions. Mrs. Blodgett's home became the residence of Vivekananda
for two months beginning in early December. With no Goodwin present, few of the many public lectures were recorded. Although no
society was founded, some continuity with this period was effected
when Swami Prabhavananda began his work in Hollywood in 1929.
The home of the Mead sisters, in which Vivekananda had stayed for
a time, was later purchased by the Hollywood organization and
maintained as a shrine. Miss MacLeod's presence in Hollywood dur-

ing her last years also preserved the impression of the time Vivekananda and she spent there with Mrs. Blodgett and the Mead family.

An invitation from the Rev. Benjamin Fay Mills of Oakland brought Vivekananda to the Bay area of California in early February of 1900. The Swami gave a series of eight lectures at the First Unitarian Church of Oakland, where Mills was pastor; by extensive publicity, some attracted up to 2,000 persons. Mills, who had spoken on interdenominational evangelism at the Parliament of Religions, had changed his course in 1895. Before coming to Oakland in 1899, he preached the social gospel in Boston under the auspices of a committee of liberals headed by Edward Everett Hale, who had also appeared at the Parliament.

Vivekananda's lectures in Mills' church led to speaking engagements in San Francisco and Alameda. The way to a permanent work was opened when Vivekananda accepted a gift of 160 acres of land in Santa Clara County from one of his students, Miss Minnie C. Boock. He immediately sought to persuade Turiyananda to come to establish a retreat, Shanti Ashrama, at the donated site.

The fevered pace of activity in San Francisco was accompanied by distressing news from other quarters. The London work was languishing; perhaps Miss Muller's decision had affected others. Sturdy, feeling that Vivekananda was not living in the West in the manner appropriate to an ascetic, had become disenchanted. Personal relationships between Abhedananda and some of the most devoted persons in New York had become strained, and Francis Leggett had severed his relationship with the Society. Vivekananda's correspondence reveals that the New York difficulty had been building up, with a Christian Science persuasion perhaps behind some of the criticisms directed towards him from London. A letter to Sturdy in September attributes to Miss Muller and a Mrs. Johnson in London the belief that no spiritual person ought to be ill. His sickness, Vivekananda stated, caused them to lose faith in him.

To Miss MacLeod, Vivekananda addressed a letter on April 10, 1900, on the trouble in New York. "I got a letter from Abhedananda stating that he was going to leave New York. He thought Mrs. Bull and you have written lots against him to me. I wrote back to be patient and wait, and that Mrs. Bull and Miss MacLeod wrote only good things about him." Another letter followed eight days later:

> ... I am so sorry Mr. Leggett resigned the presidentship. Well, I keep quiet for fear of making further trouble.
> You know my methods are extremely harsh and once aroused I may rattle Abhedananda too much for his peace of mind.
> I wrote to him only to tell him that his notions about Mrs. Bull are entirely wrong.
> ... You understand why I do not want to meddle with Abhedananda. Who am I to meddle with anyone, Joe? I have long given up my place as a leader—I have no right to raise my voice.[38]

Indeed, the leader's public work in the West was almost concluded. Worn out from his heavy schedule of lecturing, Vivekananda retired to a retreat at Camp Taylor near San Francisco for a few weeks in the late spring. It was an idyllic time of refreshment. Ida Ansell, who became a devoted follower with the Sanskrit name of Ujjvala, describes how, as he gained some respite from his illness, he delighted in cooking for the group, making an Indian curry, showing them how to grind spices, merrily laughing with them all the while. He was particularly charmed with Mrs. Hansborough, one of the Mead sisters who had come to San Francisco with him from Los Angeles. She was used to roughing it, having traveled in Alaska with less than first class accommodations. "Her care-free spirit and indifference to convention pleased him," Miss Ansell's account recalls. "One day when she was eating something, he helped himself to a portion from the same plate, and remarked, 'It is fitting that we should eat from the same plate, we two vagabonds'."[39]

But eagerness to return to India soon called the Swami back across the Continent. He had seen much during his two visits to the West, but, although his earlier fire against its materialistic values now burned low, he was still distressed by what seemed to him the superficial concerns of Westerners. He said to Sister Nivedita, "Social life in the West is like a peal of laughter; but underneath it is a wail. It ends in a sob. The fun and frivolity are all on the surface; really it is full of tragic intensity. . . . Here [in India] it is sad and gloomy on the surface, but underneath are carelessness and merriment."[40] He tarried briefly with friends such as the Hales in Chicago, Christine Greenstidel and Mrs. Funke in Detroit, and helped Turiyananda with leadership in New York until Abhedananda's return in July from lecturing in the Boston area. Then, with Abhedananda apparently stabilized in New York and Turiyananda departing for San Francisco, Vivekananda left for Europe.

There was no London visit on this occasion, perhaps owing to the tenuous relations with the earlier adherents there. But a sojourn in France occupied a three-month interlude before the return to India was resumed. Paris was holding a Congress of the History of Religions, on a smaller scale than the Parliament in Chicago and with hesitancy from French Catholicism, but still a gathering in which the Swami desired to participate. Few missionary representatives of the various faiths were present; the body was largely composed of scholars who studied the origins and history of the world's religions. Vivekananda was in attendance at a number of sessions, but spoke only twice. The Indian scientist, Dr. J. C. Bose, who was later to be closely associated with Nivedita, was present, and the two men from Southern Asia enjoyed each other's company. Others with whom he was in close contact in Paris were Sarah Bernhardt and Madame Calvé, of operatic fame, both of whom he had known in the United States. Following the Congress, Mrs. Ole Bull invited him to stay for a time at a cottage in Brittany, where they were joined by Nivedita and Josephine MacLeod.

A party assembled to accompany the Swami to Constantinople, Greece, and Egypt. He was the guest of Madame Calvé and others included Monsieur and Madame Loyson, Jules Bois, and Miss MacLeod, who was with him perhaps more than any of his Western followers throughout his travels. In Egypt the rather leisurely pace was suddenly interrupted as the Swami felt an urgency to return to India. An intuition of the death of Mr. Sevier is credited with his departure from the others. He arrived in early December at the monastery in Belur, this time with none of the fanfare that accompanied his earlier return. A few days later *The Indian Mirror* simply observed, "We note that Swami Vivekananda has returned to India."[41] He remained out of the public limelight during the nineteen months of life which were left to him. Some interpreters attributed this retreat to public opposition, which they foresaw would hasten his death. A letter of December 21, 1901, by "A Hindu," said, "Those who attempt to introduce reform meet with untimely death. Look at that truly great man, *the prophet of Rajoguna* [energy, virility], Vivekananda, prostrated by a fell disease, discarded by his countrymen, maligned not only by the Brahmins, but even by his own castemen. . . ."[42]

Contemporary sources contain little reference to such militant opposition, however, and the contrary assumption would indicate that Vivekananda had largely passed out of the public consciousness until notices of his death in July of 1902 revived awareness of his earlier acclaim. During the period following his return he was quietly active, however, in teaching and training his *gurubhais,* though he had relinquished a position of formal leadership. A few travels within India were undertaken as his health permitted, the first being the swift errand of mercy to bring comfort to Mrs. Sevier, whose husband had indeed died while the Swami was en route to India. A trip to Eastern Bengal with his mother was in part to strengthen the work in Dacca, but was also intended as a personal pilgrimage to several holy places. In February and March of 1902, he was accompanied to Bodh Gaya by a Japanese Buddhist visitor and then went on for his final pilgrimage to Benares. In response to the plea to begin a charitable work in Benares, he sent a fellow monk from Belur on his return.

His death came, by the interpretation of his followers, as an act of conscious volition, in fulfillment of a prophecy given many years before by Ramakrishna. He consulted an almanac to determine the most auspicious day and, although his disciples did not sense that the end was near, in retrospect they discerned his many allusions to his coming *mahasamadhi* (death). This came during a period of meditation on the evening of July 4, 1902. It had been a busy day, in which he devoted three hours in the afternoon to the instruction of the younger monks in Sanskrit. He walked with Premananda for some time and then conversed with his brother monks on the rise and fall of nations. "India is immortal," he said, "if she persists in her search for God. But if she goes in for politics and social conflict, she will die."[43] He retired for meditation and death came, at the age of thirty-nine.

On the following day, his fellow monks gathered, along with many others when the word became known. Nivedita came from Calcutta and stayed some time with his body, fanning it lovingly. He was cremated across the river from the site where Ramakrishna's body had been consigned to the flames sixteen years before.

Chapter Five

INDIA'S RESPONSE TO VIVEKANANDA

The years in which Vivekananda had been in the West belonged to a period of relative quiescence in Bengal. Movements for reform had largely spent their force and even the reformers among the *bhadralok* (cultural elite) showed little disposition to share their position of authority with those beneath the three upper castes. It was, however, a time of quiet before the storm. A year after Vivekananda's return, Lord Curzon was to begin his seven-year tenure in Calcutta. He began to move toward greater political efficiency shortly after his arrival, and Bengal, his headquarters province and by all admissions the most politically overgrown, was the first to feel the pruner's touch. The British felt that the Bengal *bhadralok* had become increasingly distant from the masses, and the clear objective, in the Act of Partition and measures which immediately preceded it, was to challenge elite power, to divide and rule.

Bengal, then, in 1905, became the center stage of extremist activity against British policy. Before this time, the most visible weight of *bhadralok* sentiment had been in support of Westernizing influences. Vivekananda, receiving the benefits of education, which had become the primary vehicle of mobility under the British, reflected this fascination with the West throughout his youth. Insularity from the West, according to the sentiment of this position, was responsible for India's present backward condition. There was a certain Bengali pride, for English education had enhanced Bengal's separate cultural and linguistic tradition, but little genuine national feeling on the part of *bhadralok* members. Nationalism, as exhibited in Congress Party leadership in both Moderate and Extremist wings, was concentrated in the Bombay Presidency rather than in Bengal at this stage.

What Vivekananda had to offer to Bengal upon his return was nationalism based on religious identity, a nationalism which had proved its mettle on Western soil. He had become particularly conscious during his travels in India and the West of the isolation of Bengal from the institutions of the larger Hindu tradition, among them the monastic way. His position, therefore, as an English-educated champion of Hinduism from Bengal, displayed many anomalies to the people of India. This may readily be seen in the press reports and other communications concerning him during his tenure in the West and following his return.

Publicity of Vivekananda's activities in the West, then, elicited a variety of responses in the Indian press. The early confusion as to his identity and point of origins gave way to a hesitant endorsement by those whose only knowledge of him was constituted in the reports from America. *The Indian Mirror* of July 6, 1894, said, "The Swami is a young man of learning and ability, and if he succeeded in making such a powerful impression on the American mind in favor of Hinduism, how much more would the cause of our religion gain in that antipodal world, if some of the very best representatives of the Hindu community went there, and lived and preached as Swami Vivekananda has been doing for so many months?" A certain incredulity toward the glowing reports of the achievements of Vivekananda, unknown in his own country, awakened a contrasting confidence in the innate worth of that which he had been disseminating, the Hindu faith. "Americans," so the report continued, "would, indeed, seem born to cooperate with Hindus to evangelize the civilized world, according to the tenets of the Hindu spiritual ethics."[1] Hindu pride swelled, while reservations remained towards the vehicle of this triumph, who had not been duly recognized nor delegated to his role.

The above may most closely distinguish the attitudes of what may be termed the "orthodox" community within Hinduism, although the term requires elaboration. It does not, obviously, describe those who assent to a particular set of doctrinare formulations as in certain Western faiths. Doctrinally, Hinduism is not a single consistent system but an encyclopedia of philosophy, a congeries of systems. Orthodoxy has reference to the social organization which, in essence, typifies Hinduism more than any one of the systems of thought which evolved in India. Various reformers, with something like a prophetic vision, were occupied in the nineteenth century with pointing out how local customs (*deshacaras*) of eating, drinking, marriage, and other social usages had crystallized into inviolable religious restrictions. Vivekananda became one such critic, particularly with reference to his own native state of Bengal.* Despite his apologetic advocacy of Hinduism in the West, the challenge of his violation of the code merely in voyaging to the West did not go unnoticed, as evidenced by his hostile reception at the Dakshineswar temple upon his return. Orthodoxy consisted in a rigidity of mind towards social change.

One illuminating incident upon his return to India occurred with the visit of the representative of the Cow Protection Society. In commending the man for the expressed objective of saving cows from butchers by buying them and maintaining refuges, the Swami asked if the organization was undertaking any relief for the starving in the current famine in central India. The man replied that this was not part of their program, and that the famine had occurred because of the *karma,* or sins, which the sufferers had accumulated. Vivekananda repressed his indignation and replied that he had no sympathy with an organization which had no feeling for human ills yet ministered to cows whose condition could also be accounted for by the same application of the *karma* doctrine. He made clear that his own service would be directed first of all towards human needs.

The associates of Vivekananda in the West were persons of large vision, standing, surely, at the other end of the spectrum from the orthodox. They were champions of a multiplicity of causes designed to advance the status of women and of minority groups. His relationships with persons of this character supremely unfitted Vivekananda for any merely "orthodox," "revivalist" role upon his return to India. The reformer was little in evidence in him prior to his going, and one can only feel that his association with persons of a reforming spirit in the West helped him to develop his critical perceptions towards the social order in both East and West.

*In his "Reply to the Madras Address," in 1894, Vivekananda indicted Bengal on four counts: "the curious and unorthodox custom of hereditary *gurus,"* less of an exposure to "the great brotherhood of *sannyasins,"* a dislike for renunciation (*tyaga*) among the higher classes, with a preference for *bhoga* or enjoyment, and a system of religious education which, with Madras and Bombay, he found inferior to that in northwest India. Vivekananda, *Collected Works, op. cit.,* vol. 4, pp. 336–40.

With most of the press reflecting a more liberal position toward social change, orthodoxy was not much given to a literary defense of its position in the period with which we are concerned. A few samplings, however, indicate the orthodox position. One observer conjectured that the absence of pandits from the town meeting held in 1894 in Calcutta in support of Vivekananda indicated their judgment that his attempt to integrate moral concerns with current social issues was irrelevant. Another interpreter criticized the tendency in Vivekananda, noted earlier in the Brahmo Samaj, to claim a breadth for Hinduism which distorted the particularities of its own tradition. There was a trend in the Parliament, he observed, to score most highly by adopting an amorphous posture which obscured all differences. "Vivekananda took a few cuttings from the rock of Hinduism, and he won an easy victory! Unfortunately, religion like homeopathic medicine, is not increased in power by dilutions and triturations; on the contrary, the more you make a religion broad, the more you make it lifeless, and absolutely inoperative if you go beyond its natural basis and height."[2]

The Dakshineswar incident, denying even the least courtesy towards the one who had traveled across the ocean and had intercourse with the *mllecchha* (foreigner), illuminates the inflexibility of certain of Vivekananda's countrymen, who felt that Hinduism had nothing to do with Vivekananda's activities in the West. It would seem that both the orthodox and the more radical reformers were agreed that Hinduism had had no representatives at the Parliament. Mozoomdar and his colleagues were Brahmos, not Hindus, by their own designation. Although Vivekananda claimed freedom as a *sannyasin* from restrictions on diet and foreign travel, there was no consensus that any true Hindu could do as he had done.[3]

A criticism of the orthodox position, in an editorial of May 21, 1894, in the *Indian Nation,* comments on Dharmapala's Calcutta address.

Mr. Dharmapala's enthusiasm for Hinduism was unbounded, not "sectarian Hinduism" he was careful to complain, but the pure and undefiled Hinduism such as Swami Vivekananda has been preaching in America. If that is so, Mr. Dharmapala's enthusiasm is worth nothing. The pure and undefiled Hinduism which the Swami preached has no existence today, has not had any existence for centuries, and is at the present moment only an affair of books and not of life, a thing therefore, of merely abstract interest. The only Hinduism that is practically worthwhile discussing today is sectarian Hinduism. It is that Hinduism which resents the slaughter of kine, which keeps out the English-returned Hindu, which proscribes remarriage of widows, and marriage between different castes, which makes the early marriage of girls compulsory. It is that Hinduism which is distinct from Brahmoism. It is the only Hinduism that we can admit to be real.[4]

The virulence of the attack identified Hinduism with the orthodox position. As we know, Hinduism demonstrated a plasticity which enabled it to adopt many of the reforms urged upon it by Vivekananda and other reformers. Orthodoxy, however, discerned the challenge and continued its resistance to the Ramakrishna Movement founded by Vivekananda. But the orthodox response represents only a part of the judgment of Hinduism.

Reservations of a different order came from devotional Hinduism, particularly from Bengal Vaishnavism. The organ of this movement, *Amrita Bazar Patrika,* did not immediately mount an attack, but came increasingly to feel that Vivekananda had abandoned the *bhakti* (devotional) spirit of his master, Ramakrishna, to expound a dry philosophy. In 1896 the editorial tone of this journal, moving from its earlier position of appreciative recognition, began to call Vivekananda's work into question. "We have some very great doubts as to the success of Vivekananda in the West," an editorial confessed. "His dry philosophy, in which the growth of man is based upon poverty and celibacy, is not likely to catch the fancy of any large number of people in the land of modern civilization. We want something emotional to give a proper direction to Western energies. We have a notion that the life and teachings of Shri Guaranga [Chaitanya, the Bengali devotee of Krishna of a few centuries earlier] are likely to produce the needed effect in the West."[5]

The same journal defined its own standards for success in the West in terms of the numbers of converts made to Hinduism, a measure which, as we have seen, Vivekananda was not himself hesitant to apply for a time. In interviewing Vivekananda shortly after his return in 1897, *The Madras Mail* asked, "What prospects have you, Swamiji, for the spread of your mission in England?" "There is every prospect," Vivekananda replied. "Before ten years elapse [the] vast majority of the English people will be Vedantins."[6] The understanding of what constituted conversion differed quite patently, however. Vedanta, for Vivekananda, was the universalistic dimension to be found in Hinduism, but with echoes also in other traditions. It was not to be qualified by the adoption of alien customs or with obeisance towards a personality from a different, strange culture. Conversion, for the editors of *Amrita Bazar Patrika,* meant the acceptance of a historical personality, such as Chaitanya, and of the object of his devotion, Lord Krishna of Vrindavan. "Has he [Vivekananda] been able to make any Hindu of the Christians and atheists of the West? In other words, has he been able to persuade any one of his followers to accept Sri Krishna of Vrindaban—at least, the Sri Hari of Prohlad or Dhruba? If he has been able to do that then he has done some real and solid work."[7] Again, "A Christian never becomes a Hindu by accepting only Hindu philosophy. Conversion means the acceptance of a personality. . . . If a Christian accepts the Lord Guaranga in preference to Christ, he becomes a convert to Hinduism, or more correctly, to Vaishnavism." The article judged that Sister Nivedita, Vivekananda's follower, could not be regarded as a convert to Hinduism, as her devotion to Kali was not to a personality but only to a symbol which served to make vivid certain aspects of Hindu philosophy.[8]

The official biography seeks to clarify the charges raised by the Vaishnavas and Vivekananda's defense. Back in Bengal, in conversation with a Vaishnavite, he said, "Babaji, once I gave a lecture in America on Shri Krishna. It made such an impression on a young and beautiful woman, heiress to immense wealth, that she renounced everything and retired to a solitary island, where she passed her days absorbed in meditation on Shri Krishna."[9] The Swami apparently referred to the fading actress Stella, who had been at the Thousand Islands, as related in the previous chapter. Vivekananda nevertheless justified his conscious attempt to suppress the *bhakti* temperament within himself. He told his *gurubhais* on another occasion, "I am trying and trying always to keep down the rush of *Bhakti* welling within me. I am trying to bind and bind myself with the iron chains of *Jnana* [the intellectual, philosophical way], for still my work to my motherland is unfinished, and my message to the world not yet fully delivered. So, as soon as I find that *Bhakti* feelings are trying to come up to sweep me off my feet, I give a hard knock to them and make myself adamant by bringing up austere *Jnana.*"[10]

While little of the correspondence to Vivekananda from his

fellow disciples is extant, a few of his letters to them indicate the
temper of his mind that gave rise to differences of opinion upon his
return. One, in 1894 to the monastery at Alambazar, made clear his
hesitancy toward ceremonial practices and his contrasting advocacy
of educational service:

> What I am most afraid of is the worship room. It is not bad in itself,
> but there is a tendency to make this all in all and set up that old-fashioned
> nonsense over again—that is what makes me nervous. I know why they
> busy themselves with these old, effete ceremonials. Their spirit craves for
> work, but having no outlet they waste their energy in ringing bells and
> all that.

Another paragraph delineates his desire for them to initiate an
educational mission to the poor:

> Try to have their eyes opened as to what has taken place or is taking
> place in different countries, what this world is like and so forth. . . .
> Teach them astronomy, geography, etc., and preach Shri Ramakrishna to
> them. . . . The day of gossip and ceremonials is gone, my boy, you must
> work now.[11]

A letter the following year clarified his position on the preaching
of Ramakrishna. This also was to his *gurubhais,* through Ramakrishnananda:

> It is not necessary to preach that Ramakrishna Paramahamsa was an
> incarnation, and things of that sort. He came to do good to the world,
> not to trumpet his own name. . . . Disciples pay their whole attention to
> the preservation of their master's name, and throw overboard his teach-
> ings; and sectarianism, etc., are the result. . . . Try to give up ceremonials.
> They are not meant for *sannyasins.* . . . It is impossible to preach the
> catholic ideas of Ramakrishna Paramahamsa and form sects at the same
> time.[12]

That there was no immediate acceptance of this counsel is evidenced by a conversation with the other followers of Ramakrishna
upon his return to Bengal. One of them openly challenged him with
the blunt words, "You did not preach our Master in America; you
only preached yourself." The Swami replied in kind, "Let people
understand me first; then they will understand Sri Ramakrishna."[13]
Elaborating on other occasions, he stated his intent to burst the
restrictive bonds which some sought to impose on Ramakrishna's
catholic ideas by confining his worship to a temple cult. "Do you
want," he asked, "to shut Sri Ramakrishna, the embodiment of infinite ideas, within your own limits? I shall break these limits and

catter his ideas broadcast all over the world. He never enjoined me
to introduce his worship and the like."[14]

But the charges were repeatedly made in the first few months
following his return that the Swami's ways of lecturing and inaugu-
rating programs of service to the people were Western impositions
upon the teachings of Ramakrishna. Yogananda particularly asked
him to explain how his plans could be reconciled with their Master's
example. On one occasion such a challenge gave rise to an emotional
outburst of great intensity from Vivekananda. He railed at his
brothers:

> You think you understand Shri Ramakrishna better than myself!
> You think *Jnana* is dry knowledge to be attained by a desert path, killing
> out the tenderest faculties of the heart. Your *Bhakti* is sentimental non-
> sense which makes one impotent. You want to preach Ramakrishna as
> you have understood him which is mighty little. Hands off! Who cares
> for your Ramakrishna? Who cares for your *Bhakti* and *Mukti* [salvation]?
> Who cares what the scriptures say? I will go to hell cheerfully a thousand
> times, if I can rouse my countrymen, immersed in *Tamas,* and make them
> stand on their own feet and be Men, inspired with the spirit of *Karma-*
> *yoga.* I am not a follower of Ramakrishna or any one, I am a follower of
> him only who carries out my plans! I am not a servant of Ramakrishna
> or any one, but of him only who serves and helps others, without caring
> for his own *Mukti.*[15]

His voice becoming choked with emotion, tears running from
his eyes, Vivekananda ran from the room to his own apartment,
where his disciples, entering hesitantly a few moments later, found
him absorbed stiffly in meditation in what they feared was his final
samadhi. In part fearing that another such outburst might be the
occasion for his departure before the completion of his mission, his
fellow monks refrained from further challenges, and set themselves
to work in the service of Ramakrishna, as interpreted by Vivekananda. It was no casual deference. The primary directions having been
determined, Vivekananda increasingly relinquished his own position
of authority, and later personal divergences from his ideal appear not
to have been associated with direct confrontations. A single, almost
devastating encounter had made a profound impression which could
not risk repetition.

Among reform groups the Brahmo Samaj, initially through
Mozoomdar in Chicago, was the first to exhibit a playback to
Vivekananda's presence in the West. Much of that has been depicted

as petulant, and Mozoomdar, who had a certain reputation from his
previous visits to the West, has been supposed jealous in finding himself eclipsed by the young Vivekananda who appeared out of nowhere, unannounced, to capture the attention of the American
populace. This may be to a degree justified, though most of the
supporting testimony is from Vivekananda himself. Mozoomdar
commissioned by Keshab Chander Sen, had traveled to the West in
1874 and 1883, and came again for the Parliament and for another
visit in 1900. The New Dispensation called him, with some justification, "the first Indian missionary to the New World,"[16] although
Keshab himself may have merited that distinction. When the Parliament was in the planning stage, Mozoomdar was asked to serve on
the Advisory Council and Committee for the selection of delegates
In this capacity he helped some time prior to the Parliament to
determine who would represent India. A collection of Mozoomdar'
lectures in American and other papers claims: "But when uninvited
Swami Vivekananda dressed as a monk reached America with the
expectation of joining the Parliament it was Protap Chander [Mo-
zoomdar] having known him while yet a young member of the
Brahma-Samaj, who sympathetically arranged for him to represen
the Hindu Monks."[17] Vivekananda, in mentioning in a letter to
friend Mozoomdar's presence along with four other representative
of Indian religious groups, said, "Mozoomdar and I were of cours
old friends, and Chakravarti knew me by name." Chakravarti wa
a representative of Theosophy. Again, "Mozoomdar made a nic
speech—Chakravarti a nicer one, and they were much applaude(
They were all prepared and came with ready-made speeches. I wa
a fool and had none, but bowed down to Devi Saraswati and steppe
up, and Dr. Barrows introduced me. I made a short speech . . . an
when it was finished, I sat down almost exhausted with emotion."[
Other contemporary references to Mozoomdar by Vivekananda wer
appreciative, although later, following word from his fellow monk
in Calcutta of certain rumors concerning him circulated by Mo
zoomdar, Vivekananda wrote to Ramakrishnananda the following
"I met here Mr. Mozoomdar. He was very cordial at first, but whe
the whole Chicago population began to flock to me in overwhelmin
numbers, then the fire began to burn in Mr. Mozoomdar's heart. . .
Mozoomdar slandered me to the missionaries in the Parliament (

Religions, saying that I was a nobody, a thug and a cheat, and he accused me of coming here and pretending to be a monk. Thus he greatly succeeded in prejudicing their minds against me. He so prejudiced President Barrows that he didn't even speak to me decently. In their books and pamphlets they tried their best to snub me, but the Guru is my help. What could Mozoomdar say?"[19]

The account is antithetical to the testimony of Mozoomdar, and we have no evidence to corroborate either position. A March 18, 1894, letter of Vivekananda to Mary Hale mentions that his "brethren in Calcutta" have told him "that Mozoomdar has gone back to Calcutta and is preaching that Vivekananda is committing every sin under the sun in America—especially 'unchastity' of the most degraded type!!"[20] The letter itself is not directly quoted. *Unity and the Minister,* a publication of Mozoomdar's branch of the Brahmo Samaj, is cited as the only direct evidence of Mozoomdar's charges in any of the biographical records of Vivekananda:

The Indian Mirror has published several long letters in praise of the Neo-Hindu Babu *Norendra Nath Dutt* alias Vivekananda in some of its late issues. We have no objection to the publication of such panegyrics on the *Sanyasi,* but since the time he came to us to act on the stage of the Navavrindavan Theater or sang hymns in one of the Brahmo Samajes of this city we knew him so well that no amount of newspaper writing could throw any new light on our estimate of his character. We are glad our old friend lately created a good impression in America by his speeches, but we are aware that Neo-Hinduism of which our friend is a representative is not orthodox Hinduism. The last thing which the latter would do is to cross the Kalapani [ocean], partake of the Mlechha food and smoke endless cigars and the like. Any follower of modern Hinduism cannot command that respect from us which we entertain for a genuine orthodox Hindu. Our contemporary may try to do his best to promote the reputation of *Vivekananda,* but we cannot have patience with him when he publishes glaring nonsense.[21]

There is an obvious petulant spirit and an impatience for what the author felt to be an inauthentic representation of Hinduism, but the only charges expressly made are those of transgressions of orthodox morality, scarcely "immorality" by Western standards. The author simply does not allow room for any category, such as modern Hinduism, in implying that Vivekananda should either revert to orthodox practice in harmony with his philosophical and nationalistic ideals, or openly declare himself a Brahmo or member of another reform group in consonance with his social practices. In any case, the dynamics behind Mozoomdar's position are rather patent: a degree of resentment and suspicion would naturally follow coming across a former associate (although Vivekananda was allied with the Sadharan Brahmo Samaj, under Shastri, rather than the New Dispensation under Keshab) who had vanished from the Calcutta scene for a number of years before appearing, unannounced and undelegated, in Chicago with a desire to speak at the Parliament, where he showed a much more defensive spirit against the Christian presence in India than that of Mozoomdar, who *may* have helped to sponsor his being seated. The additional motive of jealousy which Vivekananda attributed to Mozoomdar's actions is credible as well. Whatever reasons lay behind the questions raised by Mozoomdar and his colleagues in the Brahmo Samaj, Vivekananda felt a strong alienation from them at the time and his work in the West suffered because of their attacks, at least during a few months in 1894.

Upon his return to India, Vivekananda, in his addresses in Madras, expressed a kindred feeling for the reformers there, who he felt to have been less extreme in their methods than those in Bengal. As one of the earliest members of the Sadharan branch, he never sought to sever his connection with the Brahmo Samaj in Calcutta, although in his own mind he specified that his association was only that of sympathy towards their social reforms and not with their religious ideals. Two quotations from a May 24, 1894, letter to Professor J. H. Wright indicate his view of the relationship at that time.

> I had connection with Pundit Shiva Nath Shastries [sic] party—but only on points of social reform. Mozoomdar and Chandra Sen I always considered as not sincere and I have no reason to change my opinion even now. Of course in Religious matters even with my friend Punditji I differed much. The chief being I thinking [sic] *Sanyasa* the highest ideal and he, a sin. So the Brahmo Samajists consider becoming a monk a sin!
>
> . . .
>
> The Brahmo Samaj like Christian Science in your country spread in Calcutta for a certain time and then died out. I am not sorry neither glad that it died. It has done its work—viz social reform. Its religion was not worth a cent and so it must die out. If Mozoomdar thinks I was one of the causes of its death—he errs. I am even now a great sympathiser of its reforms—but the "booby" religion could not hold its own against the old "Vedanta." . . .[22]

Vivekananda does not specify what he considers to be the religious inadequacy of the Brahmo Samaj, though we may presume that it consisted in its adoption of a number of Christian ideals. He differed in his assessment of Keshab from his Master's deep appreciation of him. The clear equivocation on reform policy is evident in his endorsement in Brooklyn of a collection for Sasipada Banerjee's home for Indian widows in Calcutta and his later condemnation in Madras of the Bengal reformers as extreme.

Meanwhile, the Madras reformers were also questioning his utterances on Hinduism. The *Indian Social Reformer,* then based in Madras, wrote in editorial comment in 1894: "The religion of Vedanta and the double-distilled extract of it of Vivekananda, can undoubtedly give a good account of themselves before any faith of the world. But the Hinduism of the present day with its social incrustations and iniquities would not find the field so favorable to it."[23] *The Statesman and Friend of India* in the same year expressed its strong feeling that Vivekananda's paper on Hinduism at the Parliament whitewashed it, ignored its exclusiveness and its avarice in temples and other vices associated with grosser forms of idolatry.[24] *The Social Reformer,* in offering a critique of a message of Vivekananda in Madras upon his return, quoted him as follows:

Today under the blasting light of modern sciences, when old apparently strong and invulnerable beliefs have been shattered to their very foundations, when special claims laid upon the allegiance of mankind to different sects have been all blown to atoms and have vanished into air— when the sledge-hammer blows of modern antiquarian researchers are pulverizing like masses of porcelain all sorts of antiquated orthodoxies, when religion in the West is only in the hands of the ignorant, and the knowing ones look down with scorn upon anything belonging to religion, here comes the philosophy of India, the highest religious aspirations of the Indian mind, where the grandest philosophical facts have been the practical spirituality of the people. . . .

The editorial comments:

We must say that the Swami's words are only eloquent. When he says "all the little toleration that is in the world, all the little sympathy that is in the world yet, for religious thought, is here in the land of the Aryas, and nowhere else," we must say again that we dissent from him. From our short experience we know with what great acrimony and intolerance, one Hindu sect hates another and all of them hate the Mussulman or the Christian, and unless effeteness and indifference be synonymous with tolerance, we cannot say we are the most tolerant of all men on earth.[25]

Even with the above criticism, however, the periodical expressed sympathy with certain goals of reform which Vivekananda conveyed, but which seemed to them difficult to reconcile with the idolization of the national example as stated above.

"A Brahmin correspondent" in *The Madras Mail* (the paper to which Goodwin attached himself perhaps a year later) of February 18, 1897, also indicted Vivekananda for glamorizing Hinduism. He found lying strong and charity small, as evidenced by the slight contributions to the Famine Fund by Hindus, which the writer attributed to complacency induced by the *Karma* doctrine. "The Pariah—thanks to the Christian missionary—is coming up, and the Brahmin—his traditional occupation gone, has to struggle in life with the other castes".[26]

The Social Reformer, as time progressed, however, recognized how much of a reformer Vivekananda himself became. In comparing Mrs. Besant in 1901 with Vivekananda, the editors were much more in accord with Vivekananda. "Mrs. Besant has been a back-engine to the Hindu race, and the deadening effects of her influence have been felt not only in social reform, but along all lines of national activity. The National Congress has suffered grievously on account of her paralyzing influence."[27] Suffice it to say that Mrs. Besant a few years later also diametrically changed her position and became an active worker for social and political reform. Following Vivekananda's death in 1902, *The Social Reformer* noted the support which Vivekananda had increasingly given to reform movements, mentioning in particular his word of cordial good wishes to the Social Conference in Lahore.

It is our conviction that the Swami Vivekananda was a victim of this sophistry [of yielding to the crowd's desire to vest all its hopes in his person] in the twelve months that followed his return from Chicago. And it is, in our view, the strongest proof of the innate greatness of the man and lofty sanity of his ideal, that he was, notwithstanding, able to soon realize and to pull himself out of the slough into which he had been sinking. . . . His greatest and most abiding work was done after his reclamation from the mouths of the populace. The brilliant part of it was the least faithful to his ideal and the most wasteful to his energies. . . . It is a matter of melancholy satisfaction to us, who differed so much and so strenuously from the Swami at one period of his remarkable life, to bear testimony, at his death which we sincerely deplore, to the greatness of his ideal, the magnetism of his personality, and the depth of his patriotism. India is poorer for the loss of Swami Vivekananda.[28]

While the biographies do not mention an appearance at the Social Conference, the *Collected Works* contain "The Social Conference Address," without information as to its date and location. In this address, Vivekananda, while indicating appreciation for the inaugural address of Justice Ranade and a word of support for the program of the social reformers generally, primarily sought to establish the *sannyasin* as the person most fitted to assume the role of religious leadership in contemporary India. He felt that Ranade had slighted the status of the *sannyasin*.[29] It was not an incidental distinction. The movement which Vivekananda initiated, while it clearly combined many of the objectives of the social reformers with his own religious ideals, was a movement of celibate monks. He made more reference elsewhere to the Buddhist example, but here he derived from the Indian model of monastic leadership his observation of "Protestant England and America shaking before the onrush of the Catholic monk."[30] The monastic life style was doubtless a large part of his characteristic preference of Catholic to Protestant Christianity.

Vivekananda's relationship with Theosophy was particularly turbulent, and assessment of it requires considerable documentation. The difficulty was personal, although there were theological differences, and it stemmed from his contacts with Theosophy in Madras before departing from India and from a rejected appeal for financial assistance from Theosophical sources shortly after his arrival in Chicago. The circumstances of this appeal and its rejection, however, are subject to dispute. Upon returning to India, Vivekananda's denunciation of the Theosophical Society mentioned this earlier slight. In Nikhilananda's biography, we are told, "In a frantic mood he asked help from the Theosophical Society, which professed warm friendship for India. He was told that he would have to subscribe to the creed of the Society; but this he refused to do because he did not believe in most of the Theosophical doctrines."[31]

Vivekananda's own description of the incident, which doubtless underlies Nikhilananda's account, is related in one of his key addresses, "My Plan of Campaign," delivered in Madras upon his return. He details the opposition he encountered from various groups in the West, Theosophy among them; and the vituperative denunciation in which he indulged, as we shall see, in turn evoked widespread censure

from the Indian press. In addition to the refusal of a letter of introduction from Colonel Olcott, Vivekananda said that while in financial
extremity shortly after arriving in Chicago, he wired for help to his
friends in Madras. This became known to the Theosophists and one
of them, he charges, wrote, "Now the devil is going to die; God bless
us all."[32] In the tempest which followed in the press, particularly *The
Indian Mirror,* which Vivekananda had called "the most influential
paper in India,"[33] he was challenged to show the letter allegedly containing that sentence. A Westerner who was for many years associated
with the Vedanta Society maintains that according to Vivekananda
the letter was stolen from his room the day before he was to have produced it.[34]

In his sole reply in the press to Vivekananda's charges, Olcott
stated that although Vivekananda was known to oppose Theosophy
before leaving for America, Olcott recalled no request for a letter of
introduction. He denied other persecution from Madras and claimed
that he had offered Vivekananda free use of a bungalow in Madras
on his return, had accepted a place on the Committee of Welcome, of
which both the Chairman and Secretary were Theosophists, and had
been present at the reception to speak, although tumultuous crowds
forced the curtailment of that part of the program. The statement,
given to the press after Vivekananda's Calcutta address, concluded
with the words, "If he keeps his feet on the golden carpet of love that
he spread in his superb Calcutta address, he will have the goodwill
and help of every Theosophist."[35]

Vivekananda's pique with the Theosophists may be judged to
have been intensified by the oft-repeated suggestion that Theosophy
had paved the way for his success in the West. The editor of *The
Indian Mirror,* which was normally quite laudatory of Vivekananda,
was a Theosophist; he had made the following assertion in August of
1894: "But it must be said that the ground was prepared for his success by Theosophic workers long ago. The Hindus have, therefore, to
be permanently grateful to the Theosophical Society for the spread
of Hindu religious ideas in the West."[36] This became particularly
galling to Vivekananda.

Earlier, however, he had evinced a more irenic temper toward
Western leaders among the Theosophists and seemed to accept their

prior presence on the scene without rancor. In 1894 he had written to Alasinga, "Theosophists are our pioneers, do you know? Now Judge is a Hindu and Col. [Olcott] a Buddhist, and Judge is the ablest man here. Now tell the Hindu Theosophists to support Judge. Even if you can write Judge a letter, thanking him as a co-religionist and for his labours in presenting Hinduism before Americans; that will do his heart much good. We must not join any sect, but we must sympathise and work with each." Letters to Madras the following year reflect a markedly lower opinion of Judge, and the counsel, again to Alasinga, "Mind you, have nothing whatsoever to do with the Theosophists."[37] By this time, Vivekananda was developing his counterassertion that, far from needing to be grateful to Theosophy for paving the way, he had had to spend a great deal of his time winnowing the chaff of esoteric doctrine in Theosophy from the good grain of Hinduism which had been mixed with it. Theosophy, he felt, had sown confusion, and the public, alternately repelled and misled by its occult teachings, had to be reoriented to understand the essential truths of Hinduism.

His personal indebtedness to Theosophists in the West as in Madras, however, is incontrovertible. Vivekananda's work in England was begun and continued for several years under the leadership of Miss Muller and Sturdy, both Theosophists. At the invitation of Mrs. Besant, he spoke on *Bhakti,* at her lodge in London in 1896; Olcott was present. "I did it," Vivekananda said, "to show my sympathy for all sects."[38] The rather grudging personal appreciation of Mrs. Besant endured to mitigate somewhat his antipathy to the Theosophical organization itself. He visited back and forth in Almora with her in 1897, when she was staying at the residence of G. N. Chakravarti, who had also been present at the Parliament in Chicago. "Annie Besant," he wrote of this meeting, "told me entreatingly that there should be friendship between her organization and mine all over the world. . . ."[39]

The olive branch which certain admirers found in Vivekananda's Calcutta address, although never fully extended, doubtless reflected an awareness of the criticism that "My Plan of Campaign" had aroused. Public responses in *The Indian Mirror* of late February, 1897, include a letter to the editor suggesting that Vivekananda's Bengali admirers might rejoice in an attack such as he had made on the Theosophical Society, but, "If the Swami be true to his own Guru, he ought not to fan the flame of party spirit." A characteristically cordial editorial of the same month ventured the criticism:

As an outsider, his antipathy to the Theosophical Society may well be excused. We doubt if he is acquainted with Theosophical literature or that he has even glanced over Madame Blavatsky's books. Swami Vivekananda is still very young, and doubtless his present likes and dislikes will be considerably modified in the light of further knowledge and experience. Certainly we refuse to regard or accept his present fiery denunciations of things and persons as the final judgment of a matured sage.

An article by a "Brahman Buddhist," quoted in *The Indian Mirror* from *The Hindu*, comments on Vivekananda's characterization of all Theosophists as Europeans. He praised a supporter such as Justice Subramanya Ayer as a fellow countryman without making reference to his membership in the Theosophical Society. "While the Swami holds to his *guru,* why should he disturb or damage the quiet, sacred, and pious beliefs of others? . . . We implore the Swami to spare us such sweeping denunciations and judgments of men and things, as usually adorn his lips in every meeting now."[40]

Another letter in *The Indian Mirror,* by Dinanath Ganguli, says, "In giving vent to his feelings, the Swami went to the length of calling some of his opponents *Pariahs* and fools. This shows that, far from being a sage, he has not yet attained the position of an ordinary man of prudence. . . . His heart should be saturated with the nectar of *Bhakti.*" The letter continued with a quotation of the remarks with which Vivekananda prefaced his criticisms: "Not that I care what the result will be of these words, not that I care what feeling I shall evoke from you by these words; I care very little, I am the same *Sannyasin* that entered your city about four years ago with his staff. . . . The same broad world is before me." The writer questioned whether this was a correct interpretation of the role of the *Sannyasin,* who "must care for the results of his words."

While the Calcutta address may, then, have represented a partial concession to the public's demand for a milder course toward his opponents, a letter to Mrs. Bull on May 5, 1897, indicates his feelings:

The Theosophists tried to fawn upon and flatter me as I am the authority now in India, and therefore it was necessary for me to stop my work giving any sanction to their humbugs, by a few bold, decisive words;

and the thing is done. I am very glad. If my health had permitted, I would have cleared India by this time of these upstart humbugs, at least tried my best.[41]

It may be observed that Vivekananda's militant hostility toward the Theosophists had three bases: first, that of the personal slights which he reported they had administered to him. The evidence here is simply not conclusive, but it is clear that he had harbored for some time a deep rancor toward the actions of some of their leaders. Second, he identified the movement as Western, and he held a strong position that in religious matters, Westerners are always to be the learners from Indian teachers. Although his regard for such Orientalists as Max Müller and Paul Deussen is well known, one must search diligently to find a positive reference to any Westerner in India other than his own followers. David Hare and William Hastie are two exceptions, but he characterized Hare as outcasted by Christians and recognized only by his Bengali students; and, while he admired Hastie as a teacher, he depicted their relationship in religious matters as one in which Hastie received an influence and taught nothing of the worth of Christianity in return. Third, he objected doctrinally to the blending of occult and mystical teachings with materials from the Hindu tradition. At this point he gained support from reformers, who agreed with his stance, in contrast to more conservative Hindus, who, in valuing Theosophy's defense of the bastions of the Hindu tradition, felt that the tradition also allowed for such materials to be incorporated with it. *The Indian Social Reformer,* expressing assent to Vivekananda's opposition to the occult in Theosophy and elsewhere, said, "For centuries, we have been stuffed with the mysterious, the result is that our intellectual and spiritual digestion is almost hopelessly impaired and the race has been dragged down to the depths of hopeless imbecility never before or since experienced by any civilized community."[42]

Those who belonged to no sect, the masses of India, accepted Vivekananda as the national hero, the man of the hour. Fed for years with glowing reports of his triumphs in the West, he was singled out for adulation of a magnitude experienced by no other national figure until that time. Rammohan Roy had not returned from his visit to the West; Keshab was more urbane, reaching the intellectuals. Vivekananda was the conqueror, and he revived the national consciousness. More than a religious figure primarily, the initial mass appeal which he held was that of one who had vanquished the West and had a plan for his own people. That this plan was not fully comprehended by the people, but its hoped-for directions anticipated, is evident from this optimistic appraisal: "The Swami is not a mere religious recluse with no ideas beyond religion. An extremely powerful undercurrent of patriotism runs through all his speeches. He hinted that he had some plans for raising his countrymen from their material degradation. The plans are not yet out. But if American scientists and inventors are at his back, one may reasonably hope to see an impetus given to our industrial activities."[43] Not all of the hopes vested in him could, of course, be realized. Vivekananda himself had had to adjust his expectation of gaining financial support in the West for the material needs of India.

Spiritual reform, despite his own earlier objectives and those of many who looked to him, was to be his primary objective. "In this land of charity, let us take up the energy of the first charity, the diffusion of spiritual knowledge."[44] This was his gift. In keeping with its own inherent genius, India must persist in its spiritual quest and must then endeavor to broadcast that knowledge to the nations of the world. He wanted to contribute a consciousness of the great wealth which the nation possessed in its spiritual treasures. As the people immersed themselves in their own tradition, they would become strong, fitted for other, more secular pursuits. The organizations he intended to found, the education he sought to inaugurate were religious in character, but it was to be "man-making religion."[45]

Chapter Six

VIVEKANANDA'S EARLY WESTERN FOLLOWERS

As the Swami traveled through the cities of America and England, his following took shape from among the established, cultured, literate stratas of society. While certain personalities such as the two whom he first initiated into *sannyas* vows, Leon Landsberg and Madame Marie Louise, may have been identified with "radical" causes and thought of by some as personally unstable and given to fanaticism, most exuded an aura of eminent respectability. This is particularly striking in contrast with the current scene, in which new adherents to Eastern religious and quasireligious movements in the West seem rather uniformly drawn from those among the young who, disaffected with the expressed values of their culture, are in search of sharply alternative life styles.

Some of the wealthy homes in which the Swami was entertained may have considered him a social plum, an impressive acquisition for the drawing room. He rather resisted the proprietorship which a few sought to exercise toward him by changing residences often, as he felt befitted a *sannyasin*. He retained the management of his own mission. Although he objected in New York to the attempts of a Miss Hamlin to introduce him to the "right sort of persons," stating that not one such had turned up,[1] an external assessment by the standards of the day would discern a large assortment of such persons in his entourage. The biographies enumerate lists of personalities who became attached to him from among the most notable leaders in artistic, scientific, academic, and even business and political circles of the day. What was it that drew them?

If the Swami's personal magnetism attracted many, his message also must be credited with meeting a need in terms of religious and

97

intellectual commitment. The experience of William Ernest Hocking, whose liberal understanding of the encounter of world faiths was first given shape during his university training in the 1890's, may illustrate some of the dynamics at work for others also. Hocking heard Vivekananda at the Parliament and later in Cambridge, where he was studying with William James, whose relationship to Vivekananda has been noted. Reared in Methodism, Hocking testifies to a period of religious skepticism in his early university days, which was then modified by his contacts with Vivekananda and James. These men seemed to offer clues to a religion of maturity which could meet the challenge of philosophical skepticism.[2]

A man with a relationship to Vedanta of over forty years, who has long served as a Swami from the West, says that he chose the movement, first, because it provided him with a rational explanation for religious aspiration, and, second, because it furnished a discipline which could offer experience of spirituality.[3] These factors may have been operative for some who became followers of Vivekananda. Few were actively and meaningfully involved in main-stream Christianity, although for several, movements such as Theosophy and Christian Science were way stations between participation in the institutional Church and an identification with Vedanta. A certain estrangement from traditional Western religious forms and doctrines seems to have been normative for some, although data on previous religious affiliation is slight. Where specific denominational membership is mentioned, there is a tendency to associate it with personal rigidity and a limited ability to welcome the religious insights which Vivekananda had to share.[4]

The claim was early made that Vedanta, far from undermining previous religious commitments, rather reinforced them. The new relationship was felt to lead one to a higher experiencing of Christianity, now divested of its exclusive claims. Miss MacLeod, in answer to an invitation from Mrs. Bull to support the newly inaugurated organization in Cambridge, replied, "I doubt if the work progresses in the right way in New York without the Swami Vivekananda, and should consider the Cambridge element more congenial and fruitful soil, as it holds less to the necessity of Christianity as a saving power. Our Swami's great exposition of Vedanta Philosophy always favored rather than denied the mission of Christ, and left Christians better

Christians, and this is what essentially appealed to Mr. Leggett, and in fact to all of us."[5] It is interesting to find that Miss Mary Phillips, designated as being "in charge of the work" in New York, writes in a similar vein to Miss MacLeod and in the same year: "We are not giving up the religion of our forefathers," she claims, "nor the Christ of Nazareth. . . . It is a delving to the roots of all religions, leaving us free to worship in whatever form we choose. . . . There have been many Christs. All represent the fundamental principles of the philosophy of the Vedas. . . . So in studying this fundamental faith, we hold that we are only gathering information, so that we may better understand the religion of Jesus of Nazareth."[6] Thus the call to study other traditions as equally valid approaches to God was defended as real Christianity in both New York and Boston, the two earliest Vedanta centers in North America.

The relationship between Christianity and Hinduism becomes particularly complex when we consider the testimony of Sister Nivedita, in whom Vivekananda painstakingly sought to develop an Indian consciousness by having her attend meticulously to the practice of thousands of details of Indian daily life. He finally said to her, "You have to set yourself to Hinduise your thoughts, your needs, your conceptions and your habits. Your life, internal and external, has to become all that an orthodox Hindu Brahmin Brahmacharini's [female novice] ought to be. The method will come to you, if only you desire it sufficiently. But you have to forget your own past, and to cause it to be forgotten. You have to lose even its memory!"[7] From the time of her entry into India, she made every effort to live up to this counsel of her master. Yet a few months after Vivekananda's death in 1902, *The Madras Times* recorded the following question and response in an interview: "I suppose that your position in the Church of your early years [the Church of England] ceased when you entered upon the work you are at present engaged upon?" "No," was the reply, "I have never broken with my position as a member of the Church of England nor is there any reason why I should do so," and, she added with emphasis, "I am in no sense of the word a Theosophist."[8] Formally, it would seem, it was important not to renounce the identification with Christianity, but to interpret the new affiliation as fulfilling rather than destroying that relationship. Practically, it meant for Nivedita, as for no other Western worker, the assumption of a wholly new life style, gained at the expense of considerable pain in divesting herself of her former identity.

At one level, Nivedita's Indianization process may be viewed as a charming accommodation to the customs of Hindu life, eating with the fingers, etc., in obedience to Vivekananda's counsel, "Remember! If you love India at all, you must love her as she is, not as you might wish her to become!"[9] In another sense, that obedience seemed to compel her to abdicate critical judgment which she might have exercised. Such an abdication was noted in the Indian press shortly after her arrival, in editorial comment on her address on Kali worship:

Miss Noble, alias Sister Nivedita, believes that the nations are journeying on to the sect of the goddess Kali! There is evidently some illusion of spiritual optics here, for while we can easily behold men moving away from the dread presence of the great goddess, we see no movement in the contrary direction. This pious lady preaches that "religion is for the heart of the people. To refine it is to emasculate it. . . . The man who derives brutal satisfaction from life, or who sees no further than the surface of things, this man has a right to these satisfactions, and to make for himself a worship which shall express these instincts. The man who is violent in his modes of thought, and vivid in his apprehension of life, the man who appreciates the struggle of Nature, and is strong enough to plunge into it fearlessly, that man has a right to offer to God that which he hourly demands from life." That man *does* all these things, we know; but why he should be said to have a right to do them is more than we can understand. A worshipper of Kali, according to the doctrine, has a right to shed human blood, to violate the chastity of women, to drink spirituous liquors and to indulge in all the disgusting rites of the tantriks. This is revivalism with a vengeance![10]

While a certain lack of discrimination may be apparent in the above passage and in various works of Nivedita, such as her otherwise perceptive and intimate book *The Web of Indian Life*, her own account of the transformation which she experienced brings out the previous uncritical British patriotism in her which the Swami attacked so strongly. As she was composing his biography, *The Master as I Saw Him,* she wrote to her intimate friend, Miss MacLeod, "I think when I am really sure of having completed a chapter of Swami's life, I'll send it to you to read to Lady Betty. If your heart and her judgment are both satisfied, then I shall be at rest. What do you say? I am bringing out very strongly the element of struggle, between myself and Him, and this by the advice of the Man of Science [J. C. Bose, whom Vivekananda had met in Paris, and to whom Nivedita was closely related in the decade before her death]. It seems egotistical I fear, but I think on the whole that this is the true advice."[11] The struggle indeed emerges in the volume, particularly as it came to a time of crisis in Almora in 1898. If the renunciation which followed on her part seems to a Western observer a personal capitulation, it led to a truly heroic record of service in her writings, her educational work, and the social service which she championed. A strong, independent spirit is manifest also in the separate path which she chose following the death of Vivekananada.

The ostensible reason for her severance from the headquarters in Belur is given by the movement as her involvement in political activities, although there is a hesitant reserve as to its actual extent. Little direct evidence is cited, apart from the voicing of her conviction while on a tour of western and southern India that the British should vacate the country. Asked by Brahmananda to give up politics, she replied that she could not, and so dissociated herself from the Math and Mission, apparently at their request, on July 18, 1902, barely two weeks after Vivekananda's death. Her own account of the event is charitable in the extreme, as contained in two letters to *The Indian Mirror* of July 22 and July 31, 1902. The first was simply reported as follows: "Sister Nivedita begs us to inform the public that, at the conclusion of the days of mourning for the Swami Vivekananda, it has been decided between the members of the Order at Belur Math and herself, that her work shall henceforth be regarded as free, and entirely independent of their sanction and authority." In the second letter, her feelings were directly elaborated:

It is with the deepest pain that I hear of allusions to myself as having become—by the death of my great master, the Swami Vivekananda—leader of the order of Ramakrishna. I must ask you, therefore, to be good enough to give the widest currency at your disposal to the following statement: The Order of Ramakrishna has its headquarters at Belur Math, Howrah, and is under the absolute leadership and authority of the Swami Brahmananda and the Swami Saradananda—two of the most saintly men who one could ever meet. . . . My own position is that of the humblest learner, merely a Brahmacharini, or novice, not a Sannyassini or fully professed religious; without any pretensions to Sanskrit learning, and set free by the great kindness of my supervisors to pursue my social, literary and educational work and studies, entirely outside their direction and supervision. Indeed, since the death of my Guru, I am not likely to be much in contact with any of my fellow-disciples who are not women.

To my own mind, no mistake could be more deplorable than that which assumes that the Hindu people require European leaders for their religious life. The very contrary is the case. . . .[12]

Perhaps something of the hesitancy on the part of both Sister Nivedita and the authorities at Belur was a reluctance for male monastics to have oversight of work for women and girls. A comparable program for women was not begun by the movement for some fifty years, we know, and even then, the goal was for it to attain separate status within a stated time.[13] Nivedita's protective shielding of her girls from the male presence is conveyed in an account by H. S. L. Polak, editor of Gandhi's South African paper, *Indian Opinion*. Asked by Nivedita in 1909 or 1910 to speak on South Africa, he reported, "I discovered for the first time that I was with a *purdah* nationalist. What happened was I was asked to address her girls from behind the curtain."[14]

An incident like that does not convey the great personal warmth evidenced in some of the unpublished letters of Nivedita, particularly to "Tantine"—Josephine MacLeod—in which she relates how consciously she continued to labor in India in the light of moments which they shared with Vivekananda there. Detailing some of her concerns in Easter week, 1904, she said, "Oh Yum, I do pray that I may be allowed to go on doing this! I want never to leave India. While I am here, I am *sure* that I am in my right place. Can't you look into the future, and assure me that I shall be allowed to go on and on, quietly sowing the seed that Swamiji has left?" Later she wrote, "I am utterly satisfied, utterly at peace. . . . I feel sure at last that my feet are on the right path, the path blessed and approved by him, and that the only question now is whether I shall work adequately or inadequately along the lines he has given me. This peace comes largely from finding the written work so much more powerful than the spoken, so that I am not anxious because my work is done at my desk."[15]

Two other letters in 1906 find her reminiscing. "Oh how I wish I could run to you for a chat, whenever I wanted to stop working. Do you remember those sweet days beside the Shalimar? How wonderful love is! It makes one open out and unfold one's whole nature to the listener! How much of everyone's happiness that year, dear Yum, depended on the love *you* brought!" "Do you know why I am sitting chattering here? Just to make *that* more real. Those talks under the trees in the mornings, that evening in the verandah as the storm came on? Yum Yum we had the best, you and I, and what you and S. Sara [Mrs. Bull] have seen in his attitude to India, no other American ever had a glimpse of. . . ."[16]

In the last few years of her life a shadow was cast by the jealous contesting of Mrs. Bull's will by her daughter, who had opposed bequeathing a considerable sum to Nivedita's work in India. A number of her friends said in their letters following Nivedita's death in 1911 that her passing had been hastened by the grief which she felt over the daughter's hostility.* The will was reported to have been set aside by the courts on the ground of mental incapacity and undue influence.[17] A distance had also developed with Sister Christine, who nevertheless took up Nivedita's work following her death. Despite the formal parting of the ways from the headquarters of the Ramakrishna movement in Belur, relationships remained cordial, and leaders of the movement extended a great deal of assistance to her work in the years following, such as assisting in publishing and promoting the sale of her books.

While Nivedita's service to India seemed to fulfill the Sanskrit name given her by her Master (it may be translated as "the dedicated"), some other Western workers showed much less enchantment with India. Miss Muller, as previously intimated, was one. Her support in England and her financial assistance in India were of considerable value, but frictions began to arise between her and other workers, and with Vivekananda as well. Vivekananda had some frank counsel to Nivedita in welcoming her to India.

Again, I must give you a bit of warning. You must stand on your own feet and not be under the wings of Miss Muller or anybody else. Miss Muller is a good lady in her own way, but unfortunately it got into her head, when she was a girl, that she was a born leader and that no other qualifications were necessary to move the world but money! . . . She now

---

*The news of Nivedita's death came to those in the West via cablegram in October of 1911 by Frank Alexander to Mrs. Mary Funke in Detroit, (he had also come from Detroit to India, rather as a protege of Christine Greenstidel) and from Abala Bose of the doctor's family with whom she had been staying in Darjeeling where she died. Subsequent letters between those in the West, from Mrs. Funke, Miss MacLeod, and B. N. Dutt each seem to refer to "the terrible forces which have been set at work through all that malice, hate and envy which came out in the dreadful will case." (Mrs. Funke's letter.) The daughter is reported to have taken her own life a few years following the dispute. Other members of the family, however, such as Mrs. Bull's brother, Joseph Sharp of Cambridge, continued to support Nivedita's work. A letter from Miss MacLeod in 1915 relates that he had been sending $1,000 each year for the support of Nivedita's school. The above letters are in the files of the Trabuco Monastery.

intends to take a house in Calcutta for herself and yourself and other European or American friends who may come.

It is very kind and good of her, but her Lady Abbess plan will never be carried out for two reasons—her violent temper and overbearing conduct, and her awfully vacillating mind.[18]

Despite this opinion in the summer of 1897, Miss Muller remained attached to Vivekananda's work until late in the following year, when she left, according to Vivekananda, because she did not feel that a spiritual person ought to be ill as he was. *The Indian Social Reformer,* as previously mentioned, cited instead her conviction that social reform needed to accompany religious reform, and that she could best help in that direction by returning to Christianity. This attitude would contrast quite clearly with Nivedita's, both in the way she determined that her conclusion led her to make an either-or choice between Christianity and Vedanta and in her feeling that the structures of society were in need of a radical revision.

Goodwin's secretarial service was valuable for several months after his coming with Vivekananda, but the Swami indicated that he chafed somewhat at "the indignities of isolation which a *Mllechchha* [foreigner] is made to undergo here."[19] While Vivekananda and others continued to hold him in high regard until the time of his death, we do not know what circumstances dictated his assuming employment with *The Madras Mail* in July of 1897. Perhaps something of his feeling towards his earlier attachment to Indian religion is revealed in a letter to Miss MacLeod on May 5, 1898, just a few weeks before he died:

I wonder if you feel the same pleasure at the result of the naval battle in the Philippines as I do, or if you are too much of a Vedantist!! I believe I am about 50 percent American and the rest English (and, in a whisper please, not a bit Hindu.) I realize more and more every day that the Swami is not a Hindu . . . as Hindus go because everything must be judged by the sum-total, and the sum-total of India is meanness, and petty scheming, and *not* religion.[20]

This quality of disillusion with the social order and religious life of India caused him to dissociate Vivekananda from that climate, in order, doubtless, to preserve his high estimate of his teacher and his own judgment in following him.

A still different pattern of response is visible in Miss MacLeod who, until the time of her death at the Hollywood center in 1949, remained an unusually effective friend and international ambassador for the movement. By her own declaration, she was a friend of Swami Vivekananda and never a disciple.* Through many visits to India and contacts in the West, raising funds, stimulating interest in, among other persons, Romain Rolland—who began his research into the lives of Ramakrishna and Vivekananda after meeting her— she perpetuated the influence of her friend and his Master. Two letters of Swami Shivananda in India to Tantine in 1927 tell of Rolland's inquiries to Belur and his gratitude to her for her success in interpreting the greatness of these men of India to him.[21] Two of her letters to Mary Hale, in 1913 and 1916, reveal something of the personal warmth and vitality which made her such an effective spokesman for the movement. "No one," she writes, "who has ever been very near Swamiji or Margot [Nivedita]—are [sic] really ever far from me—Don't you feel this too? . . . Life never seemed to me so full—big fundamental things that are worth while cropping up all along the line these days. . . . When one has something active and creative to do this world seems young, doesn't it? It's only the people who follow that get bored!" Again: "Such a dear letter came

*Atulananda's letter to Ujjvala (Miss Ida Ansell), March 11th, 1939, is an unusually picturesque description of Miss MacLeod. It reads as follows: "Dear Tantine, she has helped and loved many, and no one has 'caught' her. Not even Swamiji. She plays with the work as her toy. And plays with the Lord. Really she is a great lover though she imagines she is a jnani. [Nivedita wrote Miss MacLeod in 1904 that the Holy Mother had told us that Miss MacLeod was a jnani. Trabuco files.] She loved Swamiji but always danced one step ahead of him. He never changed her external life. She loved and played and went her own sweet way—the way that suited her own game. Shakti—the dancing Kali. And Siva not even able to catch her dancing feet. I hope they will put her photo in the Math. Never shall I forget her ringing voice to a most humble devoted audience, 'Swamiji cleaned my shoes!' That is Tantine. And yet, watch her slip away to Swamiji's room and shut the door. What is she doing there, all alone, with no audience? She is fooling us all, dear Tantine. What a memory for the Math she'll be. Who, I wonder, will write her life. Who ever knew her? I guess Swamiji knew her best, as Turiyan knew you best. I am glad I have loved you both. Don't hurry off too soon. I'm still needing you, your gentleness and Tantine's strength. You must remember that Tantine always says, 'I'm not Swamiji's disciple, I'm no one's disciple. I was his friend. I never asked him a question, I never asked him for any-thing.' The other day only I heard her say, 'I feel as if Swamiji is just around the corner.'
    "Tantine once asked Nivedita what Swamiji stood for. She said, 'Re-nunciation.' Mrs. Sevier, when asked, said, 'Union.' 'To me,' Tantine said, 'he stood for Freedom.' " From the Trabuco files.

from you this last post—showing that the heart-throb of your life
is the same as mine—no matter what the external trappings may be
—That is what we all always felt in you—and that is why in our
hearts we always include you—I don't believe there can be much
of a mistake in any of our lives—in the lives of us who recognized
Him! as long as we keep that shrine. . . . I mean to be on earth
many a year yet!"[22]

Few people have been able to move so freely and with such
authenticity between the spiritual realms and cultures of East and
West as did Josephine McLeod, and the movement's indebtedness to
her is profound.

Atulananda succeeded after several attempts over some twenty
years in adapting to the customs and climate of India and spent
almost the whole of his long life after 1918 in India. He died in 1966
at the age of 97 near Mussoorie, where he had lived as a recluse
during most of his last thirty years. His passing marked the end of an
era, for few succeeded him who had known so many of the early
founders of the movement, East and West. He was born C. J. Heij-
blom to a Dutch family that had settled in America. His first contacts with Vedanta were under Swami Abhedananda in New York,
where he was ordained into *brahmacharya* (student) status with
three others on Easter Sunday, 1899. He met Vivekananda during
the latter's second visit to the West and stayed with Swami Turiyananda at the Shanti Ashrama in California for some months.

He remained a *brahmacharya* with the name of Gurudas until
1923, when he became a *sannyasin*, again being ordained by Abhedananda at Belur. Prior to that, shortly after settling permanently
in India, he received initiation from the Holy Mother in Calcutta.
He served for some time at the Advaita Ashrama in Mayavati, with
responsibilities in writing and editing, and some of his reminiscences
are included in his book *With The Swamis in America*. During the
long years in which he led the life of a recluse he acquired, according to his obituary, the reputation of deep spirituality.[23]

Some of Atulananda's writings manifest a quite negative experience of Western Christianity. Telling of the impact of Vivekananda's
teaching in the West, he says, "For those who are born in India it
must be difficult to realize what . . . [Vivekananda's teaching] meant
to us in the West, to us who had shaped our lives under the terrible

doctrines of the churches: that we are impotent, miserable creatures at the mercy of a whimsical, autocratic God, the sword of damnation always hanging over our heads, bondslaves at the mercy of a potentate to save or damn as he pleases." Again he writes, "To some of his [Vivekananda's] hearers, especially to hidebound Church members, such remarks were shocking and 'they understood not the sayings which he spoke unto them.' "[24] If such statements evidence a certain petulance towards Christianity, his letters occasionally contain critical observations of the level of spirituality which he saw in Indian religion as well.* His comments are often refreshingly candid; his model of spirituality was unconventional but not lacking in convincing character. Perhaps Sarma's evaluation, when speaking of Annie Besant and Pandita Ramabai as persons born in one culture who instinctively feel at home in another, may apply as well to Swami Atulananda, who nevertheless retained an ability to distinguish between dross and distilled wisdom in the country of his adoption.

The early experience of Miss Ida Ansell, whose Sanskrit name was Ujjvala, illustrates the difficult transition which a Vedanta devotee may encounter when the guru departs and another spiritual teacher arrives. If the leadership role is carried out differently, the problem of adjustment may be particularly acute. While this may be true with a transfer of leadership in most religious organizations, here it is compounded by the intimate relationship which often prevails. These dynamics were evidenced with the departure of Swami Turiyananda, guru to the small circle of disciples at Shanti Ashrama, and the arrival of Swami Trigunatita. Turiyananda's absence was first thought to be only temporary, but his successor appears to have been threatened by this tenuous relationship and by the strong ties of affection which still yoked most of the adherents to Turiyananda. It appears that two factions developed, one wanting Trigunatita to be permanently designated as teacher, and the other, still attached to Turiyananda and hoping for his return, opposing this. Some were leaving the society because of this difficulty. Ujjvala says that she "remained miserably neutral until a petition was sent to Swami

---

*In one of his letters, dated September 26th, 1924, for instance, he mentions that the Swamis around him are nice chaps but offer little spiritual help. He also cites an instance where thirty-seven Moslems were recently killed by Hindus to save one cow. Trabuco files.

Brahmananda asking that Swami Trigunatita be permanently as-
signed to the California work. This I refused to sign, and Swami
Trigunatita was displeased."[25] She states it much more mildly than
did his letter itself, written to her in Los Angeles on April 21, 1904:

> I understand you are behaving very badly with me and my work. . . .
> So long as I am here in this State the work belongs absolutely to me, and
> not to any of you, not even to your Swami Turiyananda. If you idolize
> Swami Turiyananda, go to him. Here he has nothing to do, so long as I
> am here. . . . You have not come to the Vedanta Society to supervise the
> management or to pass your views as the Prime Minister of the Empire;
> you have come here to learn some spirituality. If you can not get it, just
> softly move away. Go wherever you may get your spirituality. Do you
> understand that.
>
> Yours in Truth,
> Trigunatita[26]

Ujjvala wrote asking his forgiveness and received a letter which
was milder in tone, yet still sternly authoritarian.

> What is done is done. But do not try to act further against my wishes.
> If you do so, it would go against you. Just do and act most obediently, if
> you want your good. Just do what I want you to do. And then you would
> not incur my displeasure. Rather you will highly please me and please
> God, and you will prove yourself true to the cause and true to your nature.
> . . . Have faith in me. I will never ask you to do what is wrong for you.
> You never exercise your own intellect and judgment over what I will ask
> you to do. I know better than you, what is right and what is wrong for
> you. If you do not believe in me like that, you will have to suffer for that.
> And if you believe in me fully, then you will all the time be gaining and
> improving. . . .[27]

She said of the above that a letter "brought his forgiveness and
things went on as before until it was definitely settled that Swami
Turiyananda would not return. Later I wrote Swami Turiyananda for
permission to take spiritual instruction from Swami Trigunatita and
began such instructions in 1905."[28] Despite her submission, he did
not permit her to go to the Ashrama which she so loved for more than
a year.

Such authoritarian treatment of the spiritual seeker seems harsh,
even brutal, especially when we consider the description which Miss
Ansell gives of herself three or four years earlier. "I was lame, frail,
twenty-three in years, much younger in experience, having been de-
prived by various infirmities of the usual activities of youth."[29] Yet
her submission seems to have accorded to her a kind of veneration in

her later years, when she lived along with Tantine at the Hollywood shrine. Her vivid relating of the early days at Shanti Ashrama formed a continuing link with the founders of the work in the West. When newcomers learned who this small, unprepossessing woman was, a special aura of sanctity seemed to attach itself to her.

A vastly contrasting personality and different quality of response is seen in Madame Marie Louise, who, as one of the two first Western *sannyasins* of Vivekananda, was a forceful, controversial personality from the first days at Thousand Islands Park, where she received her monastic vows. Sister Christine, a chronicler of that period, attributes to Vivekananda a rather interesting motive for his decision to ordain Abhayananda and Kripananda, Marie Louise and Landsberg, respectively. As she saw it,

> The choice of [Marie Louise and Landsberg] grew out of the theory which he [Vivekananda] held that fanaticism is power gone astray. If this force can be transmuted and turned into a higher channel, it becomes a great power for good. . . . Marie Louise was, in some respects, the outstanding personality in this small community. A tall, angular woman, about fifty years of age. . . . The short, wiry hair, in the days before bobbed hair was in vogue, the masculine features, the large bones, the heavy voice and the robe, not unlike that worn by men in India, made one doubtful. Her path was the highest, she announced, that of philosophy, *jnana*. She had been the spokesman for ultra-radical groups and had learning and some degree of eloquence. "I have magnetism of the platform," she used to say. Her vanity and personal ambition made her unfit for discipleship, and useless as a worker in Swami Vivekananda's movement. She left first, and soon organized an independent center of Vedanta in California, and later, one in Washington.[30]

Christine's description of Landsberg is much more positive. Yet his defection came soon, whereas, operating rather independently as Christine says, Marie Louise continued as a leader at least until 1902, with work in the West and visits to India in 1899 and 1902, in the second of which she allied herself with Vaishnavism. After the time at the Thousand Islands, she soon began classes in her Greenwich Village house in New York. Attendance was small, and in an outraged letter to Mrs. Bull she expressed her feeling that the Society should have given her greater support. She apparently moved to Chicago rather soon after, where, in 1898, an interview was printed in *The Chicago Record* and reprinted in *The Brahmavadin*. The interview was occasioned by her ordination of Mrs. L. V. Comer, "the first of her race and only the second woman west of the orient," as a

Swami, with the name of Sraddananda. The article said of Abhayan-anda, "For some time she taught in New York but came to Chicago two or three years ago, where she continues to be at the head of the order in this country. She has quite a large following in the western city, and may be found at almost any hour in the rooms of the Advaita society in 24th street."[31] It seems rather surprising that *The Brahm-avadin,* a journal of the movement in Bengal, would have printed without comment the statement that she was head of the order in the United States, when Abhedananda was working in New York.

In her first visit to India, Abhayananda was in some contact with Vivekananda and the others, although she lectured independ-ently in Madras and Bombay before coming to Calcutta. Interestingly, Justice Ranade presided at her address in Bombay. Some apparent confusion existed in the minds of the press, however, as to her identity and relation with Hinduism. *The Mahratta* reported that she had con-verted a number of Americans to the Shaivite sect of Hinduism. "And moreover she has, under the authority delegated to her by Swami Vivekananda, herself ordained two Shaivite priests and one lady priestess who are establishing missions in the different large centers of population in the United States." The article also mentioned that "a Hindu Jain who happened to be in Brooklyn once went to hear her preach, and after attending a number of her services became her *chela* or pupil, and finally made up his mind to become a *sannyasi.* Swami Abhayananda therefore undertook to initiate him according to the Vedic ritual."[32]

The Indian Social Reformer detailed her conglomerate orienta-tion, referring to her as one "who is said to be French by extraction, American by domicile, Saiva by faith, Vaishnava in neck ornamenta-tion, Vedantin by philosophic persuasion and a Sannyasin in her mode of life." The article nevertheless saw in her a "sincere and modest seeker after truth" who appeared to have "more discrimination than some of the other European converts to Hinduism have shown."[33] *The Gujarati* objected to her adopting Indian dress and appearance with the change of faith as evidence of "denationalization." "What a dread people have for this epithet in this country, and how they try to avoid the slightest approach to it!" The same journal saw in Abhayananda a "presumptuous person who had allegedly come to India as a learner, but rather spent her time in preaching on the subjects about which she professed to be a learner."[34]

As to India's reaction to the news of Vivekananda's having ordained a woman to the role of *sannyasin, Amrita Bazar Patrika,* the journal of the Vaishnava movement with which she later allied herself, reveals a fascinating editorial change of heart, doubtless conditioned by her adoption of Vaishnavism. The initial comment on the news of the ordination of Vivekananda's first two Western *sannyasin* followers voiced reserve: "We are somewhat taken aback to learn that Abhayananda is only a woman. It is a settled thing in the Hindu philosophy that women are not so constituted as to be able to develop higher powers."[35] Announcing her presence in India in 1899, the journal said, "She is now here a Sannyasee, well versed in the Upanishads. Not knowing Sanskrit she had to take recourse to translations. Of course a woman can never be a Swami but that is neither here nor there, and these are mere technicalities. But a Memsahib in the garb of a Sannyasee is a spectacle that is not always seen."[36] An appreciative comment the following year says that she has gone back to America, but hopes that she can return and benefit the people by her spiritual discourses; there is no reference to any incongruity between her sex and status as a *sannyasin.* Then, in 1902, in the Vivekananda obituary notice, the journal goes full circle.

Though a disciple of the Paramhangsa, Vivekananda chalked out a path for himself. The Paramhangsa was a *bhakta,* but Vivekananda preached *yoga,* and there is a wide divergence between the two cults. Vivekananda also preached the Avatarship of his *Guru,* the Paramhangsa, and this led Swami Abhayananda, whom he had initiated and who is now in our midst delighting the Calcutta public by her sweet discourses on the religion of the Lord Gauranga to secede from him.[37]

The Ramakrishna Movement, at the same time, appears to make no reference to Abhayananda's activities after 1899, so that the posture of both groups toward her indicates something of a sectarian rivalry. An editorial of 1963 in *Prabuddha Bharata* observes of the initiation of the two foreigners as *sannyasins* that:

This was a very bold experiment, not only because it was entirely a new conception in the West, but also because the conservative section in India of those days would not approve of such a step. The experiment, of course, was not quite a success, for the persons he could get at that initial stage were hardly suited for the purpose. Thus Madame Marie Louise, . . . and Herr Leon Landsberg . . . both failed to come up to his expectation, though both showed much promise in the earlier months.[38]

This observation on the character of those who were early allied with Vivekananda rather counters the tenor of most of the Movement's evaluations, in which they are generally depicted as a select group, although with sprinklings of the curious and marginal. Neither the rationale attributed by Christine for his choice, nor the conjecture of a paucity of persons who were worthy, satisfactorily accounts for what subsequently happened in the lives of Vivekananda's first two Western *sannyasins*. The truth would seem to lie in the observation that among those associated with Vivekananda and other exponents of Vedanta in the West in the early years there was a significant number of creative, progressive, and yet balanced persons. The two most consistently impressive might be Margaret Noble and Josephine MacLeod. The stature of their devotion, their achievements, is unchallenged. Landsberg and Marie Louise may have been chosen or instructed too hastily. The brevity of other attachments need not indicate failure or disenchantment, however, so much as a continuing quest for objectives which no single movement might satisfy.

Within the Movement it is evident that considerably different life styles were permitted to evolve, in continuation of a tendency observed in the relationship of Ramakrishna and his first disciples. It is suggested that Ramakrishna's "specialized role as a divinely possessed teacher and nurturant father-figure, permitted his disciples to develop complementary, differentiated roles."[39] The latitude allowed in this intimate relationship, nevertheless, received some modification with institutionalization, and a person such as Madame Louise may have found, for instance, a religion more conducive to her emotional nature in Vaishnavism.

Chapter Seven

VIVEKANANDA'S SUCCESSORS IN THE WEST

For a time, Vivekananda seems to have rated the abilities of his followers in Madras more highly than those of his *gurubhais* in Bengal. His letters occasionally reflect this and the image which he had of the Bengal activities: an endless round of rituals and cere- monies.[1] Out of sorts with his followers in Bengal and Madras alike for not having produced any resolutions of endorsement, he wrote to his brother disciples in 1894, "Of course I never relied on the Ben- galis, but the Madrasis couldn't do anything either." Then he launched into an eloquent satirical treatise on ceremonials, a part of which reads as follows: "If you want any good to come, just throw your ceremonials overboard and worship the Living God, the Man-God, every being that wears a human form—God in His universal as well as individual aspect. The universal aspect of God means this world, and worshipping it means serving it—this indeed is work, not indulg- ing in ceremonials. Neither is it work to cogitate as to whether the rice-plate should be placed in front of the God for ten minutes or for half an hour—that is called lunacy. Millions of rupees have been spent only that the temple-doors at Varanasi or Vrindaban may play at opening and shutting all day long! Now the Lord is having His toilet, now He is taking His meals, now He is busy on something else we know not what. . . . And all this, while the Living God is dying for want of food, for want of education! The banias of Bombay are erecting hospitals for bugs—while they would do nothing for men— even if they die! You have not the brain to understand this simple thing—that it is a plague with our country, and lunatic asylums are rife all over. . . ."[2] Gradually, however, as correspondence was re- newed with the Alambazar Math, and as he witnessed their response to his suggestions, particularly with reference to the assumption of relief work and publishing ventures, he came to entertain a more appreciative regard for them. In addition, the men in Bengal were *sannyasins* while most of his associates in Madras, to his dismay, were householders. Thus, when other workers for the West were needed, he looked to his *gurubhais*.

Vivekananda did not dictate the choice of Saradananda, the first to come, or that of Kali (Abhedananda), who was soon to follow, but mentioned a few names from whom the group at Alambazar made the designation. Saradananda was slow in making his decision, which gave Vivekananda some initial pause. He grew so impatient as to write advising Saradananda not to come, but he was already on his way. This alleviated Vivekananda's distress with his brother monks. As mentioned before, when Saradananda arrived in London, Vivekananda felt that his manner was too timid and self-effacing for an effective leader, but excellent reports from America after Saradananda's work began there must have encouraged him. Saradananda worked mainly in New York, but he continued Vivekananda's example of representing Vedanta at the Greenacre Conferences on Comparative Religion and spoke on a number of occasions in Boston and elsewhere. While his tenure seems to have been productive, it was apparently at his initiative that it was determined he should return to India less than two years after his arrival. Vivekananda readily acceded, feeling that he could be of great value to the work in India, particularly in view of Vivekananda's own impaired health. The service which he rendered as secretary of the movement over many years, his literary achievement in producing *Sri Ramakrishna, The Great Master,* and his solicitous care of the Holy Mother and other women devotees, are recounted elsewhere. His limited Western sojourn must have enabled him to communicate a great deal to his colleagues in India concerning the problems and possibilities there.

Abhedananda (Kali) began his journey West late in the summer of 1896 and was with Vivekananda for a few months before the latter returned to India. He had not tarried, unlike Saradananda, which may have made Vivekananda welcome him with greater cordiality. His maiden address in London was an impressive debut. Still, the work there did not prosper in Vivekananda's absence and apparently Sturdy and Abhedananda did not serve well in harness. Abhedananda went on to America the following summer. With the new Swami on the scene, Saradananda may have felt that his presence was needed more in India. At any rate, Abhedananda settled into the work in New York, and on October 28, 1898, the Vedanta Society of New York was incorporated. Vivekananda was delighted to witness his success on his second visit. While Turiyananda, who had accompanied him, was left on the East coast to assist Abhedananda and to do some independent lecturing, Vivekananda, afer a few months' respite with the Leggett household at Ridgely Manor, headed west for new endeavors. Despite some personal dissension with the Leggetts and other earlier New York followers, Abhedananda's work expanded remarkably in the next several years. He began to hold classes for children, started his career as a very prolific writer on Indian philosophy and religion, and, as a powerful speaker, filled some of the larger halls in New York with extended series of addresses. Swami Nirmalananda was sent in 1903 to assist him with the expanded work, which included the opening of a center in Brooklyn. When Nirmalananda was called back in 1906 and Abhedananda followed for a visit soon afterwards, Swami Bodhananda was sent to continue the work. The public response to Abhedananda's return to India was like an encore to that accorded to Vivekananda nine years earlier.

Swami Paramananda having returned with him late in 1906, Bodhananda went to Pittsburgh to open a center which a group of followers had requested. A property for the Society on West 80th Street in New York City and a retreat at Berkshire, Connecticut, were purchased shortly after. Personal difficulties between Abhedananda and Paramananda in 1908 led to the latter's departure to begin a separate center in Boston.[3] Both men were very much in demand as speakers. Gambhirananda's history records that Abhedananda's extended absences, mostly in England and on the Continent, put the American work in dire financial straits. Abhedananda's independent income from his publishing and lecturing enabled him to purchase the Berkshire property from the Society. He offered to do the same with the property in New York, but this was averted by renting out most of the rooms for a time after Abhedananda moved out of the residence permanently. The trustees of the Movement in Belur removed Abhedananda from their roll on the grounds that by accepting permanent residence outside of India, he was in violation of the provisions for the holding of that office.[4] Christine doubtless refers to these events when she writes, quite melodramatically, to Josephine

MacLeod, on September 13, 1910, from the Leggett home in New
York:

Bhupur [?] and Swami Bodhananda are here constantly, and I love
to be with them. Bodhananda is beautiful and devotional and full of love
and loyalty to Swamiji.
I have brought with me from Detroit a boy of twenty-two who is on
fire with spiritual zeal and love and devotion to Swamiji. He wants to
devote himself, body, mind and soul, to the work and has asked Bodhananda to make him a *Sannyasin*. He has great powers of mind and heart, is
a born orator and has great literary ability. He has been Swamiji's disciple
for three years and has felt a call to the work but the way did not seem
clear to him until last Thursday when that terrible scandal about Abhedananda came up in the papers of the whole country [the writer has not
been able to verify this reference] when he felt that the call had come
and that he was to go to New York to snatch up the banner that was being
trampled under foot. To me there is something infinitely heroic in the idea
of storming New York in the name of Swamiji at the very moment when
Vedanta is being dragged in the dust. . . .

The young man, Frank Alexander, subsequently went to India,
rather as Miss Greenstidel's protege, worked in Mayavati for a time
in helping to compose *The Life of Vivekananda* by his Eastern and
Western Disciples, returned in poor health to Detroit in 1916, where
he died a year later. Miss Greenstidel, who was with him at his death,
wrote, "Three days before [his death] he told me that Swamiji was
calling him, gave me some directions, . . . In speaking of his Indian
experience, he always said, 'I have lived. What does it matter whether
the body goes now or later.' "[5]

Abhedananda nevertheless remained in America, lecturing and
writing, with several trips to Europe, until 1921, when he returned to
India. The life at Belur, after his prolonged stay in the West, seems to
have been excessively austere to him, and having operated with considerable independence for years, he started up a separate work in Calcutta, under the name of the Ramakrishna Vedanta Society. This
organization has continued, supplementing the publishing efforts of the
parent organization in Belur with a Bengali monthly, *Vishwavani,* a
recent eight-volume series of the *Collected Works of Swami Abhedananda,* and other materials. Cordial relations appear to have persisted
between the two organizations over the years. Abhedananda, the last
of the direct disciples of Ramakrishna to pass from the scene, died at
the age of seventy-five in 1939. While his health in his last several
years had been declining, he was sufficiently strong in 1937 to preside

over the Parliament of Religions held in Calcutta on the occasion of Ramakrishna's Birth Centenary. His address concluded on an affirmative note: "I hope that this Parliament of Religions will sound the deathknell of all communal strife and struggle, and will create a great opportunity for promoting fellowship among various faiths."[6] This was his last public utterance.

Abhedananda's writings include many elaborate expositions of the great themes of Indian philosophical thought. Some of his attempts to integrate it with current scientific theory met with objections from the Indian press. *The Indian Social Reformer* remained vigilant against what seemed to it naive attempts to enhance the status of Vedanta through such associations. It quoted Abhedananda's booklet on reincarnation as follows: "*Vasanas* or strong desires are the manufacturers of new bodies. The thought, will or desire which is extremely strong during lifetime will become predominant at the time of death and will mold the inner nature of the dying persons. It has the power of electing conditions or environments which will help it in its way of manifestation. This process is expressed by the evolutionists as the law of natural selection. . . ." The journal went on to comment:

We see here the Hindu revivalists obsequiously wearing the livery of Darwin and Spencer. . . . To us the adoption of Western scientific phraseology in the exposition of Hindu philosophy appears as an interesting illustration of natural selection in the intellectual world. Biologists tell us that imitation is one of the means whereby the weak protect themselves from the power of the strong. There are reptiles, for example, which assume the colour of the vegetation through which they creep. Conformity ensures safety, contrast invites risk. The instinct of self-preservation prompts Hindu philosophy to protect itself from the talons of the modern critics; it, therefore, imitates the voice and assumes of the colours of Western science, in which lies safety.[7]

The correspondence which Abhedananda postulated between the *vasanas*—operating to insure the continuity of dominant characteristics between one life form and its remanifestation—and Darwin's theory of natural selection may seem gross. However, it should be acknowledged that a near veneration of science at the turn of the century induced many writers besides Abhedananda and Vivekananda to clothe their philosophical speculations in scientific terminology. If Western science was a prestigious consort to be pursued, Abhedananda's attitude towards Western religious practices led him to draw some unscholarly comparisons which compromised the charitable regard for other faiths that the Ramakrishna Movement has historically sought to manifest. In his essay "Christ vs. Christianity" he counterpoises the myths of Christianity in regard to creation, the fall, etc., with Hindu philosophy rather than with Hindu myths, thus making the Christian myths appear absurd. Again, in making comparisons between Christian practices and Hindu ideals, he singles out the most unedifying facets of Christian history in violation of legitimate scholarship.[8] Despite such strictures, Abhedananda, with more time to pursue his literary interests, exhibits in his writings a more comprehensive and systematic development of Indian philosophical themes than does Vivekananda, who, with the exception of such series of lectures as those on the yogas, largely wrote more immediate utterances composed for specific situations.

The fourth of Ramakrishna's disciples to journey to the West, Swami Turiyananda, came with Vivekananda on his second visit. Like Saradananda, he demonstrated a considerable reluctance to leave India for Western shores, and also like Saradananda, he did not remain long. Vivekananda deeply respected the intensity of his devotional life, and felt that his spiritual qualities could have a great influence. For his part, however, as a man of meditation, Turiyananda was averse to public ministry and could not be easily persuaded. Finally, he yielded as Vivekananda put his arms about his neck and wept like a child as he pleaded, "Dear Haribhai, can't you see I have been laying down my life, inch by inch, in fulfilling this mission of the Master, till I am on the verge of death! Can you merely be looking on and not come to my help by relieving me of a part of my great burden?"[9]

During the time that Vivekananda was in California, Turiyananda lectured at the Center in New York in Abhedananda's absences, conducted the children's classes, and also gave addresses in other eastern cities. Several of these were in Boston, where he read a paper on Sankara at the Cambridge Conference. On Vivekananda's return from California in early June of 1900, Turiyananda was again reluctant to take up the work in California. Once more, Vivekananda's exhortations prevailed, as recounted by *The Life of Swami Vivekananda:*

The brother-disciple (Turiyananda) always hesitated to plunge headlong into any work—and tried to avoid all responsibilities. Devoted to meditation and austerity, he was averse to all activity. Failing to persuade Swami Turiyananda by arguments to take charge of the Shanti Ashrama, the Swami said at last, "It is the will of the Mother that you should take charge of the work there." At this the brother-disciple said jocosely, "Rather say, it is your will. Certainly you have not heard the Mother to communicate Her will to you in that way. How can we hear the words of the Mother!" "Yes, brother," said the Swami with great emotion, "yes, the words of the Mother can be heard as clearly as we hear one another. It only requires a fine nerve to hear the words of the Mother."[10]

Accepting this as indeed the Mother's authentic counsel, Turiyananda journeyed to California in July, just two weeks before Vivekananda was to return in the other direction for India. On parting from his brother monk, who was to return to Calcutta only days after his death in 1902, Vivekananda exhorted: "Go and establish the Ashrama in California. Hoist the flag of Vedanta there. From this moment destroy even the very memory of India! Above all, live the life, and Mother will see to the rest!"[11]

Before leaving San Francisco, Vivekananda had told his students there, "I have only talked, but I shall send you one of my brethren who will show you how to live what I have taught."[12] The major part of Turiyananda's work, after brief sojourns in Los Angeles and San Francisco, was to endeavor, in the intimate retreat setting of the Ashrama in the barren hills southeast of San Francisco, to teach a small group of devotees how to live the spiritual life of which Vivekananda had spoken. He was not to be the organizer of the work in the cities of the West Coast; that work, in San Francisco, devolved to his successor, Swami Trigunatita. But for training in the devotional life, in the art of meditation, Turiyananda had many gifts to give.

He could not, however, obey the counsel given him by Vivekananda to "destroy even the very memory of India." Accordingly, after less than three years in the West he returned to his homeland, partially for reasons of health. Shocked by the death of Vivekananda shortly before his arrival, he rather soon gave up ideas of returning to the West and followed his own spiritual disposition in withdrawing from active pursuits to engage in meditation in northern India for the last twenty years of his life. His only active work during that period was the building of an Ashrama with Swami Shivananda in Almora as a by-product of his spiritual quest. He acquired a reputation of considerable sanctity, and his counsel, often given in letters, was of great value to many persons. He seemed rather a model of the classical Indian saint, untouched for the most part by his brief tenure in the West. Atulananda and others who had been with him in the West cherished the opportunity to spend further time in his presence after he returned to India.

Miss Ida Ansell (Ujjvala) records that it was a great shock to discover, on a visit to the Ashrama by Swami Abhedananda, that the swamis did not always agree. Abhedananda, although he later secured Berkshire as a retreat for the devotees in New York City, did not approve of Shanti Ashrama. He felt that it was too inaccessible from San Francisco and undesirable for other reasons.[13] Trigunatita, Turiyananda's successor, seemed to agree, for he concentrated on getting the work well under way in San Francisco before venturing to the Ashrama with some devotees a few years after his coming. Given the intimacy of the ties which bound the early followers there to Turiyananda, his placing emphasis on a more formal, established organization in the city must have required a considerable adjustment. He imposed severe disciplines upon himself, and those who accepted him as their mentor also learned to expect similar regimens to assist them in the spiritual quest.

The work in San Francisco thrived so that it outgrew the private home in which meetings had been held at first. Trigunatita then began to plan the first Hindu temple in the West, a structure which was completed in 1906. Crowned with strange towers and turrets, it bears an Oriental flavor that seems quite incongruous in its setting at the corner of Webster and Filbert Streets, although it certainly catches the attention.* The building is still in use as the residence of one of the senior swamis and a few American *brahmacharins,* and its auditorium is regularly used for a midweek study service.

The third story was pressed into use by Trigunatita at the insistence of his followers, who felt that his ascetic practice of sleeping on a board in his office with a single blanket under him and another

---

*"Seeker's Haven," *Fortnight,* May 11, 1953, gives the following description of the building: "There is a gray, weather-board building crowned with a cluster of spires and turrets at the corner of Webster and Filbert in San Francisco. It is an architectural curiosity which is entered . . . through a Hindu doorway surmounted by a Moorish dome. On the roof the rounded battlements of a European castle sits cheek by jowl against the tapering spires of a Hindu shrine and squat summit of a mosque" (p. 24).

above was injurious to his health. He had, indeed, developed rheuma-
tism and agreed to move into the more commodious quarters, to
which he invited E. C. Brown, a native of Britain who had moved to
San Francisco in his youth. A monastery was soon begun, and ten or
twelve young men who had been attending services also moved in. A
rather loose initial regimen was radically altered when Trigunatita
proposed that all of them rise at 3:00 a.m. to begin preparations for
morning worship. Horrified, they agreed instead to 4:00, which was
what he had really wanted.[14]

The picture which Brown gave of Trigunatita at an address in
1955 at the Society in London balanced the severity of his discipline
towards himself and others with incidents warmly human in character. He related that Trigunatita liked festivities and shows and vastly
enjoyed being in the streets on New Year's Eve throwing confetti, etc.
Trigunatita had worked intensively to decorate the Temple for the
Panama Pacific International Exposition which was to be held nearby
in 1915, but his untimely death occurred before it opened. The
lighter side of Trigunatita rather confirms an impression from certain
incidents related by Vivekananda in a letter to his brother monk
Ramakrishnananda in Madras:

Sarada [Trigunatita] has his malaria brought over from Dinajpur. I
made him eat a dose of opium the other day without much benefit to him
except his brain which progressed for some hours towards its natural
direction, namely, idiocy. Hari [Turiyananda] also has a touch; I hope it
will take off a good bit of their avoirdupois. By the by, we have once more
started the dancing business here, and it would make your heart glad to
see Hari and Sarada and my own good self in a waltz.[15]

Trigunatita was certainly not an unrelieved portrait of severity,
and the monastic life of the *gurubhais* generally seems to have been
alleviated by lighter moments.

Utilizing his experience with the Bengali journal *Udbodhan*,
Trigunatita began to publish *The Voice of Freedom* in 1909; it was
the successor to *The Pacific Vedantin*, which the San Francisco group
had started in 1902.

Trigunatita's creative efforts extended into other ventures unique
in the history of Vedanta in the West. Among pictures and books
which the San Francisco society listed for sale in *The Voice of Freedom* was a painting entitled "Jesus Christ in His Yoga Posture." Mrs.
T. P. Oliver executed the painting from descriptions suggested by

Trigunatita. The eyes of the serene countenance are rather Japanese in appearance; otherwise, the distinctive features are the seated posture and the surrounding animals (two rabbits, two birds, a sleeping tiger, a snake, and a small lizard on His arm). The work illustrates the Scriptural quotation from Mark's Gospel printed beneath the title: "He was there in the wilderness . . . and was with the wild beasts" (Mark 1:13).[16] In addition to the monastery, Trigunatita operated a nunnery, both firsts for Vedanta in the West. In 1914, the year before his death, records indicate plans for extensive charitable work in the San Francisco area to be financed through income from a few acres of a walnut ranch and some other properties. While it is difficult to imagine how they might have been developed, these plans included not less than sixteen anticipated separate institutions.[17]

If a program of social service along these lines failed to develop in San Francisco or at any of the other Western Vedanta centers, the regular schedule of listed activities from the *Voice of India* was impressive enough. In addition to three public lectures on Sundays, an eighteen dollar yearly membership entitled persons to attend classes on the Gita on Mondays, the Upanishads on Thursday evenings, daily exercises at 10:00 a.m., private monthly lessons, with special breathing exercises and spiritual cure and care, and admittance to the Shanti Ashrama for "Yoga practices in daily life, under proper guidance, if certified."[18]

Three days after the 1914 Christmas celebration at the Temple, the Swami was conducting the Sunday service when a young man, a former student in an unbalanced frame of mind, threw a bomb at the pulpit. The young man was killed in the explosion, and the Swami, gravely injured, died thirteen days later, on January 10, the birthday of Vivekananda, as he had foretold the day before.[19] Swami Prakashananda, who had come as his assistant in 1906, continued the work which he had begun, although certain aspects, such as the monastery and the nunnery, which had been declining with Trigunatita's failing health in the last few years of his life, were suspended.

The fifth of the early Indian teachers of Vedanta in the West was only twenty-one years of age at the time of his landing in New York in 1906. When he first came to Belur, the monks felt that he was too young to enter the monastery, but Vivekananda, "perceiving the glowing soul within that youthful body, declared, 'He shall remain.' "[20]

During his brief residence there before going to Madras, he endeared himself to the other monks by his cheerfulness shown in such ways as his custom of walking about the monastery with a song always on his lips. Swami Brahmananda called him Basanta Kokhile, or Spring-Bird, and his amazingly youthful spirit persisted until the day of his death in 1940. Nivedita, visiting Madras after the death of Vivekananda, developed an affection for Paramananda. Noting a certain resemblance to Vivekananda she endearingly called him "Baby Swamiji," which rather stuck for a time. Both Vivekananda and Ramakrishnananda had wanted Paramananda to be with them after his *sannyas* vows at Belur in January of 1902, but Vivekananda relinquished his claim so that Paramananda might return to Madras where he had been serving with Ramakrishnananda.

A year after his arrival in America, and before leaving New York following the dissension with Abhedananda, Paramananda had published his first book. Laura Glenn, who was soon to become his devoted colleague over many years as Sister Devamata, records the circumstances:

It was not meant to be a book at all. I was spending the summer months in the Catskills, busy preparing Miss Waldo's notes of Swami Vivekananda's teachings given at Thousand Island Park and published later as "Inspired Talks." It was a moment of grave crisis with me and the Swami sought to sustain me in every way possible. . . . I fell in the way of copying the instructive portion of each letter in a little notebook. . . . This is, I believe, the strength of the book, that the words were written [from New York] for a single striving heart.[21]

His work in the Boston area began in 1908. At Christmas of that year he was in the home of Mrs. Ole Bull with Sister Nivedita and Mr. and Mrs. J. C. Bose. Characteristically, he was a man who seemed to feel commitments at a number of places where he was taken by speaking engagements. In 1912 and 1913 he made extended visits in beginning a permanent group in Geneva. The war curtailed his return visits, however, and following it other responsibilities prevented his resumption of the relationship. Feeling the need of a warmer clime in the winter months, however, he had already initiated a work in Washington, D.C. Typically, after Sister Devamata's return from India, she would assume charge of the work there upon his return to Boston each spring. This pattern continued until 1916, when, with the establishment of a group in Los Angeles, it rather assumed Washington's position as the second base of activities. By this time the work in Boston had thrived, and the group had moved into their second permanent home in the Fenway district.

The work in the Los Angeles area expanded with the acquisition of a retreat site nearby in 1923. The development of this Ashrama at La Crescenta effected a balance in importance between the centers on the East and West coasts, and travel between the two became a regular feature of Paramananda's life, of his associates in leadership, and of most society members as well. The Ashrama at La Crescenta overshadowed the work in Los Angeles city, which was eventually closed. Similarly, after Paramananda's death, the Massachusetts work centered in the Cohasset retreat south of Boston.

Another singular feature of Paramananda's career was the leadership role which he shared with a series of women. Besides Devamata, in the 1920's there were Sister Daya, Miss Katherine Sherwood, Miss Galeni Philadelphius, Sister Satya-Prana, Gayatri Devi, Charushila Devi, and Sister Amala. No men other than the Swami were prominent in regular leadership. Of the women mentioned at least four were American [the writer has not learned the personal background of Sister Daya or Sister Amala] and two, Charushila Devi and Gayatri Devi, were from India. Devamata and Satya-Prana met Paramananda on the day of his arrival in New York in 1907. While Satya-Prana devoted herself to silent service, Devamata gave leadership over many years in speaking and in publishing *The Message of the East* and other writings. She had studied at the Sorbonne before becoming a quiet student of Vivekananda in New York. He once remarked to her, "You come so faithfully yet you never speak a word."[22] After being a lay sister in an Anglican convent, she affiliated with the Vedanta Society under Abhedananda. Never able to draw close either to Vivekananda or to Abhedananda, it was Paramananda who became her teacher. Until he came, her friendship and work with Miss Ellen Waldo kept her attached to the Movement.

Shortly after her decision to live a monastic life, Paramananda indicated his feeling that she should have the opportunity to go to India while Ramakrishna's disciples were still living. He sent her with the words, "You are going to the land of great souls. Go in freedom, and if you should meet with one whom you would rather have for your teacher, do not be bound by any thought of me."[23]

But Sister Devamata became still more attached to Paramananda through her two years in India, most of which was spent in Madras with Swami Ramakrishnananda, the teacher of her own teacher. Ramakrishnananda had told Paramananda that he was destined to work in the West and in the last years of his life completed the training of Paramananda's foremost Western disciple.

Charushila Devi, one of the two Indian women who served with Paramananda in Boston and the Ananda Ashrama in California, returned after two years to open a branch of the Ananda Ashrama in Dacca, East Bengal; a number of women were housed and educated there. Gayatri Devi, who came to the West in 1927, is the niece of Paramananda. She continues to the present day as the leader of the movement, which severed formal ties with the headquarters at Belur after Paramananda's death in 1940. The issue at stake was whether the group would accept another Swami from Belur to replace Paramananda. But their devotion to their leader of many years was so great, and their confidence in the leadership of women who had labored with him was so strong, that the group did not feel that they could receive another swami whom they did not know. Although a formal separation from the movement was thus effected, it is striking once more to witness that fraternal ties have remained close and cordial.*

Two tributes, one written by Sister Devamata on the occasion of the twenty-sixth anniversary of Paramananda's landing in America, and the other by Swami Nikhilananda of New York after Paramananda's death, are eloquent summations of his ministry and his stature among his peers. Sister Devamata wrote:

*Sister Gayatri Devi and a few of her disciples stayed at the Ramakrishna Mission Institute of Culture in Calcutta for two weeks while the writer was at the Institute in October of 1970, as she regularly does when in India. On one evening her birthday festivity was observed with many devotees gathering. The shrine in the room contained, in addition to the customary pictures of Ramakrishna, Vivekananda, and Sarada Devi, that of Swami Paramananda as well, just as in the centers of Southern California that of Brahmananda will be included as the *guru* of the *guru* in residence. In one brief interview with Gayatri Devi, she singled out the place of women in leadership as the most distinctive contribution of Paramananda and his followers. Gayatri Devi gives the impression of forceful, yet gracious leadership, with a vitality which, like that of her uncle, Paramananda, gives no hint of the years she has been involved in the work.

Twenty-six years ago I stood on a pier in New York harbor and watched a ship cast anchor. It bore an unknown youth westward. As he descended from its decks, he seemed the embodiment of freshness, buoyancy and unworldliness. . . . Fearlessness shone in his eyes and spoke in the ease of his bearing. He seemed as much of the West as of the East. Today that unknown youth stands before you as an eminent teacher, lecturer, poet, author and executive. His name appears on thirty title pages and in various biographical dictionaries. He has founded a strong religious Centre on the Atlantic Coast, another on the Pacific Coast; and like the spider that draws its thread from within itself, he moves back and forth across the American Continent, drawing from out of his own head shining strands, with which he weaves a web of inspiration and blessing.[24]

The tribute of Swami Nikhilananda who, with Akhilananda, Satprakashananda, and Prabhavananda among recent swamis in the United States, has acquired considerable reputation as a scholar, was addressed, "To My Beloved Brother." It reads in part:

I can say without fear of exaggeration that among the teachers of the Ramakrishna Mission who came to this country after the passing away of Swami Vivekananda, he has been the most successful in disseminating the ideals of this ancient system of Hindu philosophy. . . . He imparted religious instruction in a unique way. He was full of fun, merriment and gaiety. Under his care spiritual discipline would not appear as a chore. . . . Even in the most casual remark or light-hearted action he kept intact the spiritual view of life. . . . His companionship itself was a spiritual discipline.[25]

Among Vivekananda's successors as representatives of Vedanta in the West, then, the above five men emerge as strong and vivid personalities, enormously different in the styles of their ministry, but each eliciting a deeply devoted following during his tenure in North America. Abhedananda was the orator and scholarly philosopher; Turiyananda was the retiring mystic who carried about him always the quiet serenity of the Himalayan heights; Trigunatita was the activist and stern disciplinarian, tempered with streaks of boyish frivolity; Paramananda was the eternally youthful spirit with a poetic eloquence, who offered to the movement a model of women's leadership which it still cannot accept; Saradananda was a quietly competent leader whose brief stay in the West did not permit the development of so distinctive a style as the others, but whose subsequent service as General Secretary of the Movement and author of the most comprehensive biography of Ramakrishna give evidence that his American stay, as a part of his total period of personal preparation, was not idly spent. The subsequent history of the Movement in the West bears the strong impress of these first cultivators of the ground sown by Vivekananda. Their activities likewise were a strong influence in shaping the future course of the Movement in India as well.

Chapter Eight

THE MOVEMENT IN THE WEST
IN RECENT YEARS

After the first wave of activity in the West by Vivekananda and his *gurubhais,* growth was modest for some years. Around 1930, however, a new impetus to the work resulted in the founding of several new centers in the United States.

Portland, Oregon

Among the most active in the second generation of teachers from India was Swami Prabhavananda, who had first come in 1922 to assist Prakashananda in San Francisco. His work in Portland, Oregon, was inaugurated in 1926, discontinued after he left to begin his work in Hollywood late in 1929, and revived by his visit in 1932. The Portland Society was placed in the charge of Swami Devatmananda, and its permanent home was acquired in 1934.

The Portland Society followed the pattern of San Francisco and New York in developing a retreat location. Devatmananda, deeply interested in nature and one of the first members of the American Rhododendron Society, enlisted some of his devotees, mostly women, in cultivating flowers around the center in Portland and in building the retreat. The location, above the Columbia River Valley, commands a magnificent view of Mount Saint Helens. The primary structure is an octagonal temple dedicated in 1954, with an inner shrine, also an octagon, for worship; the space between is utilized for study classes around five fireplaces. The present leader, following the death of Devatmananda, is Swami Aseshananda, who assisted in Hollywood earlier.

128

Southern California

A larger, and in many ways the most interesting among the societies in the West, was founded by Prabhavananda in Hollywood. He had come at the invitation of Mrs. Carrie Mead Wycoff (Sister Lalita), one of the three Mead sisters who had hosted Vivekananda in Los Angeles almost thirty years earlier. Mrs. Wycoff's home in Pasadena, donated to the Society, was the headquarters of the work in the first years. The Society was incorporated in 1934. The temple on Ivar Street in Hollywood was begun in 1938 and the wings and other buildings of the complex were added later.

A significant feature of the Hollywood center has been its association with leading personalities of the literary and film communities of Hollywood. The three persons, all of British origin, who have been most closely attached are Gerald Heard, Aldous Huxley, and Christopher Isherwood. Heard first met Prabhavananda at a social gathering and soon became his disciple, then interested Huxley, the "cynical sophisticate of the Twenties."[1] The influence of Vedanta on them became evident, particularly in Huxley's *Time Must Have a Stop*. Some of his initial impressions were voiced through the character Propter, modeled after Heard, in *After Many a Summer Dies the Swan*. Isherwood then met the Swami through Huxley and for some time lived a monastic life at the Vedanta Center; he still plays an active role. Many essays of these three writers have been included in publications emanating from the Society, and Isherwood has worked with the Swami in some of his translations of Sanskrit classics.[2] Other literary notables attending often and visiting the Swami, without becoming disciples, have included Somerset Maugham,* John Van Druten, and Tennessee Williams.

*While Maugham was preparing the screenplay for *The Razor's Edge*, he visited Prabhavananda a number of times, accompanied, on occasion, by Tyrone Power (as Larry), George Cukor, the director, and Clifton Webb (Elliott Templeton). An anecdote of one of these visits is related by Swami Vidyatmananda (John Yale). "The Swami naturally found it hard to visualize Tyrone Power being able to play a realized soul. Standing with his back to the fireplace, talking to the Swami, Power commenced to discuss his conception of how he planned to convey Maugham's hero. The Swami responded in unconcealed disbelief: 'And you think that you can play Larry!' Power sat down with a thump at this candid questioning of his ability to depict a man of illumination. But the two talked about the matter, and as a result Power

Henry Miller's comment on Swami Prabhavananda in *The Air-Conditioned Nightmare* may indicate something of what other personalities have found in meeting him: "The most masterful individual, the only person I met whom I could truly call 'a great soul,' was a quiet Hindu swami in Hollywood."[3] Two reporters give a more detailed description of the Swami:

A short, moon-faced little man, with the kindest expression we have ever known. In this area, where the cultist is expected, and honesty is the exception, the Swami is notable for his lack of ostentation. He goes about in sport shirts, flannel slacks, and usually a gray pullover sweater. He smokes cigarettes constantly, enjoys good conversation, and amazes his listeners with a dry, brittle humor.[4]

A series of articles by various persons in *Vedanta and the West* on the theme "What Vedanta Means to Me" dispels the idea, however, that the Hollywood center is a personality cult around Prabhavananda. The articles deal also with the fundamentals of Vedanta philosophy and their intellectual appeal, but they primarily relate in personal terms the fulfillment experienced through spiritual discovery by the practice of disciplines of meditation.

Operating, then, without fanfare, with no advertisement of services or lectures, the Vedanta Society of Southern California has evidenced stable and impressive growth. Beyond the complex of buildings in Hollywood, which provide quarters for some twenty male and female monastics, there are some twenty more residing at the Sarada Convent in Santa Barbara and the monastery at Trabuco. The total lay and monastic membership of the Society is given at around 650.

The Trabuco Center was erected in 1941 by Gerald Heard as Trabuco College, for the study of philosophy and religion. Heard and Huxley wrote a number of their books in this rather barren, isolated location. The property and its impressive Spanish mission buildings were given to the Society by Heard and dedicated as a monastery on September 7, 1949. Since that time there have usually been some six to ten men in residence. So long as three swamis from India were in residence in Southern California, public services were

studied the role and its religious implications with care, in an attempt to give as authentic a portrayal as he was capable of giving." Swami Vidyatmananda. "The Razor's Edge: Twenty-One Years Later," *Vedanta and the West*, March-April, 1966, P. 43.

held on Sundays, but with the reduction in staff, they were discontinued. In earlier days the men at Trabuco battled the alkaline soil and water shortage to produce a garden and raised chickens. These activities were found to take a disproportionate amount of time, and now the men are occupied instead with maintenance and new construction, editorial work on *Vedanta and the West* and other publications, and living the devotional life, with three stated hours spent in the chapel daily, etc. They do not wear a distinctive garb except during meditation in the chapel. Most have been residents at the monastery for some years.

In contrast to Trabuco, the convent at Santa Barbara enlists a sizable congregation of two hundred or more persons for worship on Sunday morning. The woman architect Lutah Riggs, after much research into Indian architecture, designed the temple, which was dedicated on February 19, 1956. The result is a wooden structure reminiscent on the outside of the buildings of Travancore on the Malabar Coast of south India, and on the interior of timber construction developed in India before 600 B.C. and later carried to Indonesia, Nepal, China, and Japan. The women monastics, like the men, are in four classes: 1) Postulants, those newly admitted; 2) Novices, those who have been postulants for at least six months; 3) Brahmacharis or Brahmacharinis, persons who have received their first vows, at least five years after becoming novices; and, 4) Swamis or Pravrajikas, who have received their final vows after having been in the third stage for at least five years. Provision is also made for lay membership, and the Board of Trustees of the total work in Southern California comprises six lay members elected for one year and nine monastic members elected for twelve. Both classes are eligible for reelection.

Apart from the sisters attached to Swami Paramananda who seem never to have received full recognition from Belur, the Southern California Society's example in ordaining women has been unique since the time of Vivekananda. Even here, however, the first five women who received their final vows in 1959 took them in Santa Barbara rather than in Belur as is customary with men, although authorization was obtained from Belur. The observances which accompanied the final vows began with the women performing their own funeral services to signify the cutting of all ties with family. They fasted on the day of *sannyas,* and a long ritual climaxed with the receipt of ocher robes, called *gerruas,* meaning earth-colored. The next three days they practiced symbolic begging by going to the homes of Society members and bringing food back to the Convent.

Saint Louis

A series of lectures by Swami Prabhavananda in Saint Louis in 1927 led to a temporary work there. The permanent Society did not begin, however, until Swami Satprakashananda arrived in 1938. He had come to the United States in 1936 and had assisted Swami Akhilananda in Providence briefly. His prior background in India had included three years as associate editor of *Prabuddha Bharata* and six years as leader of the Society at New Delhi.

The Saint Louis Society's present location, nestled among a group of churches in the city's fashionable west end, was dedicated in 1952. Some two hundred members are associated with the Society and several more persons in Kansas City meet regularly in the home of one of the group to listen to tapes of the Swami's lectures and to receive other spiritual counsel from him as they are able. Huston Smith, the noted scholar on world religions, was chairman of the board of the Saint Louis Society when he taught at Washington University. Swami Satprakashananda's own scholarly contributions have included a significant treatise on Indian epistemology, *The Methods of Knowledge According to Advaita Vedanta.*

Boston and Providence

After assisting Swami Paramananda briefly in Boston, Swami Akhilananda inaugurated the Vedanta Society of Providence, Rhode Island, on September 9, 1928. The permanent home of the Society was opened less than three years later in a transformed residence on Angell Street. If this group moved swiftly towards financial stability for itself, it also insured the building of the large temple to Ramakrishna at the headquarters in Belur. Swami Akhilananda, acting for the Society in Providence, proposed to meet all the expenses of the building. The generosity of Miss Helen Rubel provided most of the funds for the project. The Belur work began in 1935 and the completed temple was dedicated on January 14, 1938. Swami Vijnanananda, who had begun a study of possible designs for the temple with Vivekananda in 1897, and who had drawn its original plans, completed the act of dedication shortly before his death by placing the ashes of Ramakrishna in the completed structure.

After Paramananda's death in 1942, Providence shared its Swami with Boston. The new home of the Society in Boston was dedicated on April 1, 1942, with Professor Walter Houston Clarke of Harvard and Dean Earl Marlatt of Boston University assisting Swamis Akhilananda, Bodhananda, and Vishwananda. Akhilananda continued to serve the two centers until his death late in the 1960's, and his successor, Swami Sarvagatananda, has done so as well. Akhilananda, like so many of the other representatives of Vedanta in the West, distinguished himself through his writings, notably two books, *Hindu Psychology* and *A Hindu View of Christ*.

Northern California

Swami Dayananda, who returned to India in 1931, had only a brief tenure of two years in San Francisco, but his experience in the West was important for his subsequent career in his native land. He had been much impressed with the health services in San Francisco, especially in the fields of maternity care and pediatrics, and he hoped to work along those lines in India. After a small beginning in a rented house, helped by two American nurses who had come with him, the work grew in Calcutta. A building constructed on Sarat Bose Road in 1938-39 was the nucleus of the present Ramakrishna Mission Seva Pratishthan, one of the largest general hospitals in the city and a model for hospital and medical services now offered in various places in India by the Mission.

Swami Vividishananda, who had been assisting Dayananda, headed the San Francisco work briefly, till illness forced him to turn it over to Swami Ashokananda. Under the latter's leadership, the work in San Francisco came to rival that in Southern California, with auxiliary centers in Berkeley and Sacramento, retreats at Lake Tahoe and Olema—in addition to the earlier one still retained at Shanti Ashrama—and, in 1958, an impressive new temple and monastic quarters a few blocks from the old temple in San Francisco. The centers in Sacramento and Berkeley began moving towards

a more autonomous status following the death late in 1969 of Swami
Ashokananda. Swami Shraddhananda is in charge at Sacramento,
Prabuddhananda in San Francisco, and Swahananda at Berkeley.
Chidrupananda, an American swami, has served in an administrative
capacity in San Francisco from about 1930, even before Ashokananda came. His only leadership in worship has been a monthly
lectureship in Berkeley.

The work in Northern California for some years has featured an
extensive training program for monastics. Men are undergoing training at Olema, at the old and new Temples in San Francisco, and in
Sacramento; several women are being trained in San Francisco. A
very high proportion of the Northern and Southern California membership has been initiated, in contrast to a newer center such as
Chicago, where less than half of the members have elected to take
this step.[5] Notable in the Northern California centers is enhancement
of the natural beauty of the surroundings by cultivating extensive
garden areas. Once the members completed the buildings in Sacramento, they began to develop a large garden area at the rear of the
property.

From visits to monasteries in Southern and Northern California,
I have noticed something of a difference in emotional tone in discussions and eating meals with the monks. Without my commenting
on this, one of the monks at Sacramento volunteered, "I supposed
you've noticed a difference between us and the fellows at Trabuco.
Swami Ashokananda modeled our monastic life on austerity, and
Swami Prabhavananda on devotion." In mentioning this later to
Swami Vandananda in New Delhi, he was reluctant, from his experience, to confirm this difference, feeling that neither of the Swamis
referred to would agree that one pattern was more or less devotional
or austere than another. I would still observe, however, that the atmosphere at Sacramento seemed more sober and inhibited in the
presence of a visitor, while that at Trabuco seemed open and relaxed.
Perhaps Phabhavananda's guidance is reflected in a quotation from an
earlier interview: "Rigid rules and disciplines imposed from without
do not work in practice and cannot help spiritual growth. Why should
we follow certain rules of conduct? Because of authority? Because
so and so tells us to? Any rule imposed from without on the basis of
authority, which takes away our freedom of thinking and acting,

even though it may be the *right* rule, does not inspire man to carry it into practice. Rigid rules and disciplines of conduct can be followed only if they are self-imposed." Another earlier resident of Trabuco, however, observed to the writer that he feels Trabuco has more discipline now than when first started.

Seattle

After his health improved, in 1931 Swami Vividishananda continued a work begun in Washington, D.C., by Akhilananda. He labored in Denver from 1936 to 1938 and then inaugurated a permanent work in Seattle. The temple was dedicated in 1942. Typical of other Western centers, both a public and a private dedication service were held; the latter, referred to as the "actual" dedication service, was held earlier. The public service, again typically, consisted primarily of addresses on Vedanta philosophy that stressed the harmony of religions. The private, or "actual" service, was quite ritualistic in character, as this description shows:

> The offering of flowers, sweets and fruits, with the ringing of bells, burning of incense and waving of lights, intermingled with chants and prayers, continued for hours. The climax was the Homa ceremony, or fire ritual, which consists in consecrating and worshipping fire as an emblem of the Divine. A fire was built on a copper brazier having a layer of sand on which mystical designs were traced. Oblations of clarified butter and other ingredients were offered on the blazing flames, sacred texts being softly intoned with each offering. After the fire ritual Swami Ashokananda read aloud selected passages from the Upanishads, Bhagavad Gita and Chandi.[6]

Swami Vividishananda's long tenure in Seattle, continuing until the present, has been augumented since the early 1950's with visits to supervise a group meeting in Hawaii. The Hawaii group was founded by E. Raphael Marozzi, who, after an introduction to Vedanta from Swami Vividishananda during military service in Seattle, traveled to the holy places of India in 1950 before settling in Honolulu.

Chicago

Swami Gnaneshwarananda, who had come as an assistant to Swami Bodhananda in 1927, went to Chicago in 1929 to start a Vedanta Center in the near north side. This thrived until his untimely death in 1937, at only forty-four years of age. Besides being a dynamic

speaker, he skillfully played Indian musical instruments and organized an orchestra of Vedanta students. His successor, like Gnaneshwarananda and Prabhavananda, was a disciple of Swami Brahmananda. This was Swami Vishwananda, who conducted services for
seventeen years in rented space, until in 1955 a permanent headquarters building was purchased on East Elm Street. Following his
death in 1965, Swami Bhashyananda was appointed; his brief tenure
has been characterized by rapid expansion. A new temple was
dedicated on September 7, 1966, in the Hyde Park District in South
Chicago. Three days later a service in recognition of the seventy-
third anniversary of the Parliament of Religions was held and representatives of the various world faiths spoke.[7] Since then, this has
been a regular observance of the Chicago center.

By 1970, some nine young men in training for the monastic
life were living at the center or in the newly acquired monastic location in Ganges Township, Michigan. Six women were living in
another house acquired for the purpose a few doors from the center;
most of them had secular employment but devoted free time to work
in the center. Several of the young men traveled with the Swami to
India in the spring of 1970.

The Swami belongs to the eighth generation of temple priests
but is the first to have attended college. He received an M.A. in
Sanskrit with a minor in English literature of the romantic period.
He lived with Gandhi for several months in 1930 and 1931 as a
student preparing for nonviolent activity against British rule.[8] His
current style of ministry in the West, in addition to a full program
of activities at the center, includes an extensive schedule of speaking
engagements, mostly in schools and churches.

New York

Swami Nikhilananda arrived from India in 1931 to assist Swami
Akhilananda in Providence. Two years later, however, he opened a
second center in New York City, to be known as the Ramakrishna-
Vivekananda Center of New York. The Swami's impressive translations and volumes on Indian philosophy and religion have earned
him lectureships at Columbia and Temple University; he has gathered a strong following over the years. Currently some 130 members
are enrolled, a slightly larger group than at the earlier New York

center. John Moffitt served as an assistant to the Swami for some years and received *sannyas* vows; a Protestant minister, the Rev. Andrew Lemke, has acted as a substitute lecturer a number of times. At present, Swami Adiswarananda from India conducts most of the public ministry in Nikhilananda's near retirement.

Chester Carlson, inventor of the xerographic process and a consultant for the Xerox Company in Rochester, New York, is Vice-President of the Ramakrishna-Vivekananda Center. "Hinduism," Carlson states, "appeals to me immensely because its experimental and practical approach to self-realization and the search for God is the method any scientist uses when he wants to discover something: try and try again."[9]

Another distinguished guest delivered the Vivekananda Centenary address at the Center in 1963. This was U Thant, then General Secretary of the United Nations, who had been closely connected with the work of the Ramakrishna Mission in Rangoon, Burma. In his address, U Thant described Vivekananda's primary concerns in coming to the West as synthesizing the Eastern and Western concepts of culture and civilization, promoting tolerance in human relations, and stressing the spiritual disciplines of meditation and contemplation.

At Nikhilananda's request, the woman sculptor Malvina Hoffman made bronze busts of Vivekananda from her memory of him. The works are in the Ramakrishna-Vivekananda Center, the Trabuco Monastery and the Center in Portland.

The work at the original Society in New York was supervised for thirty-eight years by Swami Bodhananda, until his death in 1950. His successor, who continues till the present despite impaired health, is Swami Pavitrananda. This Center is in a large mansion on 71st Street just west of Central Park. The Ramakrishna-Vivekananda Center is just east of the park in a large mansion on 94th Street.

Toronto and Washington, D.C.

In addition to the established centers in North America and the two subsidiary groups in Kansas City and Honolulu, two new groups have been recently started by Swami Ranganathananda, who has served as something of an ambassador at large for the Movement in recent years. An extended lecture tour throughout North America in 1968 and 1969 took him to Toronto, where a group was organized in November of 1969, the first in Canada. Its President, who visits it when possible, is Swami Bhashyananda of Chicago. This group, unlike most other Vedanta Societies in the West, is composed mainly of Indian nationals, mostly in the professions; it gathers in the Friends Meeting House near the University of Toronto. A Washington, D.C., group, which has had Vedanta workers periodically for many years, was formed after a visit by Swami Ranganathananda during his lecture tour.

Numerically, the Movement in North America cannot count more than 2,500 members, which certainly seems a token effort. There may be reasons for the modest rate of growth, which will be explored in later chapters. A certain upturn of interest is evidenced in the last few years, with the general fascination that has grown for Eastern religious and cultural expressions. However, nothing has been evidenced to parallel the rampant growth of popularized movements such as the International Society for Krishna Consciousness or the pursuit of Transcendental Meditation as set forth by the Maharishi Mahesh Yogi. On the other hand, the teachings of Vedanta have been widely disseminated through the very extensive publishing efforts of the spiritual teachers of the Ramakrishna Movement who have come from India, as well as of persons, such as those in Hollywood, related to the Movement. The judgment of an American who has recently received his *sannyas* vows that, historically, the giants of Vedanta have been sent to the West, would seem valid. No precise measurements of their influence in North American life late in the twentieth century can be made, but it is significant. Certain indigenous movements have advanced themes which they appear to hold in common with Vedanta and which are not at all alien to the culture, such as a general feeling for the essential harmony of the world's religions. To say these movements owe such teachings to the influences of Vedanta may not be demonstrable. But there are congenial attitudes that have enabled the Movement to strike responsive chords, while retaining something of the mystique of the ancient Orient.

South America

If the Movement's numerical strength is unimpressive in North America, this is even more true elsewhere in the West. In all of South

America there is but one center, in Buenos Aires, where Swami Vijayananda was deputed in October of 1932. In 1941, the Ashrama was relocated in the small town of Bella Vista, 30 kilometers from Buenos Aires, and the Swami, who continues in spiritual leadership, is now assisted by Swami Paratparananda. The work is conducted in Spanish and in English and many of the works of Vivekananda and others in the Movement have been published in Spanish from this center.

Europe—Paris

We have observed that the group in London did not thrive in Vivekananda's absence and, despite a number of speaking engagements and lecture tours by various representatives of the Movement, no permanent work was sustained in Europe until 1933, when Swami Yatiswarananda began a work of some five years duration, lecturing and forming study groups in Germany, Switzerland, Holland, Paris, and London. A permanent center in Paris was initiated in 1936, when a group of Frenchmen inspired by Romain Rolland's works met at the Sorbonne to celebrate the centenary of Ramakrishna's birth. Swami Siddheswarananda was subsequently invited by this group to come from India to teach Vedanta. He arrived in 1937 and arranged a series of conferences at Montpellier and Toulouse and at the Sorbonne. The war years interrupted the work, and the Swami spent several years in neutral territory until 1947, when land was acquired on an old estate at Gretz, southeast of Paris. The Ashram constructed there has served as a retreat for persons interested in Vedanta from various places on the Continent. Following the death of Swami Siddheswarananda in 1957, Swami Nityabodhananda, now in Geneva, served at Gretz until Swami Ritajananda came in 1961. A few years later John Yale, who, until his ordination as Swami Vidyatmananda, had been associated with Swami Prabhavananda for some years in Southern California, came to assist with the work at Gretz.

Some fifteen persons live permanently as disciples at the Ashram. There are no caretakers, so visitors, who usually spend no more than a week at the Ashram their first time, join in the daily work with the disciples, in addition to time spent in meditation, study, and worship. Twenty francs per day is set as a minimum charge for visitors, including board and room. A program is issued from the Ashram three times per year, along with certain occasional publications. Regular lectures are given in Paris, and study groups which meet in Brussels and Wiesbaden are supervised.[10]

Geneva

Since leaving Gretz, Swami Nityabodhananda's work in Europe has been concentrated in Geneva. The group there, however, has been small, and he has had regular engagements at least yearly at Nîmes, Nancy, Basel, Avignon, Rome, and Athens. The Swami has continued, also, to teach in Paris, first at the Sorbonne and more recently in the hall of the Museum of French Monuments. Late in 1970, the work in Geneva had progressed to the stage that a permanent center was begun on the shores of Lake Geneva. Four books in French have been published by the Swami, on Yoga, Vedanta, and the Upanishads.[11] He has also held a visiting lectureship at the University of Geneva. A recent activity which he helped to promote was the Second Spiritual Summit Conference, held in Geneva from March 31 to April 4, 1970 (the first was in Calcutta two years earlier), an interfaith gathering with an impressive list of leaders of the world's religions present.

London

The Movement has long cherished a dream of a permanent center in London, but this was not begun until 1934, with the arrival of Swami Avyaktananda. By late 1948, however, his work had taken a political turn which the authorities in Belur did not approve, and he disassociated himself and his activities from the Ramakrishna Math and Mission in a letter of June 16, 1949. He stated, "I realize fully how wise it is for the Ramakrishna Math and Mission to keep aloof from the conflicting ideologies and political movements in order to serve mankind spiritually and materially."[12] Accordingly, the Swami and "Vedantic Communism," as he termed it, separated from the parent order, and a new work was inaugurated by Swami Ghanananda with the blessing of Belur. Ghanananda had stopped in England for what was supposed to be a brief series of lectures on his way back to India from a preaching tour of South Africa and the United States. He was soon able to put his infant organization on a stable foundation, with the publication, in 1951, of a bimonthly journal, *Vedanta for East and West,* and the acquisition in 1964 of a permanent home in the Muswell Hill section of London. The editorial adviser of the journal has been Dr. S. Radhakrishnan. Contributors to other books issued by the London Center, such as *Swami Vivekananda in East and West,* have included Kenneth Walker, A. L. Basham, and Ninian Smart.

The property in Muswell Hill is still retained by the London Center, but much of the work has gravitated to the location in Holland Park, the present address of the Society. Following the death of Swami Ghanananda in 1969, Swami Bhavyananda, a physician and formerly head of the Society in Shillong, Assam, came to be in charge of the work. Six men are currently in monastic training at the London Center and another, Swami Parahitananda, is serving in India at the Advaita Ashramas in Calcutta and Mayavati.[13] Subsidiary groups have recently been started in Leeds, Leicestershire, and Dover. Some two to three hundred people are members of the parent organization in London.

As was earlier observed, Vivekananda felt that, through the work of the great Orientalists, such as Max Müller and Paul Deussen, Europe was more acquainted with Vedanta than was America. Later Romain Rolland was to acquaint the French-speaking people with the life and teachings of Ramakrishna and Vivekananda. Perhaps for this reason there seemed less of an imperative on the part of the Movement to establish permanent centers in Europe. Those three which have been instituted, however, have followed a pattern somewhat similar to that in North America, *i.e.,* a rather impressive literary output emanating from and extending the influence of the centers. One may assume, thus, that in North and South America and Europe alike there are many readers of Vedanta literature who have no formal attachment to one of the existing groups. Among the many requests for literature and instruction in spiritual practice in the files of the Society in Southern California, a letter from Brazil illustrates the situation of many. After reading Swami Prabhavananda's translation of the *Gita, The Song of God,* the reader lamented not having been able to find, "in materialistic and sensualistic Brazil," more information about the Gita. In sending a sample copy of *Vedanta and the West,* along with the address of the Society in

Argentina, the Hollywood Society said, "We don't particularly stress membership from a distance. However the catalog we are sending will suggest books for you to read. The main objective is to some day meet a teacher (*guru*) and take instruction in meditation, possibly leading eventually to discipleship. This is the Hindu tradition."[14] The situation, however, remains, that there are few gurus for the sizable number of persons whose interest in Vedanta is awakened by the reading of the literature.

Part II

The Ramakrishna Movement

Tradition and Innovation

Chapter Nine

THE MOVEMENT AND THE
INDIAN TRADITION

An extremely harsh judgment of the Ramakrishna Movement, in its relation to Hinduism, is made by René Guenon, who categorizes it together with the Brahma Samaj and Arya Samaj under the heading, "Vedanta Westernized." These, he says, are "more or less akin to Theosophism," which is made the subject of more extensive vilification. After discussing the Brahma Samaj, Arya Samaj, and other less known movements, he says, "Another still more completely aberrant branch . . . is that founded by Vivekananda, the disciple of the illustrious Ramakrishna, though unfaithful to his teaching." It has become in the West, according to Guenon, a sentimental and consoling religion, with a strong dose of Protestant moralism. The intemperate character of his assertions continues:

> An altogether Western propensity for proselytism rages intensely in these organizations, which are Eastern in nothing but the name, apart from a few merely outward signs, calculated to interest the curious and to attract dilettantes by playing on their taste for an exoticism of the feeblest type. This so-called Vedanta, . . . which pleased the West all the better the more completely it is distorted, has practically nothing left in common with the metaphysical doctrine the name of which it bears.[1]

This purist approach, which suspects any dilution rising out of intercultural encounter, is sharply in contrast to the assessment made by the Indian Christian observer, Paul Devanandan. As mentioned in the Introduction, I feel that Devanandan's category of a "renascent" movement is suggestive but inadequate to describe the Ramakrishna Movement. He uses the term to express the Movement's relationship with its parent Hinduism rather than his other rubrics of reform, revival, and revolt. Devanandan notes that every historical

145

religion is characterized by a creed, a cultus, and a culture, which he defines as doctrinal beliefs, religious practices, and world outlooks. The impact occurring when a religion interacts with a larger environment is first felt in the area of culture, then in the cultus, and finally, if at all, in the credal core itself. The renascent movement interacts with forces from within as well as extraneous ones, effecting change primarily at the level of culture. While the Ramakrishna Movement indeed exhibits these tendencies in ways which will be elaborated, the basic meaning of renascent is less adequate to describe them than is the term "satellite," proposed by me in the Introduction. In addition to depicting the emergence of new life, the image of the satellite graphically conveys the interaction between the religious tradition from which it has ascended and those of the new climes which it explores. It illustrates, then, the manner by which the Movement bursts into new life, as well as the quality of that life; it says more.

Devanandan's analysis that such a movement initiates change primarily at the cultural level is not altogether accurate either for Vedanta. Change does occur, but, as we shall explore, it may best be understood as coming into being through the Movement's new models of religious reform and social service, which rubrics do not quite fit change as described by Devanandan's categories of analysis. The Movement has fostered new models. It has done so to effect the modernization and universalization of the Indian religious tradition in response to the challenge of Westernization. Guenon's judgment is apparently rendered on the assumption that nineteenth century or earlier Hinduism is accepted as the benchmark. On that basis, the Ramakrishna Movement, in the new models fostered in India and the somewhat different garb it has adopted to make its message intelligible in the West, is a fraud. Part Two of this book, however, assumes that these "new" models are not entirely new; it attempts to trace their derivation in the Indian tradition and to discuss the ways in which they have taken shape through interaction with the West. The resultant Movement bears a strong impress of authenticity, not of fraudulence, in two ways: its continuity with the tradition and its ability to reformulate elements from that tradition to meet the new situation.

Two terms must be clarified in their usage. These are tradition and modernization; universalization will be discussed in a later chapter.

In using the term "the Indian religious tradition," I am partially dependent on my teacher, Paul Younger, whose usage[2] emphasizes continuity and comprehensiveness in a way which contrasts with that of Wilfred Cantwell Smith. While Smith also emphasizes continuity, his range is narrower, so that he speaks of "the *Hindu* cumulative tradition." This may be applicable to Western religions, which have a more clearly defined dogmatic core, but it obscures the similarity of experiences in the Upanishads and early Buddhism, for instance, and the kind of "mutual irradiation" which Hinduism had with Buddhism for centuries in India. The Indian religious tradition, then, is preferable, although the religions, with this understanding, can be referred to separately.[3]

Younger's reasons for considering that the tradition proper begins with its formulation, and that what preceded (primarily Indus Valley and Rig Vedic civilizations) should be considered as background, are not to me wholly convincing, however. Younger uses the phrase "religious tradition" to mean "a conscious authoritative expression of religious experience," so that the Upanishadic-early Buddhist statements mark its formal beginning.[4]

This seems to me to do some historical violence to the earlier religious seers, however, who were themselves, as Smith notes, recipients of a "tradition" and bearers of it, with modifications, to other generations. It is difficult to do justice to them merely by considering them "background" to what came later. My usage of "tradition," then, is consciously broad, and in contrast with the above sources.

Tradition may be used in another sense as it contrasts with modernization. One often finds in India that the terms "Westernization" and "modernization" are used almost synonymously, perhaps to his revulsion. It is difficult here to make precise definitions beyond registering a strong objection to that identification. I have found, however, great personal accord with the treatment of the subject in Lloyd and Susanne Rudolph, who state their reservations about citing models of tradition and modernity before going on to list contrasts which they have found heuristically useful.[5]

Insofar as its changes have extended to credal elements, the crucial new adventures by the Ramakrishna Movement have largely been through its elaboration of the claim that Hinduism is *sanatana dharma,* or universal religion. This means, in effect, that the wide umbrella of Hinduism may be expanded to shelter even the one formerly considered as *mllechcha* (as the barbarian, the goy, or the infidel in Western traditions), whatever the precise nature of his religious belief and practice. Hinduism, thus conceived, is no single system of religious thought and practice but a congeries of systems, as wide ranging as the varied human temperaments themselves, of many cultures. This is explicitly a credal claim, so recognized by D. S. Sarma, whom Devanandan quotes in this regard. Sarma writes:

> Hinduism has latterly been content to remain only an ethnic religion. But, in the future, it should become a credal religion also, as it once was. . . . Only the creed to be enforced should be as flexible as possible. . . . There should be absolute freedom for any stranger to come into any room of our spacious mansion and make himself comfortable there. Only the person who comes in must conform to the rituals, usages and formulas of the sect he chooses.[6]

That there is a gradation of paths is implicit in Sarma's conception of the credal basis of Hinduism, whose *"sadhana* is designed for the purpose of actually taking the man who chooses a particular path to his goal and making him see and realise God under some form or other at first and then ultimately attain to the Formless." Devanandan would criticize the practical expression of the claim that Hinduism is *sanatana dharma* by calling for it to come to a recognition of the distinctiveness of the various constituent systems of religious thought and practice which it conceives, often naively, to be embraced within it. He sees a particular need for Hindus to undertake a serious study of comparative religions for this reason. Otherwise, as will be explored later, their understanding of other religious expressions may actually represent a considerable distortion of the ways in which these faiths have developed and are understood by their adherents.

To the parent body, however, the modern formulation of the *sanatana dharma* does not by itself represent a threat. Hinduism has historically manifested a capacity to absorb divergent religious expressions. In earlier days, other groups settling within the subcontinent, even as conquerors, were assimilable. Thus, within the last century, for a nation whose pride had been severely chastened, one avenue of renewal lay in religious conquest of the political conqueror. Even though this could only be achieved through the claim of intellectual mastery, it provided a powerful transfusion to national morale. To assert that the wisdom of the Hindu sages anticipated the religious insights of the ruling Europeans was to assert that the ultimate conquest belonged to India. The victory was capable of being extended beyond the subcontinent also. Vivekananda's initial skirmishes provided incipient proof that this counterthrust, in borrowed imperial language, would vanquish the world.

From within the tradition, however, questions were raised about Vivekananda's assumptions concerning cultus and culture. Was he, while apparently rendering alien Christianity innocuous as a variant *bhakti* strain from pure Vedanta, in fact importing many of its organizational models? Was he himself victimized by the West's illusory materialism in fashioning a service-oriented band of monastics and diverting them and others from the true Indian pursuit of *moksha* (salvation)? Did not his claim of exemption from caste restrictions as a *sannyasin* amount to a flaunting of those details which make up the fabric of the Hindu social order? Did he really represent Hinduism in the West?

The Statesman and Friend of India, in an obituary article on Vivekananda, commented, "His vogue was not sustained, and in India his departure from the ceremonial law of Hinduism detracted very greatly from his influence".[7] This may have been apparent to certain observers at the time, although the Movement certainly appears to enjoy an eminent respectability among Hindus today. And even then, another journal, *The Mahratta* from western India, could observe that, although Rammohan Roy possessed the gifts of genius in greater measure than Vivekananda and Keshab was far more cultured, neither succeeded in "pushing the campaign of aggressive Vedantism into the hearts of the Europeans and the Americans" so well as Vivekananda. This success the journal attributed to Vivekananda's intense love for Hinduism which both Rammohan Roy and Keshab lacked.[8]

Some lack of congruity has been noted earlier between Vivekananda's Hinduism in the West and in India upon his return. Whatever the reasons for this dissimilarity, his work in India must be judged as a piece in terms of the presence of his peers within the tradition. How, then, was the love which he bore for Hinduism manifest in India? Was that manifestation genuine Hinduism or an aberration, both there and in the West, as Guenon charges? A large key to these questions lies in our understanding of Vivekananda's ideal of the monastic vocation. His model for the religious life for everyman, insofar as he thought in such universal terms, developed out of this monastic model.

The two historic precedents within Hinduism upon which he sought to construct and legitimate his model were 1) the Vedic period, characterized by confidence, expansion, affirmation of life, and the world, and 2) the cult of Shiva as an ascetic, the mythic embodiment of the ideal of *tyaga* or renunciation. *Svarga,* the Vedic heaven, could be interpreted quiet materialistically, and its *sadhana* was well-disciplined *karma,* with the sanction of the enjoyment of present existence. The Shaivite cult did not thrive in this atmosphere, but in the Upanishadic period, *moksha* began to replace *svarga* as the end of life, and the solitary Shiva with his alternative ascetic path became more acceptable. He became associated with yogic disciplines and with *jnana,* the philosophical path, rather than with the householder's concerns. Vivekananda's synthesis of the two sought to yoke the strength and heroism of the Vedic period with that of the renunciate, celibate model of Shiva. He did not draw on the other aspect of Shiva's mythic personality, the erotic and sensual.[9]

One might question whether as the Movement developed the latter ideal might not have tended to overshadow the former, although beyond the Movement, the Vedic component fortified rising nationalist expressions. Swami Prabhavananda's initial rejection of the monastic path on the grounds that the monks were lazy was representative, doubtless, of the feelings of many. A recent Parsee critic, extolling the Vedic ideal, points out that ancient Indian civilization put *kama* (earthly love) and *artha* (pursuit of material well being) first. In support of this he quotes Sri Aurobindo, "The fullness of life must precede the surpassing of life."[10]

It is primarily the deep inferiority complex which springs from the Indo-British connection which made us reject Kama and Artha as morally degrading. We did not outlive the shame of being caught as a decadent and weak society when we first faced the West in the eighteenth and nineteenth centuries. To assert our self-esteem and our own superiority over the apparently materialistic West, we fell back on Dharma [social duty] and Moksha for a kind of spiritual superiority.[11]

The indictment contains a measure of validity; it is difficult to imagine how any monastic movement could sustain itself without some assumption, however tacit, that its path is a higher path, a nobler calling. While, therefore, Vivekananda's may not represent a perfect synthesis of the two classic modes of which the critic speaks, he must at least be judged to have attempted a synthesis. This he did with integrity to the models as he understood them, and for the purpose of establishing his own Movement. The synthesis which he attempted, in reconciliation of Vedic heroism and Shaivite renunciation, was to be realized in the monastic ideal as follows: the monks were to be characterized 1) by their single-minded pursuit of God-realization, in which all detracting attachments were to be rigorously eschewed; 2) by the transcendence of superfluous *deshacaras* (local customs) and overweening concern with avoidance of pollution in attendance upon the true essentials of religion; and 3) by a life of strenuous, service-oriented activity.

In idealizing the *sannyasin* as India's cultural hero, at once epitomizing the best in its tradition and in his exemplary life conveying the dedication through which the needs of modern India might be met, Vivekananda drew also on the example of the Buddha and his followers. There was almost a conflation of the figures of the Buddha and Shiva in the boyhood visions of ascetic figures which he related. The educational and medical services rendered by some of the Buddha's disciples make his citation of that precedent logical for his own service-oriented understanding of the monastic role. While he generally recognized the historical divergence of Buddhism from Vedic religion, some of his less systematic utterances represent the Buddha himself as a great teacher of the Vedas. "He [the Buddha] preached the most tremendous truths. He taught the very gist of the philosophy of the Vedas to one and all without distinction."[12]

Few scholars of the Indian tradition would agree with this portrait of the Buddha as a staunch advocate of Vedic philosophy or with Vivekananda's assertion elsewhere that the Vedanta philosophy is the foundation of Buddhism.[13] It is not surprising, however, in view of his tendency to consider Vedanta the substratum of even Western religions, that he would seek thus to harmonize divergent tendencies in the Indian tradition. One other factor in Buddhism was a significant referrant, perhaps, as suggested earlier, germinating from his relationship with Dharmapala. Nivedita makes the point that Vivekananda was greatly fascinated with all the historic details of the life of the Buddha and that as early as 1887 with his *gurubhais* he read the *Lalita Vistara* and the *Prajna Paramita* of the Mahayana school in the Sanskrit originals. "Chief of intellectual passions with the Swami," she says, "was his reverence for the Buddha."[14] But she also comments that there was no event in Indian history to which he referred more constantly than the great charge of Asoka to his missionaries. "Remember," Asoka has said, "that everywhere you will find some root of faith and righteousness. See that you foster this, and do not destroy."[15] The monastic ideal thus incorporated the missionary component as well, but one which must deeply respect the beliefs and practices of those to whom the monk would minister. It is the missionary component also which differentiates the Ramakrishna Movement from others which might be termed renascent, for this is one of its arms of interaction. Devanandan's discussion, emphasizing the work in India, concerns itself less with those aspects by which we may designate it a satellite movement.

The various factors, then, from the Indian tradition, which composed Vivekananda's monastic ideal were: 1) the Vedic spirit, recognizing that material well being was not antithetical to the development of spiritual strength, 2) Shaivite asceticism, enhanced by Sankara's monastic experiments and intellectual virility, and 3) the service and missionary oriented monasticism of Buddhism. A fourth factor was his personal legacy from his master, Ramakrishna, who began to weld his young followers together into a monastic group. There were, of course, also householders among his followers, such as Mahendranath Gupta, author of the *Gospel*, the intimate biographical record of the last few years of Ramakrishna's life. Thirty years after Ramakrishna's death, an incident is recorded which underscores the particularity which the monastics felt that they had enjoyed with their Master.

It was the evening of March 14, 1916, the day following the public celebration of Sri Ramakrishna's birthday. Swami Premananda and Swami Akhandananda, disciples of the Master, were seated on a bench on the eastern veranda of the Belur Monastery, overlooking the Ganges. Several other young swamis and brahmacharis . . . were seated on a bench nearby. Presently Swami Achalananda, who was one of the group, addressed Swami Premananda; "Revered sir, please tell us something about Sri Ramakrishna. To hear of him directly from you is far more inspiring and uplifting than to read of him and his teachings in the Gospel."

"Very little of the Master's teaching is recorded in the Gospel," replied the Swami. "There is too much repetition. M. used to visit the Master occasionally and would note down his teachings as he heard them. But Sri Ramakrishna taught his disciples differently, according to their different temperaments and their capacity of understanding. His teachings to the monastic disciples were given in private. As soon as the householder disciples would leave the room he would get up and lock the door and then speak to us living words of renunciation. . . ."[16]

It is clear from the above that the young monks considered themselves chosen vessels to receive the esoteric content of their Master's teaching and, from Premananda's elaboration, this often consisted primarily, as we might anticipate for monastics, of counsel on the renunciation of worldly enjoyments, symbolized by women and gold. Lust and greed, then, were the perpetual snares by which man might become attached to this illusory world. At another level, however, he often demonstrated a childlike acceptance of the world. He could be delighted with it, as his homespun illustrations reveal, in a way in which Vivekananda could not. The Vedic component which balanced his emphasis on renunciation was at the feeling level, whereas that of Vivekananda's was evidenced in a strong determination of the will, manifesting itself heroically in social service and nationalism. For both, worship of the Goddess reinforced the motif of renunciation, for through recognition of the Mother in all women, bondage to lust was to be overcome.

Sakta worshippers in Bengal at the turn of the century, however, came to be influenced more by the style of Vivekananda's reverence for the Mother than that of Ramakrishna. In Vivekananda it was linked to nationalism as well as renunciation, rather after the model of Bankim Chandra, whose stirring *Bande Mantaram* (meaning "I salute the mother") early gave voice to nationalist aspirations and has practically become the equivalent of a national anthem for India. The Mother and the motherland for Vivekananda became linked symbolically, yoking personal resolve with a nationalist cause. While Ramakrishna's death occurred before the rise of the nationalist movement, it would be difficult to imagine his having participated in it in the manner of his disciple.

The contrast is further sharpened as we view the later strategy of Gandhi, similarly interested in forwarding nationalist objectives, but in a more specifically political manner than Vivekananda. Still, his understanding of renunciation, linking it to *satyagraha* or soul-force, expressed through nonviolence, held more kinship with Ramakrishna than with Vivekananda. The Bengal *bhadralok* (intellectual elite) characteristically followed Vivekananda's more militant posi-

tion, feeling that self-assertion as taught by Bankim Chandra, Vivekananda, and Aurobindo, was needed rather than the strategy of
self-abasement which they saw in Gandhi.[17]

The positive dimension of freedom seems more characteristic of
Vivekananda's interpretation of the *sannyasin's* role than renunciation, though he extolled the latter ideal frequently. The *sannyasin's*
path, as he often exuberantly described it, seemed to some observers
at the time to celebrate an almost irresponsible abdication of social
obligations. While he exalted it as the most practical way of experiencing freedom from bondage to the world, others saw it as constituting, in effect, an antisocial appeal. *The Indian Social Reformer*
quoted Vivekananda in an early issue of *Prabuddha Bharata* as follows: "What about this marvellous experience of standing alone,
discarding all help, breasting the storms of life, of working without
any sense of recompense, working a whole life, joyful, free, because
not goaded on to work like slaves by false human love or ambition?"
It commented:

> It is glorious to work without any sense of recompense, but not to be-
> come a *sannyasin* out of a mere love of freedom from the slavery of family
> obligations. To accept the wider obligations of service to the whole society
> in lieu of the narrower obligations of a family is good; but the acceptance
> of a *sannyasin's* life, because in that kind of life there is nothing to goad
> you on to work, is just the most vulnerable point in the system of monastic
> orders. . . . While therefore, individual celibacy may be excellent, greater
> care is necessary in the establishment of an order of monks.[18]

Vivekananda's consciousness of this danger led him with his
gurubhais to make provision for what may be termed both the
cloistered, contemplative monastic life style, and the apostolic heavily
concerned with work in the larger society. A recent Western scholar,
writing on the personal and social factors in the growth of the Ramakrishna Movement, asserts, "The movement is a permanent, pro-
fessionally administered network of agencies, with scarcely any traces
of the charismatic leadership that brought it into being."[19] The writer,
from his own experience, would strongly dispute this. The service-
oriented, seemingly secularized institutions are there, but to live for
even a brief time in one or more of the centers makes one very conscious of the importance given to the contemplative life and to
devotional acts associated with what Isherwood has called the cult of

Ramakrishna. The mystical, contemplative element is not over-shadowed by the secular goals of education and medicine, although it is valid to observe that Vivekananda and his associates sought to implement their new objectives within a framework of traditional ideas. The employment of a more secular rhetoric might have severely retarded the Movement's effectiveness.

It may be that in incorporating the Vedic component as well as that of renunciation, Vivekananda actually understood the former more than many others who have traditionally, but superficially, appealed to the Vedas as the foundation of their own positions. If the Vedas really do reflect a world view which sanctions the goal of material well being, then it is not irrelevant to cite them in support of humanitarian programs such as educational and medical work, famine and flood relief, etc. Nor, on the other hand, is this dimension to be regarded as a distortion of Ramakrishna's "pure and unadulterated" Hinduism, as some suggest, but rather as a valuable modernization of it.

As to the Movement's own self-consciousness of its relation to Hinduism, a recent lawsuit is in point. According to two swamis whom I consulted, the Movement sued the government of West Bengal because of its controls over the educational institutions operated by the Ramakrishna Mission. Their case, which succeeded, was based on the constitutional provision (article 25-1) which gives all persons, subject to public order, morality, health, etc., the right freely to profess, practice, and propagate religion. The Mission claimed that, as a minority religion, its activities were exempt from interference. One of the swamis accepted the designation literally that the Ramakrishna Movement is a minority religion. The other defined it by stating that it is a minority religion within Hinduism. I suggest that the latter is probably the more normative interpretation.

The difference specified by the second swami is that the Ramakrishna Movement embodies the universalistic aspects of Hinduism, recognizing no barriers of caste, creed, or nationality, but seeking to minister to all. John Yale's report of a visit to Benares in the 1950's illustrates this. The leading community hospital, by his account, was limited to Hindus in this most traditional Hindu city, so that Muslims (and Christians?) if they were to receive any hospitalization at all, came to the Ramakrishna Mission Hospital.[20]

If the establishment of precedents from the tradition was achieved, partially for forensic purposes, it was equally true that the followers of Ramakrishna also drew on contemporary models, largely from Western religious organizations. True, the historical example of the early Buddhist *sangha* (order) might be appealed to, but there were present in India Roman Catholic monastic orders with monasteries, convents, and, to a degree, medical and educational facilities. The extreme proliferation of such institutions in the West had a staggering impact on Vivekananda. Characteristically, while many of his references to Christianity in general did not evidence a warm and charitable feeling, those to Roman Catholicism separately were benevolent. Its provision for celibacy and its comparatively minor role in the stimulation of social criticism in India may have been two reasons for his preference of Roman Catholicism to Protestantism. Interestingly, however, there is little record of personal relationships with Catholic priests in the West or in India, or of lay persons with Catholic backgrounds among his followers. The Roman Church had both the cloistered and apostolic varieties of monastic life, all the same, and it had organization. There was no acephalous, loose-knit structure such as certain sect-type religious groups manifest, but a centralized authority to which the lesser hierarchical officials and groups were ultimately amenable and to which they looked for spiritual guidance and doctrinal clarification.

The organizational model was modified in several ways: 1) Through granting a large measure of autonomy to local societies, particularly in the West, where, in conformity with democratic practices, boards of trustees usually are established locally. In India lay persons also serve on managing committees in certain centers. 2) The relative absence of a prescriptive personal regimen. From the earliest days of the organization and from Ramakrishna's example, it was determined that rigid rules of conduct would be detrimental.* 3) The lack of insistence on assent to a stated body of doctrine. Very few dogmatic controversies have arisen, and the paucity of other schismatic tendencies is rather striking. The last two adaptations modify the monastic model in the direction of the *sannyasin*, with his large emphasis on religious freedom.

*In Vivekananda's first draft of by-laws for the order, one section had been quite detailed on rules for the monks. When he proposed these to the *gurubhais*, they made suggestions for some time except for Maharaj

In addition to other precedents from within the tradition for its monastic model, the Hindu term *sampradaya* is useful in understanding other dimensions of organizational and ritual dependence. I have found Western sociological categories such as church, denomination, sect, cult, etc., of comparatively limited utility. A recent Western theorist, in addition to recognizing that the church-sect distinction is culture-bound in its almost exclusive application to Western religious organizations, questions its continued value even there. "The sociology of religion," he comments, "has tied itself to a decrepit theoretical wagon and choked on the dust in its tracks."[21] Part of the difficulty is the lack of precision in definition of terms. The absence of consensus inhibits the appearance of any sophisticated studies which might contribute to real understanding.

The term *sampradaya* would seem equally elusive initially; it is customarily used to refer to those groups which have grown up within Hinduism to provide for theistic expressions of devotion to a single deity. Weber includes traditions such as Buddhism and Jainism with certain Vaishnavite and Shaivite groups under the category of *sampradaya* and regards all of them as clearly heretical, in that they subvert caste duties.[22] Some, such as the Shaivite Lingayata *sampradaya*, may indeed attempt to set up a non-Brahmanical hierarchy of social distinctions; to this Bhattacharya gave some support in his *Hindu Castes and Sects*.[23] He is antipathetic to all such groups because he feels that they undermine the structures of society. Nevertheless, he terms Vaishnavite, Shaivite, Sakta, and other such groups as *Hindu sects* (*sampradayas*). Wach, who stresses the positive character of the term in reference to its special concepts, forms of worship, and loyalty towards an outstanding religious personality or his descendants, definitely understands that no secession from the larger group is implied.[24] Similarly, Bhandarkar, in examining primarily the doctrinal assumptions of the various systems (by which he translates *sampradaya*), emphasizes their development within the tradition. Some, as in Vaishnavism, exalt one of the varied facets of the mythological material concerning the *ishta* (chosen deity); certain movements with-

---

(Brahmananda), who was silent. "Then Swami asked, 'Raja, what is the matter? Why don't you say something? Don't you like it?' Maharaj said, 'No, Naren. I don't like so many rules and regulations.' Then Swamiji took the draft of that section and without a word just tore it up and threw the pieces away." John Yale, *op. cit.*, p. 43.

in the larger *sampradaya,* such as the followers of Vallabha, may concentrate on ceremonial expression, in contrast to the followers of Chaitanya, who typically practice devotional singing and dancing.[25] All, however, are within the tradition.

Whereas the *sampradaya* served generally to modify the syncretistic character of Hinduism in the direction of a more exclusive devotion addressed towards a particular deity, the Ramakrishna Movement, from the example of its founder, rather intensified the syncretistic spirit. As earlier suggested, the catholicity of the shrine at Dakshineswar, with temples to Radha-Krishna and Shiva in the same court as the central temple to the goddess Kali, must have been influential in shaping the devotional life of Ramakrishna. While by no means without precedent elsewhere in India, Rani Rasmoni's composite shrine vividly conveyed the ideal of coming to a knowledge of God through adoration directed towards His different forms. The various stages of his *sadhana,* as recounted earlier, illustrate his desire to experience the particular feeling-tone of each of the paths toward God-realization within the Hindu tradition. Subsequently, in what seems highly unusual for one who was basically a rustic, he sought to immerse himself deeply, if briefly, in the mystical quest of Islam and Christianity as he understood them.

Although syncretism became a hallmark of the Movement which developed around his disciples, in several respects Ramakrishna's example did not become a paradigm. First, he had a succession of gurus, and second, a succession of *ishtas* as well, although Kali retained a certain supremacy. Third, although he remained chaste and without physical desire, he was married and his wife remained in his presence for protracted periods. Finally, Vivekananda specifically counseled his followers to eschew the pursuit of the *vamachara,* or left-hand Tantric path, which Ramakrishna had followed, albeit symbolically in part. Doubtless it was felt that a more single-minded course, less fraught with temptation, was to be prescribed for persons of lesser spiritual stature than the Master. An early quotation from the *Brahmavadin* warns against excessive syncretism:

> However all-embracing and cosmopolitan one's religion may be, it is impossible to get on in secular or in religious life without belonging to a particular sect. Both society and expediency would seem to require it. A Hindu may rightly admire the lofty philosophy of Christianity and Bud-

dhism, but he continues a Hindu for all practical purposes. One cannot benefit by dreaming of Krishna, Buddha and Christ at the same instant.[26]

Such caution tempered the syncretistic temptation and preserved the Movement from the rather anomalous character of the Brahmo Samaj in its more juvenile paeans exuberantly addressed to a composite deity. For practical purposes there was some check on the facile equating of all paths; it was recognized that most devotees could not make sustained spiritual progress as dilettantes dabbling lightly in various traditions. Nevertheless, by having initiation bestowed by the monastic successors of Ramakrishna, the Movement was in contrast to most *sampradayas* of Hinduism. It resembles Tantrism rather than most devotional sects because, from his knowledge of the disciple, the guru prescribes one of a number of alternative paths which he was systematically to pursue. One of the traditional Vedic *mantras* (auspicious verses) might be enjoined, and a familiar deity out of the Hindu pantheon designated as the *ishta*. To choose the sect was to choose the *ishta* generally, although variety in worship and service rendered to the deity might be counseled.

Here the variety is extended even beyond the tradition. In the case of Western disciples with a strong continuing feeling for Christianity, the *ishta* might be the Christ or the Virgin Mary.[27] Worship of the formless Brahman, in a more philosophical manner, might also be sanctioned. Reverence for Ramakrishna himself, and to a lesser degree Vivekananda and the Holy Mother, Sarada Devi, in effect, however, tended to eclipse all other personal objects of veneration as the Movement developed. There are few parallels to this among other *sampradayas* which have remained within the tradition. The veneration afforded to such figures as Sankara, Ramanuja, and Chaitanya, was clearly secondary to the chosen mythological deities of the *sampradayas* to which they belonged. In this respect, the Ramakrishna Movement would seem to illustrate one of the prominent characteristics of Wach's category of a founded religion more than that of the *sampradaya*.[28] Viability with Western faiths, expressing a preference for historical rather than mythological figures, may have also influenced this development.

Christopher Isherwood is quite forthright in acknowledging that each Vedanta center maintains a cult of Ramakrishna, although he insists that it is not exclusive and that it points beyond itself to the realization that essentially the worshiped and the worshiper are both projections of the one Brahman.[29] The evidences of the cult are readily visible, in the pictures and statues in the centers, and in the veneration directed towards them in the inner shrines. Public services, as Isherwood also recognizes, stress the Vedantic principles rather than the personality of Ramakrishna, and one thus sees something of a creative tension in an organization which is both a philosophical society and a cult of the founder. Hindu philosophy seems clearly to be judged more assimilable by Isherwood for the non-Indian than are the devotional practices of a Hindu cult.

Although references to the teachings of Christ and the lives of Christian saints in public lectures demonstrate that the cultic elements are not exclusive, some overzealous adherents are narrow in their understanding. An example is the writer of an intolerant, patronizing account of her attempt to convert an Indian Christian. The writer, a Western woman who equates Vedanta with Hinduism, although she prefers the former term, was traveling by car with the Indian woman. In the course of the conversation she said, "I remember my Guru once saying, 'You cannot sail in two boats,' to a fellow disciple who was trying to hold on to Christ as her *Ishta,* but at the time felt a pull towards Ramakrishna." The clear implication was that the fellow disciple should give up Christ. The author later said to her Indian friend, "You know, I don't think that you are really a Christian," and concluded her remarks with the wish, "Someday I hope you will receive a *mantra.*"[30] Here Vedantin universalism seems clearly compromised —perhaps in imitation of Christian proselytizing methods—to recruit a Hindu. It is not, perhaps, an isolated example. Wendell Thomas observed earlier that Americans often became more strictly Hindu than many Hindus in India and more anti-Christian than the swamis from India.[31]

Vivekananda's satirical objections to ritual and his reservations about the mushrooming cult of Ramakrishna have been mentioned. For him there was a rather clear hierarchy of the Hindu paths, with the highest *jnana,* the intellectual, philosophical way pursued through meditation without recourse to ritual. Nevertheless, this personal preference was balanced with the recognition that ritual was important to the spiritual progress of many, and in a letter to Sturdy we find him discussing the need to develop an effective ritual for use with the new group in London.[32] His own contribution to such practices is very much in evidence in his hymns and chants used in various centers.

Some Western centers have settled for a virtual absence of ritual in the public services. In the Ramakrishna-Vivekananda Center in New York, while statuary and pictures of the founder and his chief disciple are displayed, the Sunday morning hour begins with organ music. On the occasion of my visit, the assistant Swami then entered, dressed in an ocher robe, and opened the service with a Sanskrit invocation. He then proceeded with his lecture, which was followed by a collection and concluding prayers by the Swami in Sanskrit and English. The congregation did not participate in spoken recitations, chanting, or the singing of hymns. Members in other centers have expressed the wish that some singing could be incorporated, but Western liturgical music and lyrics are not felt to be appropriate, although soloists may render classics or modern compositions. Sanskrit chanting is employed in more intimate settings, however, where Hindu ritual predominates over philosophy, in contrast to the public gatherings. Poems such as Vivekananda's *Song of the Sannyasin* or Chaitanya's *Chant the Name of the Lord* are used daily in English in the shrine rooms at Chicago and Trabuco, respectively.

The most elaborate ritual which I have witnessed in one of the Western centers is Ram Nam, observed every other Saturday evening in the Hollywood center. Following the regular evening period of meditation, in which one of the monastic men or women presides in ritual worship towards Ramakrishna, the traditional Hindu chants for Ram Nam are sung. Copies of the Sanskrit words, transliterated, are available for visitors and others who have not memorized them. The proceedings are sedate; no dancing or processionals accompany the singing. Following this, which, with the antecedent period of meditation, lasts for some two hours, the congregation gathers for a covered dish dinner, such as might be shared at many North American churches. To my knowledge, this is the closest thing to a fellowship activity regularly held in one of the Western centers. After the supper, however, socializing lasts but briefly, for those present crowd into the living room to direct questions to the informally seated Swami Prabhavananda. No other ritual accompanies this hour, but it is a time of warm and intimate fellowship, obviously treasured by those present.

The Hindu shrine ritual in Chicago, in which I also participated, is described in a newspaper account:

. . . From time to time, the student monk waved a long gray duster
to fan the air before the altar. This was to cool the air (symbolically) for
the bust of Shri Ramakrishna.

Off the floor, the student monk picked up a goblet of water and held
it as an offering. . . . Another time he held out a silver platter of sliced
oranges and dried fruit. Nearby, an incense pot sent up curls of perfumed
smoke. On each side of the altar were fresh-cut flowers. . . . During worship, he used the symbols of the five elements of the universe. These are
water, earth (food which comes out of the earth), fire (a purifying
agent), air (incense) and space (exemplified by the sound of the tin-
kling).[33]

John Yale credits a leading Swami of the Order with the observation that, just as Vivekananda was responsible for stirring people
up to physical activity and service and getting the work organized, it
was Brahmananda whose stress on spiritual practice first gave shape
to the devotional character of the Movement centering around worship
of Ramakrishna. Without this, he observes, "the movement might have
deteriorated into a kind of good works protestantism by now."[34] The
latter element clearly would not satisfy the Western Vedantin. Nor,
by itself, would it reach the people of India.

The model of the *sampradaya,* then, with its emphasis on ritual
and devotion, is one of the foremost ways in which the Movement
maintains its fidelity to the tradition. It is in this manner, also, by
which the Movement is made accessible to the Hindu masses. Whereas
ritual in the Western centers is largely reserved as esoterica, in the
inner shrines, for those deeply immersed in the Movement, it is *puja*
(acts of worship) during the conduct of morning and evening rituals
which attracts the Indian populace. The Hindu holy days are also
occasions for great throngs coming to the Mission centers. I joined
with a crowd of tens of thousands at the Belur Temple during Durga
Puja festivities in West Bengal. The particular occasion was Kumari
Puja, in which a young girl, chosen after a painstaking annual search,
was singled out for veneration as a visible manifestation of divine
qualities. The Movement appears to cherish a deep feeling for Hindu
folkways and festivities, as no mere philosophical movement or monastic order of social workers would, and the people's recognition of
this is evident.

How has fidelity to the Hindu tradition been given organizational as well as ritual expression in the West? In one of the North
American centers I witnessed a mundane incident which may illus-

trate the problem of defining this organizational model. An assistant to the Swami identified himself over the telephone to a retail store nearby by saying, "This is the Hindu Church." Historically, the two terms are incongruous. As Paul Devanandan observes, "Hinduism has never thought in terms of congregational worship [he excepts certain renascent movements], where a corporate body of believers approach God in a sense of togetherness. . . . The conception of the Church is a rock of offense to the Hindu."[35] Yet in the West, the centers, as they grow in size and duration, tend to operate much like established churches. Originally, as with other movements, the intent was to think of the infant organization as something other than a new rival sect. The coming together of the followers was chiefly to gain a new conception of religion which would enhance their understanding of their own tradition. Vivekananda was asked in London, "I am told that though you lecture here, you do not intend to found a new sect." He responded. "That is true. What I desire is to lay stress on the unity of all religions, and those who grasp what I wish to teach will carry this lesson of essential unity into their denominations."[36]

Most early followers thus continued to consider themselves Christians and maintained connections with the organized church. This tendency continues in certain smaller centers. A 1950 article observed of the Portland center members, "Some are as devout in other churches as in the society. Some are converts from a religion which they no longer consider the sole basis of salvation. But most consider themselves Christians."[37] The process by which, as the society becomes larger and more established, a more exclusive religious loyalty on the part of the members attaches them to it, appears in two observations growing out of the early years in Boston under Swami Paramananda. In 1914, at the dedication of the new home, Dr. Lanman, Professor of Sanskrit at Harvard, and Professor and Mrs. Adams spoke. The last speaker commented:

> I am glad of this opportunity to tell a little of what the Vedanta Center has been to me, and why I see fit to supplement attendance at my own inherited Church with visits to this other branch of Oriental worship. . . . I need all the help I can get. These are strenuous times for everyone, but I think the strain on women is most severe. . . . Some of us may go on the rocks if we do not carry a spare anchor. . . . I regard the Vedanta Center as one of my spare anchors.[38]

Seven years later, Sister Devamata stated:

The period of misunderstanding appears to be definitely over. People no longer feel the need to offer explanations to their friends when they choose the Center as their Church, and a convincing sign that the clergy are arriving at the same attitude of mind came recently in the form of an invitation to the Swami to join the Federation of Ministers in Boston.[39]

This represents, then, a transition from an adjunctive fellowship, complementing one's identification with an established religious body, to a group which sees itself operating in much the same manner as other such bodies and is thus entitled to claim the same "exclusive" loyalties from its adherents. This may represent something of a common phenomenon in institutionalization of religion, although it would appear more Western in character. It is further evidenced in those societies where, ironically, the Hindu practice of initiation has been stressed. The resultant intimacy with the guru in close spiritual guidance would seem to preclude simultaneous reliance on other religious leadership. Some persons have told me that it is simply a matter of having no time for other religious attachments while carrying out the disciplines prescribed by the guru.

The guru-disciple model represents a significant departure from clergy-lay relationships in Western religion. As Sister Christine's account vividly describes, Vivekananda's spiritual guidance of those who had elected to become his disciples was wholly dissimilar to his normal manner of relating to friends and acquaintances. "Friends," she writes, "might have a narrow outlook, might be quite conventional, but it was not for him to interfere. It seemed as if even an opinion where it touched the lives of others, was an impardonable *guru*, all that was changed. He felt responsible. He deliberately attacked foibles, prejudices, valuations. . . . "[40] Sister Christine elaborates the variety of tactics which Vivekananda employed to stimulate the growth of each disciple as he assessed their different temperaments and needs. The method could be gentle but also quite harsh, often involving what is depicted as a frontal assault on traditional ideas and pet foibles. His intensity was overpowering for some, who related better to other swamis who succeeded him. Christine relates that a brilliant woman later spoke of the different swamis who had come to the United States, and said, "I like Swami————better than Swami Vivekananda." To the look of surprise which met this statement, she answered, "Yes, I know Swami Vivekananda is infinitely greater, but he is so powerful he overwhelms me." Yet Vivekananda cultivated no slavish dependence. He laid down principles, but expected his disciples to make their own application of them. "Stand upon your own feet," he thundered. "You have power within you!" Christine comments, "His whole purpose was not to make things easy for us, but to teach us how to develop our innate strength."[41]

In one respect, Vivekananda's manner of relating to his followers was not typical of later patterns, for the Movement was not yet organized. Thus his counsel, as may be seen with those whom he initiated as well as those receiving vows of *brahmacharya* and *sannyas,* was compressed into very brief periods of time. Christine and Mrs. Funke had arrived late at Thousand Islands Park just before others were to be initiated. This was the occasion for unusual strategy. The Swami shyly said that, since he didn't know them as well as the others, he would like to use a power which he seldom employed, that of reading their minds. They joyfully assented, and he was apparently satisfied, for they are initiated along with the rest.[42]

As powers claimed by the early charismatic leaders were institutionalized, more formal procedures and stated periods of instruction were adopted. One swami suggested to the writer that a year of intense, regular, supervised instruction might now be normative before initiation were to be offered. Following initiation, however, the disciple is much more on his own, responsible to cultivate the skills of meditation, etc., which had been imparted to him. If his guru should depart, he might have other teachers but no duplication of the other, singular relationship.

Initiation is conferred privately, with the designation of the *ishta* and the recitation of the *mantra* which has been selected. It is thought of as a powerfully moving experience. One member told me that she had desired to receive initiation but that the swami in charge of her center had advised her that she should wait until her health improved.

Harland Hogue writes of Vedanta that, in contrast to Theosophy, it has clearly defined leadership roles, and that the persons filling them are respected both within and outside the Movement.[43] This is evidenced with similar intensity but in different manner in India and the West. For instance, I have observed the reverential taking of the dust of the feet many times in Ramakrishna centers in India. This act, called the *pranama,* is a traditional one performed by pious persons towards anyone considered holy. While it is not practiced in Western centers, the veneration and deference accorded to the swami reflect the Hindu attitude and appear much greater than in other Western religious bodies. That this veneration can become excessive is expressed in an article by a former Vice-President of the Math and Mission:

> The task . . . is how to realize this truth that the devotee, the Ishta Devata [the Chosen Ideal], and the *guru* are in reality manifestations of the same transcendent spirit. . . . The spiritual seeker should always remember that the idolizing of a human form and blind worshipping of a human personality is a stumbling block in spiritual progress, and is harmful to both the disciple and the *guru.* . . . If the disciples continue to cling to the *guru's* personality and look up to him for help and guidance at every step, he feels the drag and regrets his inability to make them attain that spiritual strength and freedom which he himself enjoys. . . . It is for this reason that a wise spiritual teacher deprecates the idea of blind personal service, which is very common in India.[44]

This counsel stands as a corrective against a too great dependence on the guru.* Apart from this relationship, however, there is evidenced a larger measure of impersonality in the Western societies than in established churches and sects, where fellowship is, if not a primary goal, at least an explicit secondary one. Some members express a reticence to speak of their backgrounds; social activities were singled out for their absence by persons in several centers. In this Vedanta would appear, like Christian Science, to have much

---

*Amiya Corbin, in an article, "Holy Mother," *Vedanta and the West,* March-April, 1947, relates how Sarada Devi's example was rather the obverse of over-dependence on the *guru.* She initiated many persons, giving *mantrams* freely in any circumstances, in a railway station, the middle of a meadow, etc. Once a disciple protested against her liberality in giving initiation: "Mother, you give initiation to so many people! A *guru* is supposed to look after the welfare of the disciple, but how is it possible for you to remember so many?" She replied that, though she could not recall all of these persons, she gave them to the Lord and trusted the power of the *mantrams* which she had received from Ramakrishna. The initiate, she insisted, was to practice *japam,* the repetition of the name of the Lord as taught in initiation. Here it would seem that, just as certain of Ramakrishna's actions were not to be taken as paradigms, so also was the example of Sarada Devi not to be pursued by lesser teachers.

more the element of *Gesellschaft* than *Gemeinschaft,* as Bryan Wilson observes, where persons are drawn by a common interest. In both, also, the system of private instruction, which Wilson terms a cult aspect, is at least as important as the stated services. [45] In Christian Science, however, this may be gained simply by reading, in contrast to Vedanta, where in centers such as Hollywood and San Francisco the guru's intimate guidance is regarded as crucial. Other characteristics of Christian Science—with which, perhaps because of its obvious indebtedness to Indian thought, Vivekananda had considerable rapport for a time—illumine similar organizational patterns of Vedanta. For example, the swami rarely performs a wedding; in Christian Science there is no official designated to perform weddings, and they are not held in Christian Science churches.

The Movement's patterns of leadership, organization, and ritual thus appear to maintain a distinctive continuity with the Indian tradition, along with certain understandable adaptations to Western customs. Rather than constituting aberrations, as Guenon has charged, these adaptations may rather indicate a willingness to adopt ways of expression which will not seem alien or incongruous while maintaining fidelity to the essentials of the tradition from which the Movement evolved. In its transcultural forms this posture reflects a responsible attempt to balance a sensitivity to and respect for the backgrounds of its new adherents with an integrity in its representation of the truths resident in Hinduism. It remains to see how the social and intellectual emphases have maintained a similar tension.

Chapter Ten

SOCIAL SERVICE AND NATIONALISM

Some Western observers such as Guenon, cited in the previous chapter, have criticized the Ramakrishna Movement for its lack of authenticity as an expression of Hinduism. Others, measuring it by the standard of what a movement purporting to be universal in its breadth of concerns should contain, have indicted it as being truncated for having no social dimension. Harland Hogue, speaking out of twelve years of "somewhat regular contact" with one of the California centers, says that he has never been able "to discover any concern for a responsible religious critique of the social order either in India or the West, on the part of the Swami." He also condemns Vedanta in India which, "although it has taken a mild concern for humanitarianism, . . . has done little to alleviate the sources of political, economic and social disorder."[1]

Indeed, this Movement, especially in contrast to those dominant in the West, clearly has not been primarily concerned with social issues. This contrast is sharpest in the Movement's Western centers; in India the obverse impression is gained, so that one must ask two questions, with a third emerging from the second. Why has the Movement in the West defined its mission almost wholly in terms of rather narrowly conceived religious and not social tasks? Second, why, in its place of origins, did the Movement develop even "a mild concern for humanitarianism"? Finally, how was social service reconciled with the strong nationalist feeling which also surfaced? In other movements studied in Chapter One, these two elements did not always work well in tandem, yet both emphases were retained in the Ramakrishna Movement. In this a convincing and consistent reconciliation or is it anomalous?

168

The dynamics of the development in the West might be construed as those of a counter-cultural expression: the prevailing understanding of religion is strongly social, with political overtones; therefore the new movement establishes a contrasting identity. Historically, however, this stance appears to have evolved out of an earlier ambivalence on the part of Vivekananda and his followers. Vivekananda initially was greatly impressed with the social institutions developed by Christianity. Nor was it mere politeness which made him gravitate first towards those who championed the social gospel. These were the liberals such as Benjamin Fay Mills, and their reception of him was much more cordial than that of the still dominant conservative Christianity, whose leadership may have been typified in the Rev. Joseph Cook. Both these tendencies in Christianity contained elements of counter-cultural thrust.

The social gospel movement condemned the social order for the "rugged individualism" by which the self-made business tycoon ran his empire in competition with his business rivals but essentially without challenge from his employees. It was not a period in which he negotiated with labor; instead he furnished those in lower socioeconomic levels with a model of what hard work and determined, if ruthless, striving could produce. The social gospel affirmed that man must exercise a conscience towards his fellows less able to assert and claim their rights as persons. Its political implication was shown in it advocacy of socialism as essentially congruent with the social character of Christianity.[2]

The counter-cultural aspect of conservative Christianity surfaced in its critique of the materialistic values which it believed ordered American society. Insisting that man is meant to aspire towards more spiritual and otherworldly goals, this interpretation of Christianity was not primarily concerned with reordering society but with reorienting man to aspire towards that which transcends society. (I believe that although its strongholds are real and visible, this understanding has receded in American Christianity, and that the social gospel has tended to dominate in the churches following the time of Vivekananda, Mills, and Cook.)

Therefore, despite the continuing accord extended by liberal Christianity, the Movement itself has increasingly moved towards the position which discriminates between the material and spiritual, the soul and the body, the ephemeral and the eternal, etc. In this it bears more likeness to conservative Christianity, although it continues to enjoy little institutional appreciation. Those who succeeded Vivekananda in the West began to emphasize the distinction between the social churches and the spiritual movement. The ostensible reason for not becoming originally involved in social service in the West was appreciation for the Western faiths, which were already capable of carrying out such work. It was almost a vote of confidence to judge that the Movement's own province of work should be complementary rather than competitive. This rationale is still stated on occasion, but the more critical stance appears to dominate. This has the effect of an alternate theology to that which informs the work in India and not merely a difference in strategy. The earlier charitable regard for the Christian social emphasis in the West, then, has more typically been replaced by an attitude which sees no spiritual dimension behind social concern in the churches. This is reflected in recent comments of Swami Ranganathananda, after his extensive tour in the West on behalf of the Movement. In response to the question, "Is world-weariness causing the average American to practice authentic spiritual disciplines and seek spiritual experience?" he writes:

> There are very few opportunities for this kind of serious religion and for attaining to authentic spiritual experience. They are not able to satisfy their hunger. The Protestant churches of various denominations, for example, do not have the capacity to give this kind of spiritual food to modern Americans, nor do they provide the right kind of opportunities. Churches are sometimes full. That is because they have changed their policy. Instead of giving religion, they recommend some social action, some protest against the Vietnam war, or some such thing. All the church programmes consist of that sort of thing—what they call social action, social involvement. At many places I had to say, people come to receive spiritual nourishment from the churches. If the churches are not meant to fulfill that function, what else are they meant for? There are other institutions to give man the other types of nourishment and involve him in other types of activity. If the churches do not give the things of the spirit, man is left empty. Even the Catholic churches have changed their approach. They also are engaging themselves increasingly in social action programmes to the neglect of the spiritual.[3]

Such a statement seems to be the logical outgrowth of the policy decision to focus on the more exclusively spiritual. In contrast to the dominant culture's understanding of religion, this has been the more normatively ascendant expression of the Ramakrishna Movement.

Here it approximates the posture of a number of metaphysical sects current in the American scene.[4] Hendrik Kraemer has observed in the West "a weariness with one's own cultural and religious world, a nostalgia for the exotic," culminating in a readiness to be invaded.[5] This phenomenon has surely intensified since the time of Kraemer's writing, as may be witnessed from the plethora of books on Indian spiritually and the varied quasi- or pseudo-Eastern expressions which have evolved in recent years. Most contain an implicit critique of the social concern found in the established churches. They appear to be offering a path which is consciously presented as a superior alternative, and not one which is merely complementary.

A number of the metaphysical movements in America appear to draw their membership from among the more affluent and well educated sectors of society. This is demonstrably true of Christian Science and Vedanta alike. Such a background might contribute to a reaction against the concern for societal reform in mainline churches, just as an identification with the socially established may inhibit the effectiveness of such groups in reaching those attracted by more recent counter-cultural religious expressions. Vedanta has experienced little expansion through the burgeoning interest in Eastern religious generally among young people. Groups have spawned prolifically from such figures as the Maharishi, Swami Bhaktivedanta, and Meher Baba, creating cells on college campuses and especially enlisting the alienated. Perhaps such persons, like lower-class sectarians, remain aloof from movements such as Vedanta because of their more formal institutional structures. At any rate, although Vedanta Centers are adjacent to major universities in Berkeley and Chicago, I know of no campus groups as such which have been attached to the Ramakrishna Movement.

A progression postulated by the writer of a recent research article on a Meher Baba group may, however, suggest a different kind of appeal for those attracted to Vedanta. Meher Baba's outspoken words against the use of drugs have enabled campus groups, such as the one at the University of North Carolina at Chapel Hill, to serve as a halfway house for those desiring to overcome the drug habit. The writer sees such persons as moving from a profile of drug hippie to Baba hippie to Baba straight, and projects that the next logical step may be that of secular (or even mainline Christian?) straight, with the individual reintegrated into society.[6]

We might see in the appeal of Vedanta a contrary progression. From the apparent presence of affluent persons in the Movement, it may be conjectured that a number of them, having achieved a measure of success in active pursuits within society, might find a contrasting solace in the mystical, contemplative varieties of religion. Thus, to choose consciously, as the Movement has done, to minimize activities and service ventures, may be to provide a compensating religious style for them. This clearly is not a counter-cultural movement both because it is not a youth movement and because the renunciation motif is somewhat muted. There may be a critique of materialism generally and adherents may orient themselves to more mystical pursuits, but this measure of renunciation is not accompanied by the appeal of "and give it to the poor." The spiritual quest itself might inspire a few persons to renounce; most would require the added social incentive as "successful" adults to adopt that radically new life style which could properly be termed part of a counter-cultural movement. I suggest, therefore, that whereas marks of material achievement are retained by most adherents of the Movement, it generally is reflective of Western cultural values. Its critique of materialism, like that of churches which have preached a similar message, becomes accepted as rhetoric; it is not sufficiently persuasive to inspire dramatic new departures. Perhaps only young people and a small handful of adults really have the mobility to become part of a counter-cultural thrust.[7] The Ramakrishna Movement may have counter-cultural aspects, but it does not emerge as a counter-cultural movement. Those in the counter-cultural movement, by remaining oustide, appear to recognize this.

In India, by contrast with the West, the Movement developed at least a "mild concern for humanitarianism." The Movement's early directions there were determined by the often competing tensions of nationalism and social reform in Bengal at the turn of the century. A portion of the Bengal *bhadralok* (cultural elite), which had attained its status through English education and governmental service, was both receptive to the British presence and sensitive to defects in the social order. Reform thus became a primary agenda item in Bengal at an early date and reform leaders there began to arouse the nation's conscience. The British presence was felt more strongly as a stimulant, but it may also be judged that reform was more urgently needed in Bengal than elsewhere, partly through British initiatives. Under the unique *zamindari* (landlord) system, which the British reinforced in Bengal, the peasant, being landless, was also largely voiceless, particularly by contrast with the peasant as operator of the *ryotwar* (small farm) in Madras and Bombay States. The reform movements initiated in Bengal may be understood as compensatory in part for the greater social distance existing there than elsewhere between peasant and elite. Reform measures of course were never fully effective. Even those considered reformers among the elite first resisted pressures from the British at the time of the Bengal Partition crisis and then later from the leadership of the National Congress to broaden the base of political involvement. A statement of Surendranath Banerjee in 1919 reflected continuing reluctance on the part of the elite to countenance any threat to their position of dominance. "The educated community," he said, "are the natural protectors of the masses, and I desire to emphasize that fact. . . . We are the natural protectors of the masses, and have always been so, because they are our people—the bone of our bone and the flesh of our flesh."[8]

Although Vivekananda and his followers also retained something of an elitist status, usually they did not exhibit this same measure of paternalism. Immediately he set his infant monastic organization to the task of ministering to the needs of the people. Had it not been for Vivekananda's overwhelming popularity as champion of India in the West, this would have been difficult for the Bengal elite to accept. One difficulty was that monasticism itself was never a familiar pattern in Bengal. Bypassing the traditional pattern of the *ashramas,* it would have been suspect also to the orthodox for its implicit criticism of caste usages in the exceptions claimed for the *sannyasin.* Bhattacharya's work from the late nineteenth century in Bengal elucidates this suspicion very clearly.[9] Even though there were models of the monastic life from earlier Buddhism and from the Hindu tradition in the institutions established by Shankara and various other more or less organized groups, their reputation certainly was not uniformly positive. Then, when this new group of monks began to foster social service in an organized way, another dimension was introduced. To allow holy men to pursue their spiritual quest through begging or in isolation in a monastery was one thing, but to see persons from high caste origins ministering indiscriminately to all sorts of persons seemed to the orthodox to contribute to still greater confusion.

Another difficulty in gaining the *bhadralok's* assent to the Movement's direction was that the traditional social order had already been effectively challenged in Bengal more strongly than elsewhere. This had come through devotional movements, primarily Vaishnavism. Thus, although Brahmins in Bengal retained a measure of the supremacy which the Indian tradition had afforded them since its earliest formulation, the devotee also had something of a competing special status. However, the leveling which occurred in such movements was not widely diffused into social roles; it had remained largely restricted to times of participation in devotional activities. Brahmins could live with such restricted challenges as this, and there was little organized opposition to the devotional movements. Many Brahmins, of course, participated in them.

The rather extra special status claimed for the *sannyasin* was of a different order, however. It reasserted the claim, dating from the time of the Buddha and the Upanishadic philosophers, of an esoteric teaching to be entrusted to a small coterie of persons. Under the inspiration of Asoka, the audacious attempt later had been made to move beyond these esoteric communities and apply the tradition to the whole of society. This attempt received its clearest defense in the Gita, where the mystical vision and the performance of the *svadharma*, one's own social responsibility, were intimately linked. The vision granted by Krishna reinforced his counsel to Arjuna to carry out his duty as a *Kshatriya* (warrior), which in turn would assist him in his ultimate spiritual quest, the attainment of *moksha* (release through Nirvana). Concern for the socio-political order to which *dharma* (duty) is the key was thus affirmed as an authentic part of the tradition, while it was also regarded as the arena in which man perfected his spiritual nature. *Dharma* was further determined with regard to the classic ordering principles of the *ashramas* and the *varnas* or classes. Therefore, to discern the *svadharma* was to understand the stages of life and the hierarchical order of society. The determination of one's own place within these was the personal affirmation of the total tradition.

Despite its reassertion of the alternative path of monasticism, the Movement did not really pursue a policy of social reform. All of the reform activities of Vivekananda and his followers were finally conceived as being more narrowly religious in character. The social order, again governed by the concept of *dharma,* was not basically called into question. The platforms of the Movement in India, then, may best be conceived as religious reform and social service. The Movement's new and distinctive contributions would appear to be subsumed under these rubrics.

Fears of a threat to the social order itself, then, proved to be unjustified by the Movement's subsequent history. The coordination of the twin policy objectives of religious reform and renewal with social service, however, have required a continuing defense. The question, surprising to the Westerner, which still surfaces is, "What does this social service have to do with religion?" The quarters from which it is raised may also elicit surprise. One such source is John Moffitt, referred to earlier as a former associate of Swami Nikhilananda in New York, and a swami in the Movement for a time. Moffitt recently wrote a two-part article, "Varieties of Contemporary Hindu Monasticism," in which he observes:

During the first decade of the present century, traditional monks usually looked down on the monks of the Ramakrishna Math for helping the poor and the sick, and those overtaken by natural calamities, as betraying the monastic ideal of bearing witness to the Spirit . . . In traditional monasteries, among all orthodox monks, it had been customary throughout Indian history for the spiritual seeker to devote himself completely to spiritual practice.[10]

Moffitt goes on to note that Vivekananda and his followers felt that the initiative for social service should come from monks, but that now, following independence, with the government encouraging lay people to assume their social responsibilities, the example of the monks is no longer needed. Thus he makes the interesting suggestion, published in one of the journals of the Movement, that the problem at present is how modern Hindu monks may return to "the original ideal of Indian monasticism, bearing witness to the reality of the Spirit":

The Ramakrishna Math and Mission—like the Roman Catholic Church in the United States [of which Moffitt is now a lay member, with his profession that of a full-time journalist and author]—must find a way to divest itself of its many worldly institutions and, of its own free-will, turn over its facilities to the public. . . . The total monastic community will be grappling with the problem of how to serve, once again, as a purely spiritual reminder that God alone is the goal.[11]

It is intriguing that this suggestion that the Order return to unalloyed spiritual pursuits comes from a Westerner who worked for many years in a land where Vedanta, unlike India, has had no involvement in social service. Operationally, we can only conclude that in India the Movement has synthesized its thought around the affirmation that work is worship, whereas the narrower definition of religion which has prevailed in the Western centers may seek to impose itself on India also. The tension, however, is in some ways preserved in both realms. *Prabuddha Bharata,* in one of the same issues in which it published Swami Ranganathananda's comments criticizing the social emphasis in Western religion, also quoted Walter Rauschenbusch, a leader of the social gospel movement in the United States when Vivekananda came at the turn of the century, as follows:

> It is true that the social enthusiasm is an unsettling force which may unbalance for a time, break old religious habits and connections, and establish new contacts that are a permanent danger to personal religion. But the way to meet this danger is not to fence out the new social spirit, but to let it fuse with the old religious faith and create a new total that will be completer. . . . There is so much religion even in non-religious social work that some who had lost their conscious religion irretrievably have found it again by this new avenue. God has met them while they were at work with him in social redemption and they have a religion again, and a call to a divine ministry.[12]

The presence in India of a modest program of social service does not, however, refute Hogue's criticism that, in the absence of a religious critique of the social order, the Movement has done little to alleviate the sources of political, economic, and social disorder. Most observers would not be so confident as John Moffitt that the model of social service has really caught on, even with governmental administration of many programs of social welfare and assistance. Such services as securing jobs, caring for widows and orphans, etc., where available, are still offered more characteristically within caste boundaries and not by religious or political institutions which reach across them. Moffitt seems to imply that the Movement's example in monastic involvement in social service has inspired the government and lay persons to take up such work themselves. The extent of this influence is doubtless also exaggerated. We may commend the work that has been done by the Movement without attributing to it a magnitude in excess of what the facts warrant.

At another level, however, it would be difficult to overestimate the contribution made by Vivekananda. This is the inspiration which he furnished to the spirit of nascent nationalism of his day and beyond. The impression grows that the nationalist image is his most lasting one. Nevertheless, with him, as with Tilak and Aurobindo, it may have qualified the development of a social critique. Although insistently apolitical, Vivekananda's stance was clearly in accord with Tilak's activist interpretation of the Gita. Each sought to cultivate in his fellow countrymen a feeling of national strength and pride. Among such leaders at the turn of the century the consciousness was growing that the nation, now weak and servile, had previously been a strong and influential power. This bred a chafing of the spirit, a deep-seated rancor against the *tamasic* or slothful qualities which seemed to infuse the blood of the nation's people. Resentment against the imperial overlords was accompanied by a fervent desire to emulate their virility. How to stir up the people to claim their great destiny, how to awaken them to a knowledge of who they were, these were the overwhelming concerns which remained always in the consciousness of men such as Vivekananda. Much of his rhetoric, once more, although apparently critical, was not designed to bring about fundamental changes in the social order but to shame India out of slumber to an affirmation of her own cultural worth. Vivekananda interpreted the Western spirit of power and energy as natural to the Yavana or Greek temperament; the Arya, by contrast, tends towards quietness and meditation. The former is characterized by enjoyment, the latter by renunciation. But then he makes the judgment, "Europe and America are the advanced children of the Yavanas, a glory to their forefathers; but the modern inhabitants of the land of Bharata are not the glory of the ancient Aryas."[13] Although he feels that the ancestral fire will once more manifest itself, it is presently buried, latent beneath ashes. These ashes are the delusion that India, believing that she is pursuing *sattva,* or truth, is actually drowning in a sea of *tamas.* His indictment continues:

Where the most dull want to hide their stupidity by covering it with a false desire for the highest knowledge, which is beyond all activities,

either psychological or mental; where one, born and bred in lifelong lazi-
ness, wants to throw the veil of renunciation over his unfitness for work;
where the most diabolical try to make their cruelty appear, under the
cloak of austerity, as a part of religion; . . . where knowledge consists only
in getting some books by heart, genius consists in chewing the cud of
others' thoughts . . . ; do we require any other proof that the country is
being day by day drowned in *tamas*?[14]

He then goes on to say that the nation and each person must pass
from *tamas* through *rajas* to *sattva*. Where he feels that the West was
almost wholly lacking in *sattva*, it is *rajas,* the spirit of energy, which
was practically absent in India. His oratorical portrait of the *rajas*
which India needs is eloquent:

What we should have had is what we have not, perhaps, what our
forefathers even had not—that which the Yavanas had; that, impelled by
the life vibration of which, is issuing forth in rapid succession from the
great dynamo of Europe. The electric flow of that tremendous power vivi-
fying the whole world. We want that. We want that energy, that love of
independence, that spirit of self-reliance, that indomitable fortitude, that
dexterity in action, that bond of unity of purpose, that thirst for improvement . . . we want—that intense spirit of activity (*rajas*) which will flow
through our every vein, from head to foot.[15]

In analyzing his nationalistic language, we also note that he was
highly sensitized to the danger of capitulation to the Western spirit,
and he extolled the keeping of the Indian ideal of *sattva* before the
nation's eyes so that it would not simply be overwhelmed by Western
rajas. His countrymen could respond to the challenge because of his
forthright denunciations of Western values during his travels in Europe
and North America. They knew him as one of their own, and, despite
his Western education and travels, there was no question of compromised loyalties. His background uniquely fitted him as a catalyst for
India's rising spirit of nationalism. Indeed, one may observe that his
continuing image in India has undergone something of a process of
secularization, with the nationalist clearly dominant over the religious
leader. The separation of these categories should not, however, be
pressed too far, for the religious contribution doubtless fortified that
of the national leader. One source comments, "It would be true to
say that Swami Vivekananda and Mahatma Ghandi have, each in
turn through their religious inspiration, awakened a love for the
Motherland such as no purely political leader has ever been able to
evoke."[16]

One source, however, portrays Vivekananda as having been more politically oriented than he is usually depicted. He is quoted as saying, "What does X know of politics? I have done more politics in my life than X. I had the idea of forming a combination of Indian princes for the overthrow of foreign yoke. For that reason, from the Himalayas to Cape Comorin, I have tramped all over the country. But I got no response; the country is dead."[17] I have been unable to determine if the author of this book was the brother of Vivekananda referred to below, but it would be intriguing to learn if he had cast his more illustrious brother's story in his own overtly political style.

Whether or not they could do so with integrity, it is clear that other political figures cited Vivekananda's example as precedent. This began rather early, with the escalation of extremist and even terrorist activity in Bengal shortly after his death. They continued, so that decades later, the great Bengali nationalist, Subhas Chandra Bose, could detail his dramatic dependence on Vivekananda. It had begun when Netaji (the title, meaning "leader," by which Subhas is usually known today) was a schoolboy of 15, in 1912. Vivekananda's fervent and heroic appeals to the nation, when stumbled upon, overwhelmed him, and he gathered a group of students around him to study the writings of Vivekananda and Ramakrishna. This clearly helped Netaji to resolve his own identity crisis, and in a more militant direction. "I no longer recited Sanskrit verses inculcating obedience to one's parents; on the contrary, I took to verses which preached defiance. . . . Vivekananda's ideal brought me into conflict with the existing family and social order."[18] Despite, then, his specific disclaimers of any political mission and the care exercised by his successors against all such connections, his words exercised a great influence on the nationalist movement. Farquhar interestingly numbers his brother, Bhupendra Nath Dutt, among a group of extremist writers, including Bipin Chandra Pal and Aurobindo Ghosh, in Calcutta after the Bengal Partition in 1905.[19] In 1908 this brother was imprisoned, as recounted by an Indian writer:

> The cult of violence was openly preached in the columns of *Yugantar*, edited by a young man named Bhupendra Nath Datta, a brother of Swami Vivekananda. When the young man was given a long sentence, his mother expressed her joy at the service rendered by her son, and 500 Bengali women went to her to congratulate her. The son himself declared

in Court that there were 300 million Editors behind the papers to take his place.[20]

Through his own familial line, as well as through the political activities of Sister Nivedita, his devoted Western follower, and many others who might be cited, Vivekananda's influence on the nationalist movement can only be judged to have been profound. Most would not feel, however, that he would have been in accord with extremist policies, for his own language and policy were not inflammatory. They contained little that could be construed as vitriolic towards the British, but rather contained a positive affirmation of the worth of the Indian heritage. Still, his posture was that of a determined defender of that heritage who could not disguise an edge of belligerence. The Indian philosopher Aurobindo, who earlier in his career more or less assumed Vivekananda's nationalist mantle in the political sphere in Bengal after Partition, writes of his qualities as a spokesman for the Indian tradition, in contrast to Nag Mahasya, a lay disciple of Ramakrishna mentioned earlier.

> There are men like Nag Mahasya in whom spiritual experience creates more and more humility; there are others like Vivekananda in whom it creates a great sense of strength and superiority—European critics have taxed him with it rather severely. . . . Each position has its value. . . . This was not mere egoism, but the sense of what he stood for and the attitude of a fighter, who, as the representative of something very great, could not allow himself to be put down or belittled.[21]

This defense would not satisfy some of the Western critics to whom Aurobindo alludes, however; they have included such men as Albert Schweitzer, who writes, "For us people of the West the great spiritual and ethical personality of Vivekananda is rendered difficult to understand by what appears to us his boundless self-consciousness and by the hard, unjust and contradictory judgments in which he allowed himself to indulge."[22] Some of his claims for India, like his sweeping judgments of the West on occasion, were notably excessive, for he asserted that India was the world's pioneer, not only in things of the spirit, but also in what Hocking has called the "clean universals" of science, mathematics, and technology.[23] Any "borrowing" which India might require of the West at this stage may, according to this perspective, be regarded as a claim for repayment of a long-standing loan.

Vivekananda was not unaware of a certain tendency toward an excess of national pride. Once, indeed, he acknowledged that his greatest weakness was his love for India.[24] Despite the evidence of this, however, we have seen that he could direct a perceptive self-criticism toward his own nation. In his more private moments, as well, such as those recorded by Sister Christine at Thousand Islands Park, he was given to protracted soliloquies on the cultural differences which he had observed, and which might inform each other to effect a higher level of human society. At Greenacre, Maine, he had taught a group of open-minded young people. "Here," she writes, "he came in contact with a new phase of American life. These splendid young people, free and daring, not bound by foolish conventions, yet self-controlled, excited his imagination. He was much struck by the freedom in the relations between the sexes, a freedom with no taint of impurity. 'I like their *bonne camaraderie,'* he said. For days he would pace the floor, in a soliloquy, thinking aloud the question this posed."

Which is better, the social freedom of America, or the social system of India, with all its restrictions? The American method is individualistic. It gives an opportunity to the lowest. There can be no growth except in freedom, but it also has its obvious dangers. Still, the individual gets experience even through mistakes. Our Indian system is based entirely upon the good of the *samaj* (society). The individual must fit into the system at any cost. There is no freedom for the individual unless he renounces society and becomes a *sannyasin*. This system has produced towering individuals, spiritual giants. Has it been at the expense of those less spiritual than themselves? Which is better for the race? Which? The freedom of America gives opportunities to masses of people. It makes for breadth whilst the intensity of India means depth. How to keep both, that is the problem. How to keep the Indian depth and at the same time add breadth.

Christine comments, "It goes without saying that this was not merely a speculative problem, mental gymnastics."[25] The incident is illustrative of the complexity of the rich personality of Vivekananda, which admits of no facile generalizations. We may observe, however, that he was given to attributing qualities to the East and West which are not always demonstrable. The Movement, following his lead, and often with less discrimination and self-criticism, has continued to foster the caricatures of the West as material and the East as spiritual. This has resulted in unhelpful nationalist expressions which border on spiritual chauvinism, such as in the article by Swami Ranganathananda cited in the previous chapter. Another passage in that article reads as follows:

> The problems of modern India are essentially problems of man's external life; whereas in the West it is the reverse.
> In many questions and answers this subject came up [during the Swami's visit to the West]. They said, "Don't you think, Swami, you have your own problems in India?" I said, "Yes, we have serious problems; but the difference between your problems and our problems in India is this: We have a soul, a pure and mighty soul. We are in search of a good and healthy body for its expression. Our former body was so weak, unfit to express the infinite soul of India. So we have to try to develop a body politic, healthy and strong. In the case of the West, you have a fine body and you are in search of a soul. Don't you think it is more difficult to find a soul than a body?" They said, "Yes."
> The problem of finding a body is easier than that of finding a soul. In two generations, we can build up our industrial strength for economic development. There is no magic about it. Western help is there. . . .[26]

This typology has been criticized by other interpreters within the movement, such as Swami Yatiswarananda, who served in Europe for a time, and Swami Prabhavananda in Hollywood. The former, insisting that "spirituality is the birthright of us all," finds in Europe and America "fine spiritual souls who would be rare even in India" and in India excellent scientists.[27] While, as Prabhavananda suggests, India's culture may have developed along a line which may be called spiritual and the West along more nationalistic and humanistic lines, East and West, in refutation of Kipling, do meet because of a common humanity which the oft-cited differences have obscured.[28]

I would judge that expressions such as those just cited are more characteristic of the Movement's central thrust. Having pointed to contrasting tendencies, it seems clear that the Movement's prevailing philosophy and practice aspire towards a transcultural expression. Whereas nationalist and universalist elements might be maintained in the person of the charismatic leader Vivekananda, the institutional decision was made rather early to focus on the universal. This was in fidelity to Vivekananda's express wishes, but more definitively than he could manage, as evidenced in the separation between the leaders at Belur and Nivedita almost immediately after Vivekananda's death. Here it seems clearly to have been felt that political activity, and thus overt nationalism, was not consistent with institutional objectives. At the same time, the Movement has persisted in a holistic understanding of religion through the inclusion of a strong emphasis on social concern. In the West this was not included for the reasons discussed, and in India it was expressed in terms of service rather than reform. The latter was not accomplished with ease, but Buddhism and Saivism provided models from within the tradition for monasticism and service which could be maintained without real challenge to the social order which was built around *dharma* and caste. These two elements of universality and holism are most significantly exemplified in the program of the Ramakrishna Mission Institute of Culture.

Swami Nityaswarupananda, who founded the Institute in Calcutta in 1938, recently returned as its director. He had assumed other duties shortly after the dedication of the Institute's present buildings in southeast Calcutta in 1961. Guiding the Institute's activities with a quiet, self-effacing competence, the Swami speaks of one of the Institute's central aims as consisting of a "plea to India as well as to Western nations to overcome one-sidedness, and, by mutual enrichment, develop equally the inner and outer aspects of life."[29] This expectation of forwarding man's spiritual and material solidarity is implicit in the Institute's varied pattern of activities. Because of West Bengal's current political instability, it has been difficult to implement the goal of bringing together a community of international scholars, but the Institute continues to foster an impressive array of educational opportunities and possibilities of intercultural exchange. A recent brochure, prepared for presentation to UNESCO in an appeal for financial support, detailed an ambitious schedule of additional objectives, which would seem to accord with the philosophy of an international enterprise such as UNESCO.[30]

The Institute's *Bulletin* of July, 1971, illustrates the Movement's very visible commitment to humanitarian concern. In addition to a lucid article and an editorial detailing the background of the refugee crisis, the issue contained an appeal for funds and a report of the camps which the Ramakrishna Mission has set up for refugees. These camps were feeding and housing at that time some 98,000 refugees. Even in consideration of the total magnitude of the refugee migration, this cannot be judged a small-scale operation. It has taken a skilled and sophisticated administration to be able to respond so swiftly to this demand, which began only in March, 1971.

The Movement, then, from its inception, and despite the immensity of its task and its limited resources, has had a leavening influence as a quickener of the Indian conscience. In such a humanitarian cause as the relief of Bengali refugees, it has helped to mobilize world compassion. The burden of responsibility, obviously, has rested with the Indian government, and in this connection the question raised earlier in this chapter of the relationship between the Ramakrishna Movement in its humanitarian concerns and the secular state must be more fully explored. Having given the example, can the Movement, as Moffitt has suggested, now extend its confidence to the secular powers to continue such work precisely through withdrawing into more exclusively spiritual pursuits? A response may be suggested at two levels.

First, having spent a great deal of energy to instill into the Indian consciousness the idea that work is worship and that service to man is service to God, a more narrow operating definition of religion at this stage would be regressive in the extreme. The Movement's schools have offered practical education, teaching Brahmin boys to work with their hands alongside young men from other caste origins. If the monks themselves were now to retreat from social service, would it not suggest that they are essentially another caste group, not unlike the Brahmins, to whom "secular" pursuits, if not demeaning, are at least distracting?

Second, to men of ecumenical vision in India's different religions, there is little idea of a common front against secularization. The latter process is rather seen as an antidote to the fanatic communalism with which the subcontinent continues to be afflicted. It is recognized that the secularist may not always be friendly to the cause of religion, and may be less enthusiastic about a shared platform against communalism, which is for him inseparable from religious influences generally. While Nehru on occasion gave tributes to leaders such as Ramakrishna and Vivekananda, and often endorsed the work of the Ramakrishna Mission, his well known secularist opposition to "religiosity" is conveyed in the following statement:

We have to get rid of that narrowing religious outlook, that obsession with the supernatural and metaphysical speculations, that loosening of the mind's discipline in religious ceremonial and mystical emotionalism, which come in the way of our understanding ourselves and the world, this nature which surrounds us in its infinite variety. . . . India must therefore lessen her religiosity and turn to science.[31]

It is quickly apparent that much of the above reflects Vivekananda's own criticisms. The latter, indeed, if we may attempt a transplant of his persuasion, would seem to have as much accord with secular humanism now as with many of the objectives of religious reform in his own day. A striking affirmation of faith is given in his profession of a desire "to worship the only God that exists, the only God I believe in, the sum total of all souls. And above all, my God the wicked, my God the miserable, my God the poor of all races, of all species, is the especial object of my worship."[32] In the final chapter we shall explore the Movement's intellectual contribution, primarily with reference to its ecumenical expression. It may here suffice to recognize that the Movement may suggest a harmony of faith at two levels, the second of which also demonstrates a solidarity with secular humanism. In its most typical linguistic usage the Movement proclaims that the world's religions are united in their common quest for the realization of God. But the second dimension, unity in the humanitarian objective of ministry to the common need, clearly is not absent. We conclude, however, by recognizing that a degree of distance remains. Western faiths do not generally satisfy Vedanta in the depth of their spirituality, nor does Vedanta seem to generate sufficient ethical and social imperatives by most Christian standards.

Chapter Eleven

THE MOVEMENT'S INTELLECTUAL CONTRIBUTION

A valid test of the intellectual virility of any movement lies in the quantity and quality of research which it stimulates. If it has substance and a core of integrity, it will provoke wide-ranging scholarly inquiry. This final chapter will attempt to apply that kind of measurement to the Ramakrishna Movement, particularly with reference to its stance towards other faiths and cultures. As a satellite movement, it has sought to reflect faithfully to a larger public the best and most viable teachings of its own tradition. Transcultural interaction, however, has also forced a reformulation and restatement of these teachings. It has been incumbent upon the Movement to understand the bases on which other faiths have conducted their own similar ventures, and to develop its own philosophy of mission in response to them.

The methodology here may duplicate this process in summary fashion by attempting to construct a platform of comparison and contrast similar to that experienced historically by the Movement. This involves looking first at the strategies of the single source with which this interaction almost exclusively developed, that of Protestant Christianity. Two representatives of Protestantism, each previously cited, will receive attention here. Their careers intersected at least as early as 1928 at the International Missionary Conference in Jerusalem, when Hocking was teaching at Harvard and Kraemer was a missionary in Java. For more than thirty years, through participation in other conferences and through their writings, these men became spokesmen for different camps in Protestantism concerning how it should relate to other faiths. Hocking was the initiator, being the author, along with the Quaker mystic Rufus Jones, of the Laymen's Foreign Missions Inquiry Report in 1930. The Report linked Christian missions with other religions in a common search for truth. This position clearly showed affinity with Vedanta's stance, but was highly offensive to many Christians. John R. Mott, a primary advocate of the missionary cause for many years came under criticism for helping to launch the report. Originally entitled *Re-Thinking Missions*,[1] it was expanded in 1940 by Hocking as *Living Religions and a World of Faith*.[2] In between, however, Kraemer had become the champion of a more orthodox stance. At the request of the International Missionary Conference, he had written his book *The Christian Message in a Non-Christian World*[3] as a study document in preparation for the Conference in Madras (Tambaram) in 1938. The Madras Conference, bearing something of the book's strong impress of continental theology, laid more stress on the authority of the faith than had the Conference a decade earlier in Jerusalem. Kraemer's leadership was established in the ecumenical movement, and in 1946 he became the first director of the ecumenical Institute in Bossey.

Briefly, the polarities of the two positions may be described as that informed by neo-orthodoxy—the position of Kraemer—which emphasized the uniqueness and authority of God's central historical act in Jesus Christ, and a stance—that of Hocking—in which dogmatics receded before the commonalities of religious experience. The latter bore a strong mystical flavor, and Hocking contrasted the term, "the nonintrusive work of God," his quiet, personal revelation, to the "mighty acts of God" by which those in the Judeo-Christian heritage felt themselves to have been made recipients of a particular historic revelation.

The two positions are not easily reconcilable. Indeed, an attempt by Kraemer to effect such reconciliation in his 1956 work entitled *Religion and the Christian Faith* illustrates its difficulty. Here Kraemer sought to clarify some issues raised in his earlier book, chiefly by way of indicating a larger identity with the theology of Emil Brunner rather than the more rigid position of Karl Barth. If the harmonization which he sought to effect seemed, however, to be pursued through partial retrenchment, it was also attempted through modifying Hocking's position, giving it a coloration more like his own. A recognition of difference nevertheless remained; Kraemer offered the criticism that Hocking's case undermined missions through putting Christianity on a par with other religions. His own insistence was on the disconti-

nuity of Christianity and other faiths, with Christ as the act of God and
not the summit of human achievement and wisdom. Still later, despite
his recognition of its need, he relegated dialogue also to a secondary
status; his reason again was that it would wear the aspect of a
counteragency to the world mission of Christianity. The Church,
first and foremost, was to fulfill her theological task of "setting her
own house in order."[4]

Hocking's thesis is encapsuled in a few key words from *The
Coming World Civilization*. "Christian faith," he says, "does not
present itself as an hypothesis competing with other hypotheses: it
exists at all only as it is verified in personal experience. This verification is affirmative: 'This Way is a way to peace.' As affirmative, it is
not exclusive."[5] This more mystical position could speak of the un-
bound Christ, who could not be confined, even by the tradition
which bears His name. Yet it did not eventuate in indifference or
relativism, a tendency which Hocking felt might issue from the position of Ramakrishna. He rejected Dewey's plea that "we must wipe
the slate clean and start afresh . . . free from all historic encum-
brances," instead affirming that "Christianity is explicitly the religion
of 'the prophetic consciousness'—that is to say of the affirmative relationship of faith to historic effect."[6]

Unwilling, then, to relinquish its historic base and the quality
of life which should emerge from it, Hocking is nevertheless aware
that its historic development in Western culture prevents Christianity
from becoming genuinely a world faith. In quest of such a faith, he
seeks to remove the stigma of syncretism, specifically citing meditation, serenity of spirit, and impersonality as elements not presently
contained in Christianity which such a faith could glean from Eastern
sources. While, therefore, it should retain its historic consciousness,
Christianity, in its attempt to attain the stature of a world religion,
must separate itself from identification with Western culture. "Christianity dictates no policy and joins no party."[7]

It should be recognized that the positions of both Hocking and
Kraemer are attempts to verbalize the universal character of Christianity. For Kraemer, this character is seen to emerge from the fidelity
of Christianity to its own nature. For Hocking, it cannot emerge apart
from conscious recognition of its own cultural limitations, coupled
with a willingness to expand through incorporation of elements matured in other traditions. The dialectic between these two positions has

been intellectually fertile, and it has also added a stimulating ferment to conversation with other faiths and to the internal quest for identity by those faiths.

No recent movement in the Indian religious tradition has exhibited the intellectual virility of the Ramakrishna Movement. Some of the latest movements, in fact, have been quite consciously anti-intellectual, for example, the International Society for Krishna Consciousness or the Maharishi's movement of Transcendental Meditation. These expressions, while they may with varying authenticity represent devotional and psychological facets of the Indian tradition, clearly do not aspire to be catalysts for scholarly research. From its inception as a movement, however, the Ramakrishna Movement has sought to articulate a philosophy of universalism. Its apologists have been many and their literary output voluminous, if uneven in its intellectual weight. Much, indeed, would seem naive and trite, consisting of re-iterations of the assertion of a facile harmonization of paths, i.e., "We're all going the same way."

Any quick judgment, however, that statements of this character are uniformly shallow would be far wide of the mark. There is a large measure of sophistication behind certain assertions of this aspect of the Movement's stance towards other faiths, a broad equivalence of paths. In support, we may cite the conclusions of a recent interpreter of Ramakrishna, A. C. Das, writing on the theme "From Dogmatism of Philosophies to Democracy of Religion." Das understands Ramakrishna as concluding that "the spiritual forms in which he [God] reveals himself are finite, though infinite in number." "Reality cannot be exhausted by a finite being in any spiritual experience."[8] It is this quality of finiteness or relativity of the various paths by which we may gain knowledge of the Infinite which affirms a plurality, and not a hierarchy, of religions.

Das's call for the recognition of a genuine plurality, and not a disguised, dogmatic hierarchy, finds support in the writings of two of the literary community who have so interestingly attached themselves to the Vedanta Center in Hollywood, Christopher Isherwood and Aldous Huxley. Isherwood writes in refutation of a narrow definition of religion set forth by Professor Irwin Edman, who regards ritual and dogma as anti-intellectual flights to authority. Isherwood feels, by contrast, that properly understood many cultic practices, rituals, and even dogmatic assertions are not antirational. He insists, for instance, that rituals may be seen as acts of recollection and self-dedication.[9] Dogmatic statements, he suggests, are really hypothetically accepted truths. Isherwood's defense is significant as a refutation of any trace of anti-intellectualism in the Movement's patterns of activity.

Isherwood is apparently also referring to a line of thought suggested a bit earlier by Aldous Huxley, in what may be seen as a Western modification of Vedanta philosophy (though it accords with Das's position again). Its teachers have usually characterized Vedanta as being nondogmatic in contrast to Western faiths, and thus more experience-centered. For Huxley, it is more true to say that each of us lives by working hypotheses, that some faiths tend to make these rigid and excessively dogmatic so that persons under their authority tend to discover only what they were initially taught to believe. With sentimental humanists, by contrast, who require only a little bit of Wordsworth for a working hypothesis, there is no motivating force impelling them to make more arduous experiments, and they progress little in charity. Huxley instead proposes a "Minimum Working Hypothesis," "for those of us who are not congenitally members of an organized church, who have found that humanism and nature-worship are not enough, who are not content to remain in the darkness of ignorance, the squalor of vice or the other squalor of respectability . . ."[10] The content of such a hypothesis, Huxley suggests, "would seem to run to about this":

> That there is a Godhead, Ground, Brahman, Clear Light of the Void [Huxley's preferred term for the Absolute], which is the unmanifested principle of all manifestations.
> That the Ground is at once transcendent and immanent.
> That it is possible for human beings to love, know and from virtually, to become actually identical with the divine Ground.
> That to achieve this unitive knowledge of the Godhead is the final end and purpose of human existence.
> That there is a Law or Dharma which must be obeyed, a Tao or Way which must be followed, if men are to achieve their final end.
> That the more there is of self, the less there is of the Godhead; and that the Tao is therefore a way of humility and love, the Dharma a living Law of mortification and self-transcending awareness.[11]

Huxley's impersonal conception of the Absolute, which also seems to lack a historical dimension, may be unsatisfactory to many

Westerners but, beyond his content, the scientific model of a working hypothesis may have an appeal. Actually, Huxley may be seen as enlarging on yet another strand of syncretistic thought, that of modern science, which Vivekananda and his successors also wanted to weave into their philosophical schemes. That they were able to do so rather convincingly may be illustrated by pointing to relationships which leaders of the Movement have sustained with noted scientists and philosophers, East and West. Vivekananda's associations with William James and the scientist Nicholas Tesla in the West and with J. C. Bose in India have been noted. Bose and his family remained particularly devoted to Sister Nivedita all her life. For the physical scientist, the appeal of a monistic philosophy, with an impersonal conception of the Absolute, such as Brahman or a Ground of Being, is evident, and for persons working in psychology, the yogic disciplines which may contribute to psychic wholeness offer a fascinating area for study. In the latter realm, Swami Akhilananda interestingly continued the pattern established by Vivekananda and Saradananda in their associations with William James by being in close professional and personal communication with such Boston area psychologists as Gordon Allport and Hobart Mowrer of Harvard and Paul Johnson of Boston University, and through participation in the Institute on Religion in a Age of Science.* Allport wrote an introduction to one of Akhilananda's two significant volumes on Hindu psychology; Edgar S. Brightman, professor of philosophy at Boston University, contributed the foreword.

The universalism which asserts a commonality, first, with other faiths and, second, with other intellectual disciplines, receives institutional expression at the second level in the network of schools operated by the Ramakrishna Mission in India. This clearly represents a considerable departure from the initial example of Ramakrishna, who detested mathematics and was generally averse to "bread-winning education," which only detracted from the primary pursuit of spiritual realization. His universality lay wholly in the realm of the religious. In elaborating his teachings, the Movement which has succeeded Ramakrishna has seen implications for other

---

* This organization, of which the writer is a member, is largely composed of persons from the New England area, most of whom are affiliated with Unitarianism and other free religious persuasions.

academic pursuits as well. Vivekananda's forceful insistence largely
determined this direction.

Another strain of contemporary philosophical thought, also
with implications for a wider, more expansive understanding of
religion, is reflected in an article by Swami Nityabodhananda. The
Swami, who has resided in Europe for over ten years and has established connections in a number of cities in addition to his headquarters in Geneva, writes on the subject of "Desacralization." His
thesis is that if Western thought and striving today appear to be
merely secular and do not clearly manifest much that is essentially
religious, it is partly because of the barriers which man has constructed around the sacred.

This is man after the second fall (when the symbols created after
the first fall are dead). He does not want to be God, for he wants to be
man choosing as his companions in this journey the spirit of independence
and the faculty of wonder.
The sacred which wants to universalize itself "desacralizes itself."
(Which means passing beyond the divisions of sacred space and sacred
time.) . . . It is man who constructed the limits round the holy and when
he finds that the holy overflows its limit in an effort to annex the unholy,
for him holiness is destroyed.[12]

It is initially jarring to behold a Swami, even of a satellite
movement from Hinduism, using terminology we tend to associate
only with current Western philosophy. It is impressive, however, to
see that the Order has fostered and promoted this kind of transcultural investigation. To move beyond our own expendable, culture-
bound trappings and address the universals of human experience is
a particular challenge to any religion; and our success, East or West,
in this venture is inconstant. It recalls Hocking's judgment on Christianity's alliance with Western cultural norms. Much of the genius of
Christianity in relating its insights to social issues derives from this
alliance. Vedanta, Hocking feels, by contrast is almost wholly non-
local.[13] Here Hocking would seem to be in support of Vedanta's
claim to be the distilled essence of religion itself. Thus, while Hinduism is very much yoked to the particularities of the Indian culture,
the intent of Vedanta would be to attend to the intrinsic substance
of religion itself.* One way in which it has sought to preserve its
concentration on the spiritual universals is, as has been noted, to
remain wholly aloof from political considerations.

* The question arises, "Is it possible for any person living in the

At this point, however, we have moved to the other side of the Movement's intellectual statement of universalistic philosophy, that which bears a more dogmatic flavor. The contrast emerges in an article by Swami Prabhavananda written two years after Huxley's. The Swami says, "God is not merely a hypothesis, He is. God can be realized and must be realized in this very life." The Swami then goes on to cite the experience of Ramakrishna, who "experimented with the existing religions and found that they are all true, inasmuch as they are the ways, the paths, to realize the one God."[14]

This is not a casual difference between the Indian teacher and his sophisticated Western disciple who desires to harmonize Vedanta and modern scientific methodology. Das, in underscoring the finiteness of the spiritual experience, would seem to accord more with Huxley's hypothetical approach. Prabhavananda's assertion concerning "the one God" may rest on a quite definite understanding of the nature of the divinity thus revealed and of the true religion which should be directed towards him. This understanding in fact has emerged. The difference in the two positions is explicated still more clearly in three addresses given at the Institute of Culture in Calcutta by Pravas Jivan Chaudhury. Dr. Chaudhury contrasts the making of ontological assertions in Vedanta with the scientific stating of postulates. This contrast he specifies as "the only major difference between Vedanta and our present [scientific] philosophy. We postulate this cosmic spirit and do not speak of proving it as true. But Vedanta believes that its assertions are true by virtue of the direct verification

---

West, to live the Hindu life?" Some would see such an intimate connection between the religion and the Indian society that they would answer in the negative, thus making the judgment that the religion, by itself, is not exportable. J. Milton Yinger, for instance, in *The Scientific Study of Religion* (London: The Macmillan Co., 1970), says without equivocation, "Hinduism as a religious term separate from Indian society is a Western idea" (p. 212). He defines it as a diffused ecclesia rather than an institutionalized one as is Western Christianity (pp. 262-3), and thus, by analogy, not packageable for transplant elsewhere.

This very judgment, however, makes necessary another category such as the one we have chosen, that of the satellite movement. The group itself seems to have felt the necessity of a more universalistic term than Hinduism. The choice of Vedanta may not, by its larger classic association in the Indian tradition, seem justifiably appropriated by a particular movement, but it is intended to convey both that which is rooted in the Indian tradition and which has the possibility of life beyond the Indian culture.

of them in the extraordinary experiences of the Vedic sages."[15] Dr.
Chaudhury had earlier elaborated this distinction in two previous
addresses at the Institute. In "Deontological Vedanta" he states:

> We believe that Vedantic statements, which are expressed in declara-
> tive statements as ontological assertions, may as well be rendered in a
> prescriptive form. The statement, "The world is illusory, Brahman alone
> exists," may be rendered as, "Experience the world as illusory and
> Brahman as the only existent." The statement, "That thou art," may be
> rendered, "Realize yourself as That." In effect, the speaker, while saying,
> "X is," means, "X is considered by me, the speaker, to be important, and
> is thus an elliptical expression for a value judgment."[16]

In "Vedanta as Phenomenology" Chaudhury says:

> Phenomenology as a method of philosophy stresses directness of the
> knowledge of objects said to be discovered by the phenomenologist, but
> it does not speak of the existence or ontological being of the objects,
> which are said to be but appearances or phenomena for this reason.
> Existence or reality of objects is bracketed or suspended by the pure
> phenomenologist, who merely describes the various stages of his intuiting
> of objects which are but products of this intuitive act.[17]

Dr. Chaudhury is clearly conversant with major strains of
phenomenological thought, in such writers as Husserl, who invokes
the principle of *epoche,* the bracketing or temporary suspension of
one's own conceptions of truth, as a necessary precondition to dialogue.[18] From this vantage point, our own convictions and mental
categories may inhibit listening to our interlocutor, whoever he is,
from whatever faith. But Chaudhury is also correct in differentiating
this position from classic Vedanta and from Vedanta as interpreted
by the Ramakrishna Movement, at least in many of its utterances. The
tendency here may not be directly parallel to Kraemer's insistence on
the radical uniqueness of one's own position, but it is none the less
dogmatic. It consists most typically in an extension of its own definition of religion, chiefly mystical, to other faiths. The resultant harmonization discerns a common core in the world's religions and
through this recognition appears to extend its arms in conciliation
towards other communions. While more humane than the overt
claim of superiority often extended by Western faiths, the blanket pro-
jection of one's own understanding of religion onto others often
results in distortions.

Kraemer's observations are useful at this point. He speaks of
the relativism of indifference, in which certain persons may be de-

lighted to find, in the sea of competing doctrines, an affirmation that the various paths all amount to the same thing.[19] This stance of premature unitarianism may effectively forestall a depth commitment to a particular tradition as well as inhibit any analytical study of other faiths. When Vedanta therefore asserts that all the major religions are striving to offer their adherents a realization of God it strikes a note of popular appeal, but with attendant dangers. The recognition of a true plurality of faiths, a democracy of religions—on which certain spokesmen for Vedanta such as Das insist—would require that the terms "realization" and "God" be definitively understood as their meanings have been developed within each tradition. If, again, Vedanta assumes that mysticism is the kernel of each faith, then it would be strongly disputed by historical evidence, as the concentration on contrasting models such as Weber's category of inner-worldly asceticism is witnessed in Western Christianity, for instance.

In lieu of its own more characteristic frontal confrontation, Christianity has also on occasion attempted to effect a harmony of sorts in this fashion, *i.e.*, through projecting its doctrinal interpretations onto other faiths. There is much that may contribute, for instance, to a mature, trustful dialogue in P. D. Devanandan's writings, but the very title of one of the major articles cited, *Christian Concern in Hinduism,* is a clear imposition, and one can readily imagine the resentment which it would provoke among Hindus. Similarly, Swami Prabhavananda's *The Sermon on the Mount According to Vedanta,* while it does not claim to be the only interpretation which may be given the passages cited, would seem to most Christians a distorted, historically unjustified attempt to cast Jesus's words into the mold of Vedanta philosophy, in continuation of Vivekananda's propensity for assuming that all of the world's great religious teachers were essentially advocates of Advaita. This, again, is the position that there exists, not a plurality, but a hierarchy of religions. It is the attempt to effect a harmony by representing the highest insights of each faith as being in agreement with one's own conception of the *summum bonum* of religious truth, and relegating other contributions of those faiths to a lower level of meaning.

Just as Christian advocates, then, such as Hocking and Kraemer, have differed in their understandings of the normative relationship which Christianity holds with other faiths, so the Ramakrishna Movement has not spoken with a unified voice in these matters. That such differing opinions have emerged and have been published by the Movement may indeed be taken as a sign of healthy intellectual ferment. Earlier the position that the insights of Vedanta were the essential substratum uniting the world's faiths predominated. It may be termed Vedanta's classic stance towards the issue of universalism and is still the most characteristic. In recent years, however, both in India and in the West, alternative solutions, incorporating sophisticated perceptions from science, psychology, and phenomenology, have been voiced by persons associated with the Movement. They indicate the confidence and openness of a movement come of age. As they are greeted by persons of similar spiritual maturity from other faith communities, there is promise of trustful encounter and productive cooperation.

A third stance should also be noted, however, before we are persuaded that a new millennium in ecumenical understanding has dawned. There is a more militantly aggressive posture in contrast to both of those already described. It stands as a continuing indictment against the excesses of Protestant missionary zeal and as an indication of the strong residue of resentment and suspicion which these have left upon the people of India. A particular incident serves as an illustration: In 1953 Dr. K. N. Katju, then Indian home minister, was quoted by the *Bulletin of the Ramakrishna Mission Institute of Culture* as having clarified article 25 of the Constitution with respect to the profession, practice, and propagation of religion. The article states: "Subject to public order, morality and health . . . , all persons are equally entitled to freedom of conscience and the right freely to profess, practice and propagate religion."* Dr. Katju's interpretation said, "Everyone in India is free to propagate his religion, but the government does not want people from outside to come and do that." The discussions with Dr. Katju revealed that it had been made clear to all foreign missionaries working in the country that if they were engaged in social welfare work, medical work, and education, they were welcome, but if they indulged in proselytization it would be undesirable. "If they come here for evangelical work," said Dr. Katju, "the sooner they stop it the better."[20]

* This is the article cited in the previous chapter in which the Ramakrishna Mission argued and was supported in its position that its

Commentary which follows from the Institute's *Bulletin* recognizes what it calls the apparent contradiction of the Constitution, but then it attempts to clarify what the term "evangelism" has meant in India. Despite missionaries' insistence that evangelism is to be contrasted with proselytism as motivated by love rather than prideful desire for increase, the article feels that, while more subtle, it still aims at conversion. This is felt to have negative value, primarily because of the separate counter-culture, composed mostly of the poor and illiterate and antithetical to the general social and political structure, which it has created in India. The artificial inducements offered for conversion, so the article continues, have produced a restlessness and a condemnatory stance towards previously held values, chiefly those of the Hindu religion. Vedanta, by contrast, promotes harmony and unity; it fulfills and does not destroy, and its representatives in the West thus merit a different reception than evangelizing Christians in India, whose activities result in exclusiveness and divisions. Thus, while the article recognized the immense amount of social service rendered by the missionaries, service which the Hindu community itself should have provided, it judged that the resulting divisiveness had outweighed this good.

Other apologists for the Movement do not aver that it has been wholly successful in focusing on the universals of religion. Isherwood remarks that as the cult of Ramakrishna is still in its infancy in the West, it therefore remains surrounded by the external symbols of the Hindu religion. There may be many who enjoy Sanskrit chants, wearing saris, and performing *pujas* (acts of worship) according to ancient Indian rituals and find these helpful in picturing Ramakrishna and his followers in their own cultural setting; however, to insist on such practices would be to prescribe that Westerners become synthetic Hindus in practicing Vedanta.[21] Another person who, with Isherwood, serves actively on the Hollywood Center board, speculates, "Possibly, even probably, as years pass, Vedanta will take on outward forms less alien to the Westerner."[22] Among other things, as mentioned earlier, this might conceivably involve a readiness to accept Westerners in positions of leadership, a rare occurrence in the first seventy-eight years of the Movement's tenure in the West.

schools were not subject to governmental interference because of the constitutional protection afforded to activities of minority religious groups.

One may laud Vedanta's expressed intent to embody universal religious themes while questioning the practicability or even the desirability of such a goal. The Movement, in creative tension with its universalist, transcultural aspiration, has also cherished the historic particularities which have brought it into being. Copious research into the lives of the founders, Ramakrishna and Vivekananda and their associates, has provided followers with a rich tradition which most would not regard as expendable. It is no mere concession to weakness to exalt this specific heritage. Related expressions, artistic, literary, symbolic, from the wider Indian culture serve to enhance the possibilities of spiritual growth for the aspirant rather than to threaten only to inhibit and restrict him. At higher levels of spiritual progress one may postulate the transcendence of such matters; practically, they give shape to the aspirant's quest and a feeling of identity with a religious community.

Persons in this Movement, then, are eminently justified in entertaining a profound appreciation of the heritage which is their own and are likewise to be commended for keeping in our common vision the possibility of a higher measure of spiritual concord. To return to the suggestions offered earlier in this chapter by A. C. Das, I would hold that, in the latter regard, the idea of a genuine "democracy of religion" may hold promise. Qualities of defensiveness and aggression which earlier were perhaps a historical necessity in establishing the Movement may yield to other attitudes in implementation of the present task. Das's ideal calls for a relational plurality, not merely an agreement to go our separate ways. It entails a willingness to study other faiths. It involves a further readiness by Eastern and Western religions alike, to accept the differences which emerge out of such study. Another, perhaps even more demanding corollary task may lie in the redefinition of one's essence and existence in the light of this deep pondering of the other. This is essentially Hocking's call for reconception. The basis for such a total encounter of trust lies in the latent, undogmatized fellow-feeling at the center of the religious impulse.

To persons in the Ramakrishna Movement, the dimensions of the present challenge may seem encapsulated in Ramakrishna's parting commission to Vivekananda. This conveys the greatness of the trust which energized him, and which has continued to inspire feelings both of confidence and humility.

Thou art the bearer, in this storm-tossed world, of the message of universal love, sympathy, joy and fraternity. It is thy sacred role, proud privilege and bounden duty to radiate peace, order and unity in the whirlpool of dissensions and wrangles into which people have feverishly thrown themselves. Be thou like the wide-spreading banyan tree in whose cool and soothing shade thousands of souls, weary and wounded in the struggle for existence, come for shelter, healing, solace and peace. The great mission of liberating people from all kinds of bondage and suffering devolves on thee.[23]

NOTES

Notes to Introduction

1 Woodbridge O. Johnson, "Non-Christian Salvation," *Journal of Bible and Religion,* vol. XXXI, no. 3, July, 1963, p. 217.

2 P. D. Devanandan, *Christian Concern in Hinduism* (Bangalore: Christian Institute for the Study of Religion and Society, 1961), pp. 14-16.

Notes to Chapter One

1 Eric Stokes, *The English Utilitarians and India* (Oxford: Oxford University Press, 1959), p. 34.

2 *Ibid.*

3 P. J. Marshall, *Problems of Empire: Britain and India, 1757-1813* (London: George Allen and Unwin, 1968), pp. 72, 73.

4 David Kopf, *British Orientalism and the Bengal Renaissance* (Berkeley: University of California Press, 1969), p. 4.

5 Percival Spear, *A History of India,* vol. 2 (Baltimore: Penguin Books, 1965), p. 122.

6 Stokes, *op. cit.,* p. 44.

7 *Ibid.,* pp. 45, 46. See also, L. S. S. O'Malley, ed., *Modern India and the West* (London: Oxford University Press, 1941), p. 325.

8 Sir Percival Griffiths, *The British Impact on India* (London: Macdonald, 1952), p. 250.

9 S. Natarajan, *A Century of Social Reform in India* (New York: Asia Publishing House, 1959), pp. 33-35.

10 Editorial, "The Quarter," *Calcutta Review,* Vol. 114, April, 1902, p. 399. See William Paton, *Alexander Duff, Pioneer of Missionary Education* (New York: George H. Doran and Co., 1922), pp. 140-2.

11 Kopf, *op. cit.,* See Eustace Carey, *Memoir of William Carey* (Lon-

don: Jackson and Walford, 1836), *passim,* and John Clark Marshman, *The Life and Times of Carey, Marshman and Ward,* 2 vols. (London: Longman, Brown, Green, Longmans, and Roberts, 1859), *passim.*

12 Charles H. Heimsath, *Indian Nationalism and Hindu Social Reform* (Princeton: Princeton University Press, 1964), p. 53.

13 H. D. Keene, "Religion in India," *Calcutta Review,* no. 68, 1879, p. 207.

14 K. M. Pannikar, *Hinduism and the West* (Chandigarh: Panjab University Publishing Bureau, 1964), p. 24.

15 *Ibid.,* p. 25.

16 F. Max Müller, *I Point to India,* ed. by Nanda Mookerjee (Bombay: Shakuntala Publishing House, 1970), p. 41.

17 For differing assessments, see D. S. Sarma, *The Renaissance of Hinduism* (Benares: Benares Hindu University, 1944), pp. 75-6, and Marshman, *op. cit.,* vol. 2, pp. 238-9.

18 Griffiths, *op. cit.,* p. 249.

19 Paton, *op. cit.,* pp. 68-74; Kopf, *op. cit.,* pp. 259-62.

20 Max Müller, *op. cit.,* pp. 56-7.

21 Max Weber, *The Sociology of Religion* (Boston: Beacon Press, 1963), particularly pp. 46-7.

22 Gouri Prasad Mazoomdar, *Keshub Chunder Sen and the Schools of Protest and Non-Protest* (Calcutta: The Art Press, n. d.), pp. 49-54. Also, Dwijadas Datta, *Behold the Man* (Calcutta: Dwijadas Datta, 1930), pp. 135-40.

23 Sarma, *op. cit.,* p. 112.

24 Heimsath, *op. cit.,* p. 19.

25 Heimsath, *op. cit.,* pp. 184-5.

26 Heimsath, *op. cit.,* p. 122.

Notes to Chapter Two

1 R. R. Diwakar, *Paramahansa Sri Ramakrishna* (Bombay: Bharatiya Vidya Bhavan, 1964), p. 63.

2 *Ibid.,* p. 252.

3 Swami Saradananda, *Sri Ramakrishna the Great Master* (Madras: Sri Ramakrishna Math, 1952), pp. 35-41.

4 Sankari Prasad Basu and Sumil Bihari Ghosh, eds., *Vivekananda in Indian Newspapers, 1893-1902* (Calcutta: Dineshchandra Basu Basu Bhattacharyya and Co., 1969), p. 389.

5 Saradananda, *op. cit.,* pp. 140-1.

6 Saradananda, *op. cit.,* pp. 185-203, 529-30.

7 M (Mahendranath Gupta), *The Gospel of Sri Ramakrishna* (Ma-

dras: Sri Ramakrishna Math, 1964), pp. 503-4. See also, Saradananda, *op. cit.*, pp. 332-3, 254, 338, 470-1.

8 Saradananda, *op. cit.*, pp. 169, 881, 890-1.

9 Basu and Ghosh, *op. cit.*, (from *Amrita Bazar Patrika*), p. 298.

10 F. Max Müller, *Rammohan to Ramakrishna* (Calcutta: Susil Gupta Ltd., 1952), pp. 65-6.

11 R. R. Diwaker, *Paramahansa Sri Ramakrishna* (Bombay: Bharatiya Vidya Bhavan, 1964), p. 256.

12 *Ibid.*, p. 258.

13 Joseph Cook, *Orient* (London: Ward, Lock and Co., 1885), p. 109.

14 *Ibid.*, p. 283.

15 *Ibid.*, p. 255.

16 M, *op. cit.*, p. 599.

17 Jadunath Sinha, *Ramaprasada's Devotional Songs* (Calcutta: Sinha Publishing House, 1966), p. 139.

18 M, *op. cit.*, p. 588.

Notes to Chapter Three

1 Sister Nivedita, *The Master as I Saw Him* (Calcutta: Advaita Ashrama, 1923), p. 193.

2 Romain Rolland, *Prophets of the New India* (London: Cassell and Co., 1930), pp. 177-8.

3 Swami Pavitrananda, *Talks with Swami Vivekananda* (Mayavati, Almora: Advaita Ashrama, 1946), pp. 122-3.

4 Swami Vivekananda, *Collected Works,* vol. 3 (Calcutta: Advaita Ashrama, 1926), p. 242.

5 Rolland, *op. cit.*, p. 179.

6 *Ibid.*, pp. 178-9.

7 *Ibid.*, p. 180.

8 Rolland, *op. cit.*, p. 183.

9 Swami Nirvedananda, "Sri Ramakrishna and Spiritual Renaissance," *Cultural Heritage of India,* vol. 4, ed. by Haridas Bhattacharyya (Calcutta: The Ramakrishna Mission, 1956), p. 693.

10 See David G. Mandelbaum, *Society in India* (Berkeley: University of California Press, 1970), vol. I, pp. 58-61.

11 See Leo Schneiderman, "Ramakrishna: Personality and Social Factors in the Growth of a Religious Movement," *Journal for the Scientific Study of Religion,* Spring, 1969, pp. 68-9.

12 Philip Spratt, *Hindu Culture and Personality* (Bombay: Manaktalas, 1966). See also Rajni Kothari, *Politics in India* (Boston: Little, Brown and Co., 1970).

13 Romain Rolland, *The Life of Vivekananda and the Universal Gospel* (Almora: Advaita Ashrama, 1931), p. 300.

14 *Ibid.,* p. 298.

15 Romain Rolland, *The Life of Vivekananda and the Universal Gospel, op. cit.,* p. 284.

16 Nirvedananda, *op. cit.,* p. 687.

17 R. C. Majumdar, *Swami Vivekananda: A Historical Review* (Calcutta: General Printers and Publishers, 1965), p. 19.

18 Swami Nikhilananda, *Vivekananda: The Yogas and Other Works* (New York: Ramakrishna-Vivekananda Center, 1953), pp. 944-5.

19 Nivedita, *op. cit.,* p. 172.

20 *Ibid.,* p. 170.

21 Swami Vivekananda, *Letters of Swami Vivekananda* (Calcutta: Advaita Ashrama, 1960), p. 485.

22 See Erik H. Erikson, *Gandhi's Truth* (New York: W. W. Norton and Co., 1969), pp. 42-3.

23 See Carl Jung, *Psyche and Symbol* (Garden City, New York: Doubleday and Co., 1958), pp. 1-22. Also, Carl Jung, *Memories, Dreams, Reflections* (New York: Pantheon Books, 1961), pp. 185-8.

24 Franklin Edgerton, trans., *The Bhagavad Gita* (New York: Harper Torchbooks, 1964), p. 21. In the quotation from Edgerton, I have retained the word *dharma* which he renders "duty." The reference is from the Gita, 3:35.

Notes to Chapter Four

1 Romain Rolland, *The Life of Vivekananda and the Universal Gospel, op. cit.,* p. 33.

2 Taken from the two primary sources, J. H. Barrows, ed., *The World's Parliament of Religions,* two vols. (Chicago: The Parliament Publishing Co., 1893), and Walter Houghton, ed., *The Parliament of Religions and Religious Congresses at the World's Columbian Exposition* (Chicago: F. T. Neely, 1893), *passim.*

3 R. C. Majumdar, *Swami Vivekananda: A Historical Review* (Calcutta: General Printers and Publishers, 1965), p. 49.

4 Eastern and Western Disciples, *Life of Swami Vivekananda* (Calcutta: Advaita Ashrama, 1960), p. 312.

5 See Barrows, *op. cit.,* vol. one, on Dharmapala, pp. 95, 123, and 169. With respect to Mozoomdar, see p. 86 and pp. 113-4. Houghton's record substantiates this on pp. 51 and 596. Marie Louise Burke, *Swami Vivekananda in America: New Discoveries* (Calcutta: Advaita Ashrama, 1958), quotes *The Critic* as saying, "The most impressive figures of the Parliament were the Buddhist priest, H. Dharmapala of Ceylon, and the

Hindoo monk, Swami Vivekananda." She also notes that *The Advocate* of Sept. 9, 1893, after saying of Vivekananda that his knowledge of English was remarkable, further stated, "This is equally true of Mozoomdar, who however is a man of far greater spirituality and profounder religious conviction." (Pp. 83-4). P. C. Mozoomdar, *Lectures in America and Other Papers* (Calcutta: Navavidhana Publication Committee, 1955), records tributes from the contemporary American press, in addition to the one cited by Miss Burke, establishing secular appreciation of his stature *(passim)*.

6 Burke, *op. cit.,* at, *e.g.,* pp. 63-4, p. 73.

7 Conrad Wright, ed., *Three Prophets of Religious Liberalism* (Boston: Beacon Press, 1961), p. 97.

8 Joseph Cook, *Orient* (London: Ward, Lock and Co., 1885), p. 331.

9 *Ibid.,* p. 288.

10 Barrows, *op. cit.,* vol. 1, p. 542.

11 *Ibid.,* pp. 538, 540.

12 *Ibid.,* p. 971.

13 An article from *The Boston Transcript* of Sept. 30, 1893, however, mentions that Vivekananda distributed some pamphlets on Ramakrishna at the Parliament. If one of these reached Cook, it did not, to our knowledge, initiate a personal relationship.

14 Eastern and Western Disciples, *op. cit.,* p. 297.

15 Nikhilananda, *Vivekananda, a Biography* (New York: Ramakrishna-Vivekananda Center, 1953), p. 66.

16 Earlier he seemed rather charmed by his experiences as a fund raiser. Compare the accounts in Burke, *op. cit.,* pp. 95, 104, with those on pp. 393 and 423.

17 D. S. Sarma, *Studies in the Renaissance of Hinduism* (Benares: Benares Hindu University, 1944), p. 134.

18 See Burke, *op. cit.,* pp. 494-536. In defending Vivekananda and Dr. Janes against the assertions of Mrs. McKeen, she rather idolizes the lot of Hindu women, somewhat as Nivedita did in India. Swami Nikhilananda, *op. cit.,* indicates a better awareness on the part of Vivekananda of the inadequate status of women in India at the time. See p. 74.

19 See article by M. A. DeWolf Howe in *Dict. of American Biography* (New York: Scribner's, 1930), pp. 16-18.

20 Basu and Ghosh, *op. cit.,* p. 23.

21 *Letters of Swami Vivekananda, op. cit.,* pp. 96-97.

22 From *The Indian Mirror* of July 6, 1894, Basu and Ghosh, *op. cit.,* p. 29.

23 See Burke, *op. cit.,* pp. 395-413.

24 Nikhilananda, *op. cit.,* p. 85, identifies this person as Dr. Wright of Harvard, which seems not to be tenable.

25 Vivekananda, *Letters, op. cit.,* p. 289.

26 *Ibid.,* p. 291.

27 Nikhilananda, *op. cit.,* p. 94.

28 Marie Louise Burke, "Swami Vivekananda in New York," *Prabuddha Bharata,* April, 1963, p. 145.

29 Vivekananda, *Letters, op. cit.,* p. 353.

30 *Ibid.,* p. 351.

31 *Ibid.,* p. 351.

32 Basu and Ghosh, *op. cit.,* p. 104; p. 125; p. 134; p. 145.

33 *Ibid.,* p. 184.

34 *Ibid.,* p. 192.

35 Romain Rolland, *Prophets of the New India, op. cit.,* p. 342.

36 Basu and Ghosh, *op. cit.,* p. 452.

37 Eastern and Western Disciples, *op. cit.,* p. 645.

38 Vivekananda, *Letters, op. cit.,* p. 502, p. 505.

39 Ida Ansell, "On Recording Vivekananda's Lectures," *Vedanta and the West,* Jan.-Feb., 1955.

40 Rolland, *The Life of Vivekananda and the Universal Gospel, op. cit.,* p. 353.

41 Basu and Ghosh, *op. cit.,* p. 214.

42 *Ibid.,* p. 218.

43 Rolland, *The Life of Vivekananda and the Universal Gospel,* pp. 368-9.

Notes to Chapter Five

1 Basu and Ghosh, *op. cit.,* p. 27.

2 From the *Amrita Bazar Patrika,* Sept. 16, 1894, Basu and Ghosh, *op. cit.,* pp. 299-300.

3 *Ibid.,* p. 38.

4 *Ibid.,* p. 345.

5 Basu and Ghosh, *op. cit.,* pp. 309-10.

6 *Ibid.,* p. 700.

7 *Ibid.,* pp. 312-3.

8 *Ibid.,* p. 323.

9 Eastern and Western Admirers, *Reminiscences of Swami Vivekananda, op. cit.,* pp. 162-3.

10 *Ibid.,* p. 508.

11 *Letters, op. cit.,* p. 117.

12 *Ibid.,* p. 300.

13 Nikhilananda, *op. cit.,* p. 127.

14 Eastern and Western Disciples, *op.cit.*, p. 504.

15 *Ibid.*, p. 507.

16 P. C. Mozoomdar, *Lectures in America and Other Papers, op. cit.*, p. ii.

17 *Ibid.*, p. v.

18 Eastern and Western Disciples, *op. cit.*, p. 303.

19 Burke, *op. cit.*, p. 396.

20 *Ibid.*, p. 397.

21 *Ibid.*, p. 401.

22 *Ibid.*, p. 407.

23 Basu and Ghosh, *op. cit.*, p. 421.

24 *Ibid.*, pp. 645-50.

25 *Ibid.*, p. 431.

26 *Ibid.*, pp. 715-7.

27 *Ibid.*, p. 459.

28 *Ibid.*, pp. 464-65.

29 *Collected Works*, vol. 4, pp. 303-7.

30 *Ibid.*, p. 307.

31 Nikhilananda, *op. cit.*, p. 58.

32 *Collected Works*, vol. 3, p. 209.

33 Burke, *òp. cit.*, p. 409.

34 Personal interview with John Moffitt, for many years assistant to Swami Nikhilananda in New York City. The interview was on Oct. 25, 1970, at the Ramakrishna Mission Institute of Culture in Calcutta.

35 From *The Indian Mirror*, March 12, 1897, Basu and Ghosh, *op. cit.*, p. 183.

36 *Ibid.*, p. 39.

37 *Collected Works*, vol. 5, pp. 37-8; p. 98.

38 *Ibid.*, p. 111.

39 *Collected Works*, vol. 8, p. 453.

40 Basu and Ghosh, *op. cit.*, p. 145; p. 147; p. 152; p. 155.

41 *Collected Works*, vol. 7, pp. 502-3.

42 Basu and Ghosh, *op. cit.*, p. 432.

43 From *The Gujarati*, May 2, 1897, Basu and Ghosh, *op. cit.*, p. 403.

44 *Collected Works*, vol. 3, p. 222.

45 *Ibid.*, p. 224.

Notes to Chapter Six

1 From a letter to Mrs. Bull, April 25, 1895; *Collected Works*, vol. 6, pp. 306-7.

2 William Ernest Hocking, "Recollections of Swami Vivekananda," *Vedanta and the West,* Sept.-Oct., 1963, pp. 58-63.

3 Personal interview with Swami Chidrupananda, the San Francisco Vedanta Society, June 4, 1970.

4 As for instance with Mrs. Dutcher, Vivekananda's hostess at the Thousand Islands, who was "a conscientious little woman, a devout Methodist."

5 Sept. 17, 1896, letter from Miss MacLeod in England to Mrs. Bull. From the files of the Trabuco Monastery, Trabuco, Calif.

6 From *The Indian Mirror,* July 3, 1896, Basu and Ghosh, *op. cit.,* pp. 102-3. *The Hindu Patriot* of Dec. 28, 1896, however, reprinted an interview from a London newspaper in which Vivekananda was asked if his message would make people attend Church oftener. He replied, "I scarcely think it will. Since I have nothing whatever to do with ritual or dogma, my mission is to show that religion is everything and in everything." Basu and Ghosh, *op. cit.,* p. 294.

7 Sister Nivedita, *Notes of Some Wanderings with the Swami Vivekanada* (Calcutta: Udbodham Office, 1957), p. 310.

8 From *The Bengalee,* Dec. 28, 1902, Basu and Ghosh, *op. cit.,* p. 283.

9 Article by Nivedita in *The Bengalee,* a reprint from *The Hindu,* Sept. 10, 1902, Basu and Ghosh, *op. cit.,* p. 273.

10 *The Indian Social Reformer,* May 21, 1899, *ibid.,* p. 454. The full text of the address, from the *Prabuddha Bharata* of April and July, 1899, is in Basu and Ghosh, *op. cit.,* pp. 620 ff.

11 March 6, 1906, letter from Nivedita to Miss MacLeod, files of the Trabuco Monastery.

12 Basu and Ghosh, *op. cit.,* pp. 225-6.

13 See John Yale, "The Order of Ramakrishna," *Vedanta and the West,* July-Aug., 1954, p. 38.

14 H. S. L. Polak, "In Honour of Her Memory," *Vedanta for East and West,* March-April, 1953, p. 125.

15 Margot (Nivedita) to Miss MacLeod, Wednesday of Easter week, 1904, and Jan. 24, 1906. Trabuco files.

16 Margot to Yum (Miss MacLeod) from Calcutta, Feb. 21, 1906. Trabuco files. Second reference between same persons in June, 1906.

17 Wendell Thomas, *Hinduism Invades America* (New York: Beacon Press, 1930), p. 120.

18 Vivekananda, *Letters of Swami Vivekananda* (Calcutta: Advaita Ashrama, 1906), p. 434.

19 Vivekananda, *Letters,* p. 436. Letter to Mrs. Ole Bull, Aug. 19, 1897.

20 From the Trabuco files.

21 Sept. 21 and Nov. 2, 1927. Trabuco files.

22 Dec. 28, 1913 and Feb. 8, 1916. Trabuco files .

23 *Prabuddha Bharata,* Sept. 1966, p. 400.

24 Swami Atulananda, "Swami Vivekananda's Mission in the West," *Prabuddha Bharata,* July, 1970, pp. 261-2.

25 Letter in Trabuco files.

26 From the Trabuco files.

27 Trabuco files.

28 Trabuco files.

29 Ida Ansell, "Memories of Swami Turiyananda," *Vedanta and the West,* vol. XV, Sept.-Oct., 1952, p. 134.

30 Eastern and Western Admirers, *op. cit.,* pp. 164-5.

31 Article by Delia Davis, *The Brahmavadin,* Aug. 15, 1898, Basu and Ghosh, *op. cit.,* pp. 534-5.

32 *The Mahratta,* March 5, 1899, Basu and Ghosh, *op. cit.,* p. 380.

33 *The Indian Social Reformer,* Feb. 5, 1899, *ibid.,* p. 454.

34 *The Gujarati,* March 12, 1899, *ibid.,* p. 415.

35 *Amrita Bazar Patrika,* March 18, 1896, *ibid.,* p. 304.

36 *Amrita Bazar Patrika,* March 28, 1899, *ibid.,* p. 320.

37 *Amrita Bazar Patrika,* July 7, 1902, *ibid.,* pp. 324-5.

38 Editorial, "Swami Vivekananda's Achievements in the West," *Prabuddha Bharata,* June, 1963, p. 328.

39 Leo Schneiderman, "Ramakrishna: Personality and Social Factors in the Growth of a Religious Movement," *Journal for the Scientific Study of Religion,* Spring, 1969, p. 61.

Notes to Chapter Seven

1 See, *e.g.,* letter dated Nov. 30, 1895, Vivekananda, *Collected Works,* vol. 5, pp. 53-4; letter of 1894, vol. 6. p. 264.

2 Vivekananda, *Collected Works,* vol. 6, p. 264.

3 The two relevant sources are *Swami Abhedananda in America,* by Sister Shivani (Mary Le Page) (Calcutta: Ramakrishna Vedanta Math, 1947), and Sister Devamata's *Swami Paramananda and His Work* (La Crescenta, California: Ananda Ashrama, 1926-41).

4 Gambhirananda, *History of the Ramakrishna Math and Mission* (Calcutta: Advaita Ashrama, 1957), pp. 178-80.

5 From Trabuco Monastery files.

6 Gambhirananda, *The Disciples of Ramakrishna* (Calcutta: Advaita Ashrama, 1955), p. 177.

7 *The Indian Social Reformer,* Dec. 9, 1900, Basu and Ghosh, *op. cit.,* p. 456.

8 Swami Abhedananda, *The Complete Works,* vol. 2, pp. 213-9.

9 Gambhirananda, *The Disciples of Ramakrishna, op. cit.,* p. 216.

10 Eastern and Western Disciples, *op. cit.*, p. 672.

11 *Ibid.*, p. 673.

12 Gambhirananda, *The Disciples of Ramakrishna, op. cit.*, p. 218.

13 Miss Ida Ansell, "Memories of Swami Turiyananda," *Vedanta and the West*, Sept.-Oct., 1952, p. 141.

14 E. C. Brown, "Vedanta in America: My Reminiscences," *Vedanta for East and West*, July-Aug., 1959, pp. 190-2.

15 Vivekananda, *Letters, op. cit.*, p. 447.

16 *The Voice of Freedom*, June, 1911, inside cover.

17 From the files of the Trabuco Monastery.

18 *The Voice of Freedom*, Dec., 1909.

19 Gambhirananda, *The Disciples of Ramakrishna, op. cit.*, pp. 247-8.

20 *Message of the East*, Fall, 1940, p. 142.

21 Sister Devamata, *Message of the East*, Nov., 1924, pp. 211-2.

22 From the obituary review of Devamata, *The Message of the East*, Spring, 1943, pp. 36-7.

23 *Ibid.*, p. 37.

24 Sister Devamata, *The Message of the East*, Jan., 1933, p. 20.

25 Swami Nikhilananda, *The Message of the East*, Fall, 1940, pp. 169-70.

Notes to Chapter Eight

1 Robert Joseph and James Felton, "Hollywood Swami," *Script Magazine*, Feb., 1948, p. 19.

2 These have included *The Song of God*, a translation of the Gita, which has been through many printings, Patanjali's *Yoga Aphorisms*, and Sankara's *Crest Jewel of Discrimination*. Prabhavananda, with Frederick Manchester, earlier translated *The Upanishads*, and he has independently translated the *Srimad Bhagavatam*, along with many other books on Vedanta philosophy. Interesting titles among these include *The Spiritual Heritage of India*, with Manchester's assistance, and *The Sermon on the Mount According to Vedanta*. Isherwood has separately written a historical study, *Ramakrishna and His Disciples*.

3 Brahmachari Prema Chaitanya (John Yale), "What Vedanta Means to Me," *Vedanta and the West*, Nov.-Dec., 1955, p. 28.

4 Joseph and Felton, *op. cit.*, p. 19.

5 Joseph and Felton, *op. cit.*, p. 18.

6 From interviews with Swami Bhashyananda and Swami Chidrupananda, of the Chicago and San Francisco centers, respectively.

7 *Vedanta and the West*, May-June, 1942, p. 121.

8 I spoke for Christianity at this service.

9 "A Convert Takes Path to Hindu Monkhood," *Chicago Sun-Times,* July 10, 1967.

10 "Hinduism in New York: A Growing Religion," *The New York Times,* November 2, 1967, p. 55.

11 From information in interviews with Swamis Ritajananda and Vidyatmananda, August 23, 1970, and brochures issued by the Gretz Society.

12 From information in an interview with Swami Nityabodhananda, August 26, 1970, and brochures of his work in Geneva.

13 Gambhirananda, *History of the Ramakrishna Math and Mission, op. cit.,* p. 403.

14 From interviews with Swami Bhavyananda and Brahmacharya Buddha Chaitanya at the London Center, Aug. 29, and Sept. 2, 1970, and from informational materials provided by the Society.

15 From the files of the Hollywood Vedanta Society.

Notes to Chapter Nine

1 René Guenon, *Introduction to the Study of the Hindu Doctrines,* trans. by Marco Pallis (London: Luzac and Co., 1945), pp. 322-7.

2 *The Indian Religious Tradition,* (Varanasi: Bharatiya Vidya Prakashan, 1970).

3 William Cantwell Smith, *The Meaning and End of Religion* (New York: Mentor Books, 1962), pp. 142-5.

4 *Op. cit.,* pp. i-iii.

5 *The Modernity of Tradition* (Chicago: The University of Chicago Press, 1967), pp. 3-4.

6 P. D. Devanandan, *op. cit.,* pp. 125-6.

7 Basu and Ghosh, *op. cit.,* p. 663.

8 *Ibid.,* p. 395.

9 For an excellent discussion of both facets of Shiva, see Wendy Doniger O'Flaherty, "Asceticism and Sexuality in the Mythology of Shiva," *History of Religions,* vol. 8, no. 4, pp. 300-37; vol. 9, no. 1, pp. 1-41.

10 A. D. Moddie, *The Brahmanical Culture and Modernity* (Calcutta: Asia Publishing House, 1968), p. 87.

11 *Ibid.,* p. 88.

12 Vivekananda, *op. cit.,* vol. 8, p. 97.

13 *Ibid.,* vol. 5, p. 97.

14 Sister Nivedita, *The Master As I Saw Him, op. cit.,* p. 247.

15 *Ibid.,* p. 245.

16 Swami Omkareswarananda, "In the Society of the Holy," *Vedanta for Modern Man* (New York: Collier Books, 1962), p. 202.

17 J. H. Broomfield, *Elite Conflict in a Plural Society; Twentieth Century Bengal* (Berkeley: University of California Press, 1968), pp. 147-8.

18 "Single or Married?" an article in *The Indian Social Reformer,* March 24, 1901, Basu and Ghosh, *op. cit.,* p. 457.

19 Leo Schneiderman, *op. cit.,* p. 61.

20 John Yale, "The Order of Ramakrishna," *Vedanta and the West,* May-June, 1954, pp. 31-2.

21 N. J. Demerath, "In a Sow's Ear: A Reply to Goode," *Journal of the Scientific Study of Religion,* Spring, 1967, pp. 82-3.

22 Max Weber, *The Religion of India* (New York: The Free Press, 1958), pp. 23-4.

23 Jogendra Nath Bhattacharya, *Hindu Castes and Sects* (Calcutta: 1896).

24 Joachim Wach, *Sociology of Religion* (Chicago: University of Chicago Press, 1944), pp. 127-30.

25 R. G. Bhandarkar, *Vaisnavism, Saivism and Minor Religious Systems* (Varanasi: Rameshwar Singh, 1965), pp. 82-3.

26 Quoted in *The Indian Social Reformer,* Nov. 3, 1901, Basu and Ghosh, *op. cit.,* p. 461.

27 Related in a personal interview with Swami Vandananda, New Delhi, Nov. 7, 1970.

28 Wach, *op. cit.,* pp. 130-41.

29 Christopher Isherwood, editor, *Vedanta for Modern Man* (New York: Collier Books, 1962), pp. 9-13.

30 Phyllis Austin, "A Conversation," *Vedanta for East and West,* Nov.-Dec., 1966, pp. 25-6.

31 Wendell Thomas, *op. cit.,* p. 107.

32 *Collected Works,* vol. 8, pp. 356-7.

32 "Convert Takes Path to Hindu Monkhood," *Chicago Sun-Times,* July 10, 1967.

34 John Yale, The Order of Ramakrishna," *Vedanta and the West,* May-June, 1954, p. 26.

35 Devanandan, *op. cit.,* p. 102.

36 *The Hindu Patriot,* Dec. 28, 1896, quoting a London newspaper. Basu and Ghosh, *op. cit.,* p. 295.

37 George Holcomb, "He Swallows No Blades," *The Oregon Journal,* July 16, 1950.

38 *The Message of the East,* June, 1914, p. 135.

39 *Ibid.,* Jan., 1921, p. 42.

40 Sister Christine, *op. cit.,* p. 210.

41 *Ibid.,* pp. 212-3.

42 *Ibid.,* p. 169.

43 Harland E. Hogue, "The Christian Church Confronts the Cultists," paper written for the Pacific Theological Group, April 29, 1955, p. 9.

44 Swami Yatiswarananda, "The Guru Cult: A Warning," *Vedanta for East and West,* March-April, 1964, pp. 79-80.

45 Bryan R. Wilson, *op. cit.,* pp. 167-8.

Notes to Chapter Ten

1 Harland E. Hogue, *op. cit.,* p. 9.

2 See, *e.g.,* Walter Rauschenbusch, *Christianizing the Social Order* (New York: The Macmillan Co., 1913).

3 Swami Ranganathananda, "A Traveller Looks at the World," Part III, *Prabuddha Bharata,* Sept., 1970, p. 435.

4 See J. Stillson Judah, *The History and Philosophy of the Metaphysical Movements in America* (Philadelphia,: The Westminster Press, 1967), pp. 12-18.

5 Hendrik Kraemer, *World Cultures and World Religions, the Coming Dialogue* (London: Lutterworth Press, 1960), p. 18.

6 Thomas Robbins, "Eastern Mysticism and the Resocialization of Drug Users," *Journal for the Scientific Study of Religion,* Fall, 1969, p. 311.

7 On the characteristics of the counter-culture, see, generally, Theodore Roszak, *The Making of a Counter-Culture* (Garden City, New York: Doubleday and Co., 1968).

8 J. H. Broomfield, *op. cit.,* p. 160.

9 Jogendra Nath Bhattacharya, *Hindu Castes and Sects* (Calcutta: No publisher listed, 1896), pp. 276-90 ff.

10 John Moffitt, "Varieties of Contemporary Hindu Monasticism," Part 2, *Vedanta Kesari,* July, 1970, p. 134.

11 *Ibid.,* pp. 135-6.

12 Walter Rauschenbusch, "Social Christianity and Personal Religion," quoted in *Prabuddha Bharata,* July, 1970, p. 291.

13 Vivekananda, *Complete Works,* vol. 4, pp. 402-3.

14 *Ibid.,* p. 405.

15 *Ibid.,* p. 404.

16 C. F. Andrews and Girija K. Mookherjee, *The Rise and Growth of Congress in India, 1832-1920* (Calcutta: Meenakshi Prakashan, 1967), p. 2.

17 Bhupendranath Dutta, *Swami Vivekananda, the Socialist* (Khulna, Bengal, 1929), p. IV (quoted in C. F. Andrews and Girija K. Mookherjee, *The Rise and Growth of Congress in India, 1832-1920* (Calcutta: Meenakshi Prakashan, 1967), p. 2.

18 Subhas Chandra Bose, *An Indian Pilgrim* (London: Asia Publishing House, 1965), pp. 31-35. Later, however, Netaji and his friends became somewhat more critical of policies taken by the Ramakrishna Mission. "In our group we had always criticised the Ramakrishna Mission for concentrating on hospitals and flood and famine relief and neglecting nation-building work of a permanent nature, and I had no desire to repeat their mistake." (p. 75).

19 J. N. Farquhar, *Modern Religious Movements in India* (New York: The Macmillan Co., 1915), p. 362.

20 Pattabhi Sitaramayya, *History of the Indian National Congress,* vol. 1, 1885-1935 (Delhi: S. Chand and Co., 1969), p. 70.

21 Sri Aurobindo, *On Yoga: Tome Two* (Pondicherry: Sri Aurobindo Ashram, 1958), p. 478.

22 Albert Schweitzer, *Indian Thought and Its Development* (New York: Henry Holt, 1936), p. 221.

23 Cited in Kraemer, *op. cit.,* p. 339.

24 Swami Pavitrananda, "Swami Vivekananda and the Future of India," article in R. C. Majumdar, ed., *Parliament of Religions: Swami Vivekananda Centenary* (Calcutta: Sree Saraswaty Press, 1964), p. 87.

25 Sister Christine, "Swami Vivekananda as I Saw Him," *op. cit.,* p. 219.

26 Ranganathananda, *op. cit.,* p. 436.

27 Swami Yatiswarananda, *Vedanta and the West,* Sept.-Oct., 1941, p. 29.

28 Robert Joseph and James Felton, "Hollywood Swami," *op. cit.,* p. 28.

29 Swami Nityaswarupananda, "On the Eve of a Western Tour," *Bulletin on the Ramakrishna Mission Institute of Culture,* May, 1962, p. 150.

30 Swami Nityaswarupananda, *Education for World Civilization* (Calcutta: The Ramakrishna Mission Institute of Culture, 1970).

31 Nehru, quoted in S. J. Samartha, "Major Issues in the Hindu-Christian Dialogue Today," Herbert Jai Singh, *Inter-Religious Dialogue* (Bangalore: The Christian Institute for the Study of Religion and Society, 1967), p. 157.

32 In Nikhilananda, *Vivekananda: A Biography, op. cit.,* pp. 129-30.

Notes to Chapter Eleven

1 Wm. Ernest Hocking, *Re-Thinking Missions* (New York: Harper, 1932).

2 Wm. Ernest Hocking, *Living Religions and a World Faith* (London: George Allen and Unwin, 1940).

3 Hendrick Kraemer, *The Christian Message in a Non-Christian World* (New York: Harper, 1938).

4 Hendrick Kraemer, *World Cultures and World Religions: The Coming Dialogue* (Philadelphia: The Westminster Press, 1960).

5 Wm. Ernest Hocking, *The Coming World Civilization* (New York: Harper and Bros., 1956), p. 138.

6 *Ibid.*, p. 117.

7 Hocking, *Living Religions and a World Faith, op. cit.*, p. 129.

8 A. C. Das, "From Dogmatism of Philosophies to Democracy of Religions," *Prabuddha Bharata,* Feb., 1971 pp. 63-4.

9 Christopher Isherwood, "Religion Without Prayers," *Vedanta and the West,* July-Aug., 1946, p. 15.

10 Aldous Huxley, "Minimum Working Hypothesis," *Vedanta and the West,* March-April, 1944, p. 39.

11 *Ibid.*, pp. 38-9.

12 Swami Nityabodhananda, "Desacralization," *Prabuddha Bharata,* July, 1970 (75th anniversary issue), pp. 331-2.

13 *Living Religions and a World Faith,* p. 197.

14 Swami Prabhavananda, "Sri Ramakrishna and the Religions of Tomorrow," *Vedanta and the West,* Sept.-Oct., 1946, p. 159. This article and the one by Huxley are reprinted, respectively, in *Vedanta for Modern Man* and *Vedanta for the Western World,* edited by Christopher Isherwood.

15 Pravas Jivan Chaudhury, "A Scientific Approach to Vedanta," *Bulletin of the Ramakrishna Mission Institute of Culture,* Calcutta, July, 1961, pp. 235-43.

16 Pravas Jivan Chaudhury, "Deontological Vedanta," *Bulletin* [of the Institute], Aug., 1959, p. 179.

17 Chaudhury, "Vadanta as Phenomenology," *Bulletin* [of the Institute], March, 1958, p. 61.

18 As discussed also by Swami Abhishiktananda (a Christian), in Herbert Jai Singh, *Inter-Religious Dialogue,* pp. 86-7.

19 Kraemer, *World Cultures and World Religions, The Coming Dialogue, op. cit.,* p. 153.

20 Editorial, "India's Attitude Toward the Christian Missionary," *Bulletin of the Ramakrishna Mission Institute of Culture,* June, 1953, p. 127.

21 Christopher Isherwood, *Vedanta for Modern Man* (New York: Collier Books, 1962), p. 243.

22 Platt Cline, "What Vedanta Means to Me," *Vedanta and the West,* July-Aug., 1968, p. 57.

23 R. K. D. Gupta, "Swami Vivekananda's Gospel of Divine Humanism," article in R. C. Majumdar, ed., *Swami Vivekananda: A Historical Review,* p. 211.

INDEX

215